WITHDRAWN

5937209024426 FTBC

WORN, SOILED, OBSOLETE

Praise for

CREATURES OF WILL AND TEMPER

"There has never been a better time for a spirited, feminist reinvention of *The Picture of Dorian Gray*. Molly Tanzer has taken a wickedly sensuous classic and transformed it into a lively supernatural tale featuring lovestruck teenagers, diabolical botanicals, mysterious paintings, and — oh, yes — demons. *Creatures of Will and Temper* is a wild ride from start to finish, beautifully and boldly written, and a most worthy successor to Oscar Wilde's scandalous novel."

—Amy Stewart, author of *Girl Waits with Gun*

"Decadent Victorians clash with dueling demon-hunters in this page-turning reinvention of Oscar Wilde's classic tale. I loved it!"

— Charles Stross, award-winning author of *The Delirium Brief*

"Molly Tanzer's *Creatures of Will and Temper* is a smart, gorgeously written book about passion, loyalty, and love in many forms. And if that's not enough for you, it has demons and terrific fencing scenes! I loved this book, and you will too."

— Kat Howard, award-nominated author
of *Roses and Rot* and former competitive fencer

"A perfectly queer homage to *The Picture of Dorian Gray* ... A timely story, and one that I think we all need right n

— Sarah Lynn Weintraub, Pandem̶ ̶ ̶ ̶ ̶ ̶ ̶ ̶ Games

"Tanzer mixes Oscar Wilde's *The Pic̶ ̶ ̶ ̶ ̶ ̶ ̶ ̶* queer romance and demonology in thi̶ ̶ ̶ ̶ ̶ ̶ ̶ ̶torian-era fantasy novel ... The perfectly̶ ̶ ̶ ̶ ̶ ̶ ̶ ̶ ̶ between the sister [protagonists] takes c̶ ̶ ̶ ̶ ̶ ̶ ̶x (though never overplayed) web of art, swor̶ ̶ ̶ ̶ ̶ ̶, much to the sisters' surprise, actual demons. G̶ ̶ ̶ ̶ ̶ ̶ortrayed three-dimensional characters and sensual prose ̶ ̶ ̶ ̶ this smoothly entertaining story to an emotionally affecting end."

— *Publishers Weekly*, starred review

CREATURES OF WILL AND TEMPER

CREATURES

OF

WILL

TEMPER

Molly Tanzer

A John Joseph Adams Book

MARINER BOOKS

HOUGHTON MIFFLIN HARCOURT

BOSTON   NEW YORK

2017

Copyright © 2017 by Molly Tanzer

All rights reserved

For information about permission to reproduce selections from this book,
write to trade.permissions@hmhco.com or to Permissions,
Houghton Mifflin Harcourt Publishing Company,
3 Park Avenue, 19th Floor, New York, New York 10016.

hmhco.com

Library of Congress Cataloging-in-Publication Data is available.
ISBN 978-1-328-71026-0

Book design by Chrissy Kurpeski

Printed in the United States of America
DOC 10 9 8 7 6 5 4 3 2 1

For Nick

Author's Note

In his preface to *The Picture of Dorian Gray,* Oscar Wilde said, "There is no such thing as a moral or an immoral book. Books are well written, or badly written. That is all." Readers disagreed —*Dorian Gray* was widely condemned; one critic even went so far as to say it would "taint every young mind that comes into contact with it."

It was the homosexuality in *Dorian Gray* that was of paramount concern at the time, a motif that Wilde elected to elide in later editions. But another reason critics expressed dismay was over the lack of "punishment" for the eponymous character. Dorian Gray may die at the end of Wilde's novel, but he faces no retribution. Dorian's death comes not at the hands of some righteous avenger, but rather by his own.

Wilde also said, "The moral life of man forms part of the subject-matter of the artist, but the morality of art consists in the perfect use of an imperfect medium." To his mind, then, art's purpose —its obligation—is to be *good,* even if the result is a work fundamentally at odds with the desires of the morality police when it comes to establishing (or maintaining) social order.

The author of *this* book agrees that art ought to exist for its own purposes—that if there is any "ought" to art at all, it is that art's primary motivator ought not to be pedagogy. For that reason, Wilde's *The Picture of Dorian Gray* was the perfect template upon which to base *Creatures of Will and Temper.* After all, *Dorian Gray* is fundamentally a moral novel. If it truly were amoral, as Wilde maintains, Dorian's excesses would not corrupt his perfect painted image. Either that or the reader would feel no sympathy for the innocent victims of Dorian's outrages.

But what if Dorian had no victims? What if his quest for aesthetic experiences were not portrayed as a journey into a moral and spiritual underworld? As in life, matters would not be nearly so clear-cut, nor would they be so easily and neatly resolved.

While this novel diverges in several significant ways from Wilde's, the author intends for it to honor the spirit of the original, if not its content. Oscar Wilde once described *Dorian Gray* as a "fantastic variation" on Joris-Karl Huysmans's amoral, decadent novel *Against the Grain*. In that tradition, *Creatures of Will and Temper* is a fantastic variation on *The Picture of Dorian Gray*—or at least one envisioned through a glass . . . not darkly, but brightly.

—MT, 2017

PROLOGUE

What love, violence, art, and sport are to many,
diabolism is to few: simply a method of procuring
extraordinary sensations.

—*On the Summoning of Demons*

T HE FRENCH DOORS STOOD OPEN, letting in a breeze that
stirred the plants on the veranda like playful fingers, but it
remained stubbornly, oppressively hot in Basil Hallward's
studio. The heat intensified the odor of oil paints, canvas, and tur-
pentine, as well as the heavy perfume of crushed flowers, but it was
such a pleasure to look upon her friend as he painted that Lady
Henrietta Wotton did not stir from the divan upon which she lay,
a cigarette dangling between her fingers, the smoke of which carried the curiously potent odor of fresh ginger.

Basil did not speak as he worked, as was his custom—and
while it was hers to comment on matters of the day as he dabbed
and daubed, today she only watched. She was content to simply
hearken to the muffled rumblings of London that filtered faintly
into the room from beyond the little oasis of Basil's townhouse
and patio garden.

The reason for Lady Henry's quietude was respect for her
friend's recent poor health, as well as for his subject matter. Basil
was hard at work on a portrait—in fact, was very close to finishing it. It was a unique piece—Basil typically painted only from
life, and yet, much to their mutual dismay, the subject of this picture was no longer counted among the living. Even so, the painting

had the startling appearance of vitality; its colors were not those of grief, nor was its subject somber in his funereal portrait. The slender man was laughing, just as he had done in life, standing carelessly against a pillar with his hands in his pockets, his expensive suit as artfully rumpled as his fair hair. And though said hair had a touch of gray in it, he was consummately youthful in appearance, and seemed as untouched by sorrow as a boy half his age.

Basil, however, looked years older than when he had begun to paint the piece, though it had only been a few months since he had applied gesso to the canvas.

Lady Henry raised the fragrant cigarette to her lips and inhaled deeply. As the mingled essences of the tobacco and ginger hit her bloodstream, she felt the independent presence that always lurked at the back of her mind stir slightly, acknowledging what she saw—seeing for itself, but through Lady Henry's eyes. A sense of appreciation and longing touched her consciousness as the colors intensified. The shapes became more shapely; the beauty, more beautiful.

I miss him so much, she thought.

The presence lovingly acknowledged but did not partake of her sorrow. She did not expect it to. The demon that had been her constant companion for over a decade could not feel regret. It was not a part of its nature. Currently, it was more concerned with the painting. It really was as perfect a reproduction of the man as was possible. Lady Henry would know, for she had known the subject all his life. He was—or rather, he had been—her brother. Her twin, in fact. The only person in the world who might have known him better was the one who painted him now—the dark, brooding Dionysus to the brilliant Apollo on the canvas. Now that there was more silver mixed in with the black of Basil's hair, he was even more the night, if the man in the painting was the day.

With a heavy sigh, Basil set down his brush and stepped back.

"Are you finished?" asked Lady Henry.

"I've done as much as I can today without risking muddying it," he replied.

"Well then, let's step outside and have a cocktail," she suggested. "Or champagne? I don't think it's too early to celebrate your triumph. It's your best work yet." She paused. "Though before I get excited, I suppose I should ask if you have any decent champagne in the house?"

"By whose standards—yours, or mine?" It made her heart glad to hear him chuckle, even if it was only an echo of his former hearty laugh. "Decent enough to mix with absinthe, I'd imagine."

"Lovely," said Lady Henry. "Let's do that."

She rose as Basil rang the bell, and in a cacophony of crackling joints, stretched her arms, back, and legs. Lady Henry was wiry and fair, like her brother had been—youthful, but clearly in her middle years—and she, too, cut a dashing figure in her sack coat and trousers. Even before her brother's death Lady Henry Wotton had scandalized London society by wearing men's clothing in public, but while she and her twin had been built along the same lines, Oliver's suits had been too large in the shoulder and too tight in the hips. She knew, for she'd tried them all on in hopes of pinching them.

After his death, she had had his wardrobe tailored to her own measurements, and not just because Oliver's taste had been impeccable. She missed her brother every day, and it comforted her to wear his clothes.

A maid appeared without a sound, bearing a chilled bottle in a bucket filled with ice, and then departed just as silently as Basil uncorked it with a faint hiss. After splashing absinthe in two coupes, he topped them off with the champagne and handed one over to Lady Henry.

"To your finest work yet," said Henry, toasting her friend as she admired the painting from afar. "I do hope when you're finished you'll bring it round and show it off to our colleagues? Give us the first look, before you send it anywhere?"

"I don't think I shall send it anywhere . . . at least, not for some time," answered Basil, his back to the painting. Henry wondered if he was trying not to look at it.

"Why on earth not?"

"Don't laugh at me, but it is too personal. The wound is too fresh. I cannot have it judged by anyone, or remarked upon by common people. Or uncommon people, for that matter . . . save for *you*."

Henry gave him a playful smile. "Really? *Only* me?"

Basil looked a bit uncomfortable. "Yes, though I know, of course, that you are never truly alone."

The demon stirred again in Henry's mind, hearing itself referred to, though obliquely.

"Neither was Oliver," said Henry gently.

"I know, I know, but neither does that mean I am eager to show off this canvas to my former social circle."

Henry almost choked on a swallow of champagne. "Former! But surely you do not mean your absence at my gatherings to be a permanent one?"

Basil did not answer; instead, he wandered onto the veranda. Henry followed him. She had designed the garden herself, and was pleased to see that enough light came in through the fronds and branches to keep the patio bright, while still creating the illusion that they were in a country garden rather than the heart of Chelsea.

"Baz," she said, now as serious as she had moments ago been playful, "tell me truly. Do you mean to leave us forever?"

"And what if I did? Would you compel me to return?"

"Never," she said. "It is not our way." The presence in her mind heartily agreed, but she did not tell Basil this. "But . . ."

"But?"

"But I will miss you! We all would. Your absence has been noticed, and not just by us."

"Do not speak to me of that *thing!*" Basil hissed, whirling around, spilling his drink all over his hand. He cursed, and hastily sucked his fingers dry. "My apologies, Harry," he said, his voice low lest they be overheard, "but surely you must see why it is impossible. Really, I'm astonished you remain in contact with *it* after Oliver—after he, after *they* . . ."

Henry put her hand on her friend's shoulder and squeezed gently. "My dearest Basil, if there is one person in this world who regrets Oliver's death more than you do, it is I. I was only his sister; the two of you, well, calling you *lovers* seems like an insult, given the depth of your connection. Oliver and I shared a womb, but the two of you shared a *life*."

She wandered away from Basil and set her drink down on a low table in order to withdraw another cigarette from the silver case in her breast pocket. She did not offer Basil one, and though he did not as a rule mind smoke, he wrinkled his nose when she lit it. Out of courtesy, when she exhaled, she blew away from him.

"That said," she continued, "he and I did share something, something that made us closer than siblings. When we decided to summon it, to invite it into our lives, our bodies, our minds, we knew what we were doing. And when Oliver did what he did . . . perhaps it does not comfort you, knowing he chose his fate, but he *did* choose it. You know as well as I that unlike others of its type our demon is not the sort to require *that* sort of sacrifice. Thus, I choose to remain a hierophant of that which has let so much beauty into my life. Beauty, after all, is the only thing that matters."

Agreement flooded her, body and soul, as she spoke these words. She and the demon were well suited; they were literally of one mind about most things.

"I know he chose, Henry—I just don't understand *why*."

"No one understands anything, not really. We only think we do. I have nothing but respect for scientists and doctors and others who study the world, but even the most rigorous among them are only looking through a keyhole of what truly *is*."

"Be that as it may, I could not bear to lose you too," said Basil. "Oh, Harry, if *you* . . ."

"You will not lose me, but try to understand that you have not *lost* Oliver, not really. Death is an illusion, just like anything else— like distance, for example, or time, or the separateness of one thing from another. The whole universe is only matter forming and re-forming itself, endlessly, beautifully. Nothing is ever really lost. Oliver is still with us, even if—" She saw tears standing in Basil's eyes, and amended her speech. "Oh, Baz. I meant to speak comfort to you, but I see I've made you miserable. Just, know this: Oliver and I may have looked the same, and shared similar interests, but I did not condone his choice, not when he first expressed his desire to me, nor when he followed through with it. How I argued with him! But he was always so damned stubborn."

The presence in Henry's mind neither agreed nor disagreed with her; it accepted what was, what had been, and what would come to pass without judgment—only with eternal, unwavering interest. She picked up her drink again, taking a delicate sip before continuing.

"The thing is, Oliver was also less of a sensualist than I. I love this life and its pleasures too much to abandon it a moment earlier than I must. But let us leave off with this conversation. This is to be a celebration, not a wake! Even if we are celebrating the completion of a memorial."

Basil nodded, dashing the tears from his eyes with an unsteady hand. "When are you going to the country?" he asked, his voice hoarse.

"My aunt will likely require me within a fortnight," said Henry languidly, her casual tone hiding her eagerness to be done with their previous conversation. She wandered under the boughs of a potted laburnum. Its blossoms brushed over her hair and shoulders, gilding her with their pollen. "What a shame I have no excuse to put her off! I don't like leaving my greenhouse during the growing season, or the patios of my friends. None of you really appreciate the hard work I put into cultivating these little London landscapes; it all goes to seed while I'm away. Can't be helped, I suppose."

"A fortnight . . . too bad. You'll miss my niece arriving," said Basil. "Ah well, I assume you'll be back before I pack her off again."

"Which niece? The younger or the elder?"

Basil gave Lady Henry a stern look. "Perhaps you *should* stay away. I won't have you corrupting innocents I've promised to protect."

"I've never in my life corrupted an innocent," said Henry, her eyebrows quirked up nearly to her graying hairline. "That is a *common* thing to do, and I am not a common sort of person. And even more importantly, it's impossible."

"How is that?"

"True innocents are incorruptible. It's only people who *pretend* to be innocent who have that chink in their armor that let wicked people like me inside."

"You are not to become familiar with my niece's armor, thank you very much," said Basil. "She's only seventeen, and I have no desire to find out if she's truly innocent, or simply a pretender."

"Seventeen! Oh, you have nothing to worry about." Henry shook her head, and finishing her cigarette, tossed it into the brazen Turkish bathing bowl Basil used as an ashtray. "Women under the age of twenty are all unspeakably boring—and I thought that even when I was under twenty myself, a lifetime ago. No, the wee duckling is quite safe from me, no matter what dirty-minded old men like you might think. I was hoping the one closer to thirty was coming to visit you. She's still unmarried, isn't she?" Henry leered at her friend.

"I will thank you not to make lecherous remarks about *either* of my nieces," said Basil primly.

"Come now—I never objected to you pursuing my brother, did I?"

"I knew your brother before I knew you!"

"Ah, but you'd never have known he felt the same about you without my intervention, would you?"

Basil blushed. "Perhaps not. Still, Dorina Gray is off limits, Henry. Completely. Do you understand me?"

"Gray? She's not a Hallward, like you?" Henry lit another cigarette, ignoring Basil's rebuke just to annoy him. "I wonder if she's as pretty as her name?"

"I know you are only baiting me because it pleases you to do so," said Basil. "You are the sort of woman who is ashamed of your own virtue. You pretend to be utterly without morals, but I've yet to see you do anything immoral, not really."

"The artists of today! Why, I'm astonished you're not driven out of the city with scourges. Claiming a *diabolist* has never done anything immoral! Your ilk are truly beyond the pale."

"Hush!" he shushed her. "Don't say that word aloud! Not out here. You can hear *everything*," said Basil, looking about furtively. "Trust me, I know—a young married couple has moved in, and it's most inconvenient."

"I apologize," said Henry. "Well, so your niece is coming to town. How nice. She's staying with you the whole time?"

"Yes. It's a treat for her. She wants to be an art critic one day, and—"

"She *what?*"

"It's not a typical girlish dream, but there it is. She's apparently begged her parents for a year to come to London and . . ." He blushed, to Henry's surprise.

"And what?"

"You'll laugh, but she wants to study me. She wants to write a monograph on my art, in the hopes of getting it published in some journal or other."

"Perfectly reasonable. You and your art are completely fascinating. It's why I spend so much time here. Is she out?"

"Out in society? Dorina? Not formally. Her parents have agreed to let her come because it's the summer, and she should be safe enough from predatory young men."

"To be sure," said Henry drolly. "Hmm. Perhaps I *do* have a good reason to deny my aunt . . . I can't allow you to bungle this. A man, in charge of a seventeen-year-old girl! I've never heard of such a thing; it's most irregular. I shall remain and guard her virtue. She'll have never had it tested before! Anybody can be virtuous in the country. There are no temptations there. London is another story."

"Henry—"

"You'll be doing me a favor, Baz, if you will but insist that I help."

The afternoon had waned as they spoke, the evening breeze picking up enough to detach and scatter a handful of heavy blossoms from the trees. They skittered over the Italian tile of the veranda floor before spilling in through the door to Basil's studio. A bee buzzed past, desperately nestling itself in the center of a pink rose before bumbling away again. Basil sighed, and Henry turned away, smiling to herself. She'd won, and she knew it.

"I suppose I *could* use the help," he admitted, "but I can't have my sister upset with me. You don't know what she's like when she's upset. And even more than that, it would be on my conscience forever if you, ah, injured Dorina. Don't you smirk at me—I realize by saying that, I shall pique your curiosity and set your mind thinking of chinks and armor and goodness knows what else. You mustn't spoil her, Henry. She is a simple thing. If you influence her, I cannot imagine it would be for the better."

"I say! If I'm smirking, it's because I'm eager to meet this child. When was the last time you saw her? I've never known a girl of seventeen to be simple or unspoiled."

"You're not exactly instilling me with confidence," said Basil.

"Be confident that I shan't do anything that will necessitate my leaving London," said Henry. "The only place I have to go is my aunt's, and we've already discussed how little I want to go there."

"I'll just have to trust you," said Basil, his words as heavy as the laburnum blossoms that yet shook in the breeze, in danger of following after their fellows.

"You don't *have* to do anything, save for finishing that painting. That, I insist on."

"Oh?"

"You mustn't leave your greatest work unfinished. It was fine for Mozart and for Raphael, but these are modern times. It's the dawn of a new century—at least, soon it will be, and no harm was ever done by being ahead of the times."

"You've changed the subject. I really would like your promise that you won't behave scandalously around Dorina."

"I make no promises to anyone, even friends as dear as you," said Lady Henry, and taking her friend by the arm, she led him back into his studio. "But I can assure you, if she's as simple as you claim, I'll be too busy yawning to consider anything scandalous."

"I suppose that will have to be enough," Basil said with a sigh. He looked even sicker in that moment, like an old shell bleached by the sun. Henry couldn't abide it, and felt compelled to make a joke in the hopes of bringing a smile to his face.

"Why are artists all so gloomy?" she quipped while faking a yawn, her words muffled by the pale hand over her red mouth. "To think, your niece wants to study you! Her parents must be wiser than I thought; seeing you mumbling over your morning paper in that awful housecoat you refuse to replace will disillusion her as to the alleged glamour of the art world in no time at all." She grinned at Basil. "Perhaps I shall ask her to one of my gatherings? If she's interested in art criticism, I'm sure she'd jump at the chance to meet with individuals so committed to living a life of pure beauty that they're willing to — oh *do* stop glowering at me like that!"

She left off, for Basil was looking daggers at her.

"As I said, Dorina is safe from me," Henry continued. "Likely she'll want to go do and see every silly thing once she gets here and that's a scene I cannot endure for long."

"She may surprise you."

For once, Henry's demon agreed with Basil — but she didn't tell *him* that.

"I doubt it," she said instead. "Now, if it were the older one coming, that would be a different matter. She will have lived enough to be interesting — to know the ways of the world. An unmarried woman approaching thirty can retain no illusions about justice, and goodness, and right as compared to wrong. She will have learned the way the world really works. Her mind will be flexible, and it's almost guaranteed to contain something other than pious ignorance and animalistic cravings for male attention."

Basil laughed. "You think you know everything about women."

"I know I'm a curious specimen, but in the end, I can claim to be one of the population."

"I'm a curious specimen of a man, and make no claims to understand men. Perhaps I'll invite Evadne to visit too . . . I'd be interested to see your theories tested. But you *must* behave yourself."

"When have I not?" said Lady Henry, the picture of innocence.

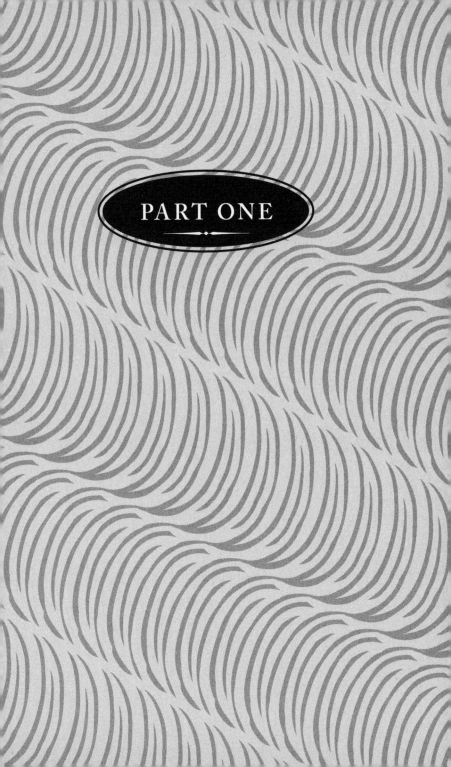

PART ONE

1

The behavior of demons, while occult, is neither surface nor symbol. The behavior of men is just as occult ... and wholly surface and symbol.

— *On the Summoning of Demons*

I F THERE WAS ANYTHING in the world sweeter than the ring of steel sliding over steel, it was Freddie Thornton's grimace when Evadne parried his attack. Even the rich odor of roses carried on the light summer wind, and perfume of the lilac, and the pink-flowering thorn were nothing to the sight of his bared teeth, and the beaded sweat of his forehead running down the bridge of his nose, over his full lips.

She had him. She could see it in his eyes, the set of his shoulders. A tactician, Evadne had let Freddie exhaust himself with fancy maneuvers in this match; had saved herself for this moment, knowing it would come. Deepening her stance, she threw her weight into her riposte and sent his sword spinning away into the ornamental shrubbery.

"Do you yield?" she asked, ripping off her fencing mask before pointing her dulled epee at his blue-veined throat.

"Of course I yield," he said, knocking it aside with the back of his broad hand.

"Good match." She slapped him on the shoulder as he removed his own mask. She knew it was bold to touch him, so she kept the motion rough and perfunctory. "You've been practicing."

"So have you," he said, rubbing at where she'd struck him. "With whom, I can't imagine, out here in the country. Have you found a master?"

"I already have a master." Evadne pretended interest in the finches that twittered gaily as they flitted among the topiaries of the formal garden. It was not a typical place for a fencing match, but she'd often used the wide gravel lane for practicing her forms.

It was also beautiful, isolated, and a bit romantic . . .

"Oh, you long ago mastered any knowledge I managed to pass on to you," said Freddie. "What a pity you're a woman! They'd have made you captain of the Oxford fencing team, I'm certain of it."

Evadne tried to cover her dismay with the sort of laugh her younger sister, Dorina, managed so easily: light and lively, as if she'd neither a care in the world nor a thought in her head. It came out all wrong, however, like it always did, and she stopped, knowing she sounded more like a braying ass than a tinkling bell.

"Ah well," said Freddie, to cover the momentary awkwardness. "Where's my sword? It's time we got back."

"One more match," urged Evadne. The last thing she wanted was to go back to the house and make herself ridiculous by forcing her short, stocky body into a frilly tea dress and her sun-bleached hair into some sort of feminine pile of twists and excrescences. Her grace came to her only when she held an epee in her hand and her limbs were encased in canvas and leather. With Freddie just returned home from inspecting the living he'd been given in the north of England she wanted to make as good an impression as possible — and that would be out here, in the healthy sunshine, not inside a dull, dim parlor.

"I think I've been humiliated enough for one day." Horrified, Evadne realized she should have let Freddie win a match or two. She'd not impressed him with her display of prowess; she'd annoyed him. She stammered an apology, but he waved her away. "I'm parched, that's all. A cup of tea is what I need."

"Oh, me too," she gushed as they reached for his sword at the same time. Of course, instead of their hands meeting over the hilt, like in one of Dorina's stupid novels, Evadne very nearly bowled him over.

"You're a beast, Evadne. You know"—he looked her up and down appraisingly—"the Greeks had it all wrong. Athena's no soft, stern beauty—she'd look like you right now, dirty as a beggar, and all brawn and sweat and determination."

Evadne wasn't pleased by this description of her person, or the goddess he'd selected to compare her to. If the love of her life was going to compare her to a deity, Evadne would have preferred one who wasn't a perpetual virgin, even a martially inclined one. She tried to toss her hair that fetching way she'd seen Dorina manage a thousand times, but just ended up spraying Freddie with sweat.

"Sorry!" she stammered, mortified. "I meant to say . . ."

"What's that?" asked Freddie, dabbing at his eyes with his handkerchief.

"It's just, I'm fairly certain I didn't spring fully formed out of my father's head."

"No," he said, looking at her strangely.

"Tea?" Evadne gestured toward the house. Perhaps conversing in a drawing room would be better than standing around in the heady perfume of the garden. At the very least, holding a cup of tea would give her something to do with her hands.

"Actually, I must away." Freddie took her sword from her, and then offered her his sweat-soaked arm. She took it, and they began to amble back to the house. "Mother will be wondering where I am."

"We'll send a servant," said Evadne. "It's no trouble. You've been gone for so long and . . ." She embarrassed herself by blushing. *I missed you,* she wanted to say. "And you've only just returned."

"I know it's terribly uncivil of me," he said gently. Evadne's heart sank. If she had been Dorina, she would have known what to do, how to manipulate him with her feminine charms. Unfortunately, she was herself, and thus unequipped to charm anything but a blade. "But never fear—you'll see me soon. It wasn't just to spar with you that I came today."

"No?"

"I'm supposed to extend an invitation, for you to dine with us tomorrow night." He grinned at her. "You and your family, naturally, but I hope *you* specifically will deign to eat the humble fare of Vicarage House?"

"Nothing would give me greater pleasure." She shot him a sly look. "It's you who surely must resign yourself to plain fare. What will they feed you on up in the north, I wonder? Oaten cakes and nettle wine? That doesn't sound so bad, actually," she hastened to add. "Appropriate for doing God's humble work."

"You've always had the stomach of a goat," he said as he guided her toward the stables. Again, Evadne wasn't quite sure his compliments were actually compliments. "You won't need one tomorrow night, though. Mother's planning a feast. It's to be a celebration!"

Her heart fluttered. Could Freddie be working up to a proposal, at long last? "Oh? Are we celebrating your success?"

"Yes, and . . ."

"And?"

"And there's someone I want you to meet."

"Oh?" A relative—perhaps a grandmother or aunt who insisted on approving of her darling Freddie's choice?

"Yes," said Freddie, his voice studiously neutral. "My fiancée."

Evadne had grown up tramping over hills and through woods with her father, but now, on this sunny afternoon, walking arm in arm with the young man she'd loved since he was a boy stealing jam out of the pantry, she felt like she might faint senseless to the earth.

"Fiancée," she murmured, then realizing she ought to at least pretend to be happy, forced another laugh. It sounded yet more dreadful than her first attempt. "But you're so young!"

"It's high time I settled down. I'm thirty-three, Evadne. I'm in my prime!"

"I'm just surprised. I had no idea you were thinking of marrying. Is she a northern girl?"

"No, her family lives in Oxford. We met when I was still at school. There has been an understanding between us for some time, but I wanted to leave her free until I could offer her a comfortable life."

An understanding! Until just a few moments ago, she had thought an understanding existed between the two of *them*. After all, Freddie had spoken freely to her of his ambitions, hopes, and plans, had asked her advice, and seemed to value her approval.

It had always been Freddie's dearest wish to find a small parish in need of a kindly shepherd to guide its flock, and to marry a respectable woman, thereby setting an example for the common people. All this had sounded completely lovely to Evadne. She even enjoyed attending services. Religion had always been a comfort to her, assuring her as it did that her faith was what distinguished her, not her looks or her manners. And living somewhere a bit wilder than Swadlincote would have freed her from needing to dress and act like a gentlewoman; would have gotten her away from her insufferably perfect little sister; would have given her more time to practice her swordsmanship, especially considering she had wanted for a regular partner as good as Freddie while he was at school. She had long dreamed of the day they would keep chickens, spar every day, and tend their small garden. She would make him tea while he wrote his sermons, and they would be wildly happy together.

But none of that would happen. *Ever.* Freddie was going to marry some Oxford girl. All he wanted Evadne to do was to meet her.

"Well!" said Evadne brightly. "She must be a treasure. Constant, patient, and willing to serve her husband and God in the north, away from everyone she knows—"

"She has an aunt in a neighboring county."

"So much the better! A local aunt is always such a delight to a young married couple." Freddie frowned at her flip remark, and she hastily backpedaled. "I very much look forward to meeting her."

"I'm glad." Freddie grinned, his ill humor forgotten. "I hope you like her."

"Why?" The question came out before she could stop it. Likely he had meant the sentiment rhetorically.

"Your opinion matters to me, Evadne. I know you will tell me the truth."

They had reached the stables. Freddie handed over the two swords and his mask to one of the grooms and called for his big bay to be saddled.

"The truth, eh? Well, we Grays are old friends of your family," she said. "We can't let just *anyone* spirit our Freddie away. She must be exceptional for us to release you."

"Oh, she is! She's the very picture of feminine grace, and so domestic! And as for her beauty, I might be biased, but other than your sister she's the best looking girl I ever saw in my life."

"That's quite a compliment," said Evadne, doing her best to keep the sourness from her voice.

"Sisterly affection requires you to defend Dorina, I know, but I shall play Paris's role in this matter." Evadne winced to again be reminded of how he had judged her Athena, not Aphrodite, as Freddie swung himself onto his waiting horse. "Tomorrow, then?"

"Tomorrow." Evadne shook his hand, standing on her tiptoes to reach.

"Please give your mother my regards, and explain my absence at tea?"

"Of course."

"Then farewell, Evadne!"

Evadne kicked a clod of dirt and stalked out of the stables as Freddie cantered away. Knowing she would be wanted at tea,

Evadne resigned herself to washing up and pretending nothing was wrong. She took a step toward the house, and then veered off toward the ornamental lake, specifically for the folly on the bank, where it sat dark and shadowed by a walnut grove. A brisk walk and a quarter-hour's peace — she deserved it.

Dorina adored the folly, of course, and had nicknamed it "The Mouldering Mausoleum." A vine-covered Gothic structure that looked a bit like the turret of a castle, it had been erected by one of the previous generation of Grays when such things were fashionable. Evadne couldn't understand its purpose, or the expense of keeping it appearing forlorn and neglected yet still comfortable for picnics, but today she was grateful for the stupid thing when it came into view. It was out of sight of the house, to give the visitor the impression of "perfect loneliness" as Dorina once put it. There, Evadne would be unobserved — at her liberty to let flow the disappointed tears that she felt gathering behind her eyes, heavy and humid as a summer storm.

Her footfalls were muffled by grass as she approached, and perhaps she did feel a bit of "perfect loneliness" as she put her hand on the cool stone. Instead of falling from her eyes, Evadne's tears gathered in her throat, tight and hot, disappointed and angry.

The wind shifted. Evadne was startled when she smelled a whiff of cigarette smoke, and heard an unmistakable giggle. Dorina must be nearby.

Another giggle, though not Dorina's, and then a low, sensual moan accompanied the next waft of smoke. Evadne was intrigued. The noise and odor were definitely emanating from above her. Dorina and a companion must be secreted atop the turret!

It was long past the hour when the family assembled for tea. What was Dorina doing out here? And who was she with?

Quietly, Evadne made her way up the folly's spiral staircase, her hand on the ornate wrought iron banister. Taking every care, she poked her nose around the corner, and gasped.

Looking as comfortable as a sultan on his throne atop a pile of pillows lay Dorina, languidly smoking a cigarette as another girl—Juliana Lennox—alternated between kissing her sister's lips and neck.

Evadne had always suspected her sister preferred the company of women. While that might have bothered some, what actually annoyed Evadne in that moment, as she looked upon the couple, was how happy they seemed.

Dorina had all the luck. A happy surprise, conceived long after the Grays had given up on a son following their daughter's birth, Dorina had been coddled by their parents, cherished by their nursemaid, treated like some rare hothouse flower.

Evadne, on the other hand, was as common as a yew tree, and just as self-sufficient. No one had ever doted on *her*. Dorina had been a lady from the day she was born; Evadne, a sow's ear not even Rumpelstiltskin could spin into a silk purse. The irony was that Dorina's easy manners were mere illusion. Her sister's beautiful smile, her winning laugh, the sincerity she could evoke whenever she needed to apologize, managed to hide her stubborn, secretive, and willful nature. And while Evadne was perpetually disappointed, Dorina had always gotten everything she wanted.

"Dorina Gray!" cried Evadne as she emerged from the stairwell. The two girls shrieked and fell apart. Juliana Lennox looked genuinely terrified; Dorina, after seeing it was Evadne who had rumbled her orgy, looked merely amused as her elder sister strode toward them to loom over them and deliver her scolding. Evadne so rarely felt tall—especially next to her longer-limbed sibling—but now she had the high ground.

"What do you think you're doing here!"

"Don't you know?" Dorina leered back at her. "Don't tell me you really were *fencing* with Freddie all morning?"

"Dorina!" Juliana at least seemed to understand the seriousness of their situation.

"You think it's funny?" Evadne snarled as she snatched the cigarette from her sister's fingers. How she *hated* being laughed at! And Dorina was always doing so—poking fun at her lack of grace, her fencing, her piousness. She could not bear it, not today!

"So you *were* fencing with Freddie?" Dorina smirked at her, and Evadne felt her face go red. "Too bad."

Her sister could not have known it was exactly the wrong thing to say. In that moment Evadne resolved that if she could not be happy, neither would Dorina. "Too bad for *you*," said Evadne. "I'm going to tell Mother *exactly* what I found her daughter doing when she ought to be drinking tea with her family. I think she'll be interested to hear you have no sense of responsibility—no judgment —none of the consideration for others a young woman should exhibit, *especially* given her ill-advised decision to send you off to London on your own. I wonder if she'll ever let you out of her sight again!"

"No!" Dorina's nonchalance turned to panic. She obviously hadn't anticipated this. "Don't—"

"Be quiet! It's my *duty* to tell them." Evadne was already descending the spiral stair.

"Let's talk about this!" cried Dorina as Evadne reached the bottom of the stairs and took off running for the house. But in running, Evadne had the advantage, in spite of being a decade older —her years of training had strengthened her legs and chest, and she quickly outpaced her younger sister.

"Oh, we'll talk about it," she shouted over her shoulder. "With our mother!"

"You wouldn't!" cried Dorina, already falling behind. "Evadne!"

Evadne quickened her pace. As it turned out, there were certain advantages to not being a picture of feminine grace.

2

The natural diabolist is he who feels keenly the pleasure
of a double life.

— *On the Summoning of Demons*

WILL SHE REALLY TELL YOUR PARENTS?" Juliana
sounded as if she might burst into tears.

"Probably," said Dorina—the wrong answer, even
if it was the truthful one. Juliana's fragile control broke, and she
collapsed onto the grass in hysterics, clutching at Dorina's skirts.
Though Dorina knew they must look beautiful to the observer,
like some opulent Pre-Raphaelite painting, she stepped back from
her companion's display.

"We'll be ruined!" the girl sobbed.

"We will not," snapped Dorina. Juliana might be beautiful and
fun, but she wasn't especially bright. "We shall be inconvenienced."

Juliana stared up at Dorina with wide eyes as full of hope as
tears. "What do you mean?"

"Neither of our families are stupid enough to let a single word
of this get out. The worst that might happen would be them separating us." And that wouldn't be *too* terrible—it would save Dorina the trouble of breaking things off with Juliana, who, truth be
told, had already begun to bore her. Most of Dorina's other conquests had understood that a dalliance was by nature casual, but
Juliana *would* go on about finding a way to stay together forever.

"But what, what if they stick us in a"—fat tears began to roll
down Juliana's plump cheeks—"a *convent?*"

What, Dorina wondered, had she ever seen in Juliana? Her eyes strayed to Juliana's ample lace-covered chest, now spattered with damp tear marks, and answered her own question.

"You think they're stupid enough to send us to live with a bunch of women?" said Dorina, exasperated.

"What if they call a priest?"

"Why would they do that?"

"To exorcise us!"

Dorina actually laughed.

"My c-cousin was exorcised," sniffled the girl.

"Really?"

"She was twitching and screaming and cursing . . . They said it must be a *demon*."

"Was this cousin from the fourteenth century? I never heard of anything so barbaric. Who believes in *demons* anymore?" Dorina shook her head. "Was she cured?"

"No," admitted Juliana. "It was some sort of bad mushroom she'd eaten."

"See? Likely our families will attribute our activities to bad habits we learned at school, and we'll be sent to live for a few months with some ghastly maiden aunt or other who won't have novels in her house." Dorina sighed. "And I won't be allowed to go to London."

Juliana's mood shifted immediately. "Oh yes . . . Evadne said. You're going to London? You never told me . . ."

Dorina winced. It was true, she hadn't told Juliana of her imminent departure; neither had she told Juliana of her aspiration to pen a monograph on her uncle and burst onto the scene as a young, brilliant lady art critic. Juliana had no comparable aspirations, and was possessed of a jealous disposition, so it had been easier just not to mention any of it.

Really, how could Dorina be expected to explain her desires to someone who cared nothing for art? Though an avid reader, Juliana considered pictures "childish" and saw nothing of note in the natural world beyond it being "pretty." Dorina, on the other hand, had studied prints of landscapes, but all she had to compare them to was Swadlincote. She was ready, *so* ready, to see more of the world. She longed to observe the city scenes that inspired Toulouse-Lautrec, Renoir, Morisot; to see for herself the paintings of Redon and Matisse; to stand before a real Rodin, Canova, or Van der Stappen. She was tired of living vicariously through journals; she wanted to be at the heart of the London art scene, visiting galleries and exhibitions on opening night, not reading about them after they'd long since closed. No periodical would accept a piece on an exhibition that everyone had already seen and experienced and remarked upon—she knew, for she'd submitted and had rejected those sorts of essays. It was essential to be there for the event itself, and this monograph on her uncle's work would be the stepping-stone from which she would launch a tremendous career.

"I'm just going to visit my uncle," she said. "At least, I was."

Juliana wasn't falling for it. She'd gained her feet, and had her fists pressed to her hips. *"When?"*

"It doesn't matter now, does it?" Dorina grabbed one of Juliana's hands and kissed the knuckles. "Anyway, let's go in. No use dreading what's to come when we can go and find out easily enough."

"Should we tidy the folly?"

"The servants will get it all." It didn't matter now if they found her carefully hoarded tobacco and papers. Dorina could scarcely believe Evadne would omit that particular detail.

As they walked back to the Grays' house Dorina wondered if perhaps she'd misjudged Evadne. Would she *really* rat her out? They'd never gotten along, that was true, but Evadne must know that to follow through on her threat, actually tattling on Dorina to their mother, was a gross breach of sisterly comradeship.

Then again, of the two of them, Dorina had always been the more concerned with things like "sisterly comradeship."

They drew near the ivy-covered back wall of Swallowsroost, the white door peeking through the green expanse like an egg in a nest.

"Should I go in with you?" asked Juliana.

Dorina considered this. "If you leave, you'll have no idea if there's a problem before my family descends upon yours to cry havoc and let slip the dogs of righteous indignation."

"Maybe I'd better stay."

Dorina glanced at her companion. It was obvious Juliana wanted nothing more than to run off. Dorina couldn't blame her. And really, if Evadne had indeed betrayed them, Juliana's hysterics would make the whole scene incredibly ugly, loud, and—worst of all—boring.

It would also be far easier to talk her way out of trouble if Juliana wasn't there, weeping at every accusation.

"On second thought, you should go."

"But—"

"Trust me," she said. "It'll be better if I'm on my own."

"Well, if you think it's best . . ." That gleam in Juliana's eyes! The chit was thrilled to have Dorina throw herself on the sword while she ran away home to her bread and butter.

"I really do. Now go on—I'll send word if I'm able. All right?"

Juliana turned back perhaps half a hundred times and blew twice that many kisses before she was out of sight. Such a mawkish display made it almost a relief for Dorina to finally duck inside.

The house was quiet when she entered. Dorina ambled toward the drawing room, her shoes shuffling on the thick carpet of the hall as she listened for any hint of raised voices, but silence prevailed. Betsy, one of the maids, emerged from where her family usually gathered for tea, bearing an empty tray. Surprised, the girl almost dropped it when she saw Dorina; upon recovering, she stammered that Dorina's mother and sister were expecting her *upstairs*. The way she said it, Dorina knew immediately that something was afoot, but she smiled and nodded—keeping up appearances and all that. She did remember to mention that a footman ought to be sent to the folly to collect her picnicking detritus. The maid curtsied in response before scurrying off.

In spite of everything she'd said to Juliana, Dorina was still surprised to find that her sister had really and truly betrayed her. It hurt her feelings more than she cared to admit, but she would not show it—not to her sister, not to anyone. She pushed an errant lock of dark, wavy hair out of her eyes, shook out her skirts, and composed her face into a winning smile. She wished she had time for a strengthening cup of tea and maybe a strawberry tart, but as Betsy had said, she was expected.

When Dorina opened the door, she found their mother seated, elegant in her lavender tea dress; the traitor Evadne was leaning against the wall, looking surly but also smug in her ridiculous fencing outfit. Dorina tried to read them like a painting—if an artist had arranged them, how should their positions be interpreted? What intrigues could be presumed, given their attitudes, their expressions? What was represented by the streak of afternoon sunlight spilling over the carpet, dividing her from them?

Interpretation was inherently fascinating to Dorina, whether it was art or people. Just the same, she'd rather know the facts.

"Mother, you're looking lovely today, and Evadne, you're looking particularly . . . healthy," she said brightly, breaking the silence. "But I can't help wondering why we're assembling here, leaving poor Father to drink his tea all alone?"

"Dorina," said their mother. "You won't talk your way out of this one."

Under ordinary circumstances, Dorina would have dismissed the idea that she could not talk her way out of something. But their mother was already on her guard, which made things tricky —and even worse, Evadne was there. Dorina had never been able to effectively charm her sister.

Just the same, she had her wits even if she didn't have the element of surprise.

"Talk my way out of what?" she asked, all innocence.

"Do be serious!" Her mother indicated the chair across from her. "Sit. Now. I want to hear exactly what went on between you and Juliana this afternoon. I've heard Evadne's side of things, and now I'd like to hear yours."

Dorina sat obediently. "May I hear Evadne's side?"

"You know very well what I saw," said Evadne primly. For being the only woman in the room dressed in trousers, she was acting like England's most proper young lady.

"I recall you interrupting my picnic . . ."

"Is that *all* I interrupted?"

"Give Dorina a chance to speak," said their mother.

Mrs. Lorelai Gray had been a celebrated beauty in her youth; now in her middle years she was a lovely, elegant, charming woman. When asked what her secret was, she always replied it was marrying for love. Dorina had been told she favored her mother in looks, which was a fine compliment, but she had always been more pleased about inheriting her mother's skill with people.

Dorina decided to start with a bit of the truth. "Juliana and I were together, yes."

Their mother's forehead dipped into her palm as she shook her head. "Oh, Dorina. I really don't know what to say."

Dorina knew what she wanted her mother to say: she wanted to know what her punishment would be. But to ask would be cheeky.

"I'm sorry."

"Sorry for being caught," muttered Evadne.

It took every ounce of Dorina's willpower not to roll her eyes. She'd never understood why exactly, but it had always been like this between the two of them. In spite of Evadne being the elder, she was—in Dorina's opinion—profoundly less mature. Perhaps all the medical journals were right, and exercise did cause women's wombs to wander about their bodies, confusing them and making them subject to queer moods and notions. Dorina looked at her mother, appealing to her with her eyes, but to no avail.

"A whim." It was time to spin a believable yarn. "Juliana's school friend lent her a—I suppose you'd call it a *risqué novel,* and we were just so curious. It won't happen again, I promise."

It was a half-truth. Juliana had come by a sort of periodical called *The Pearl,* and some of the stories contained salacious descriptions of women doing interesting things with women. It had been an eye-opening read for Juliana, to be sure. Not so for Dorina, who had won the hearts of a baker's dozen of Derbyshire's more attractive and discreet young women, from a lowly if lovely milkmaid to Miss Lavinia Ferguson, whose beauty was rivaled only by her dowry. Even so, Dorina had pretended alarm and fascination when Juliana showed her the forbidden book. She had also said all sorts of rot to make Juliana amenable to her advances: "It might be fun to try—are you certain?" "I suppose it couldn't hurt, if we kept it to ourselves." "Will we still be virgins, afterward?"

Dorina could be very persuasive, even when pretending to feel doubtful. That act had worked for her before, and likely it would work for her again. Yes, again—she had no intention of cutting romance out of her life, no matter what she might tell her mother.

Mrs. Gray sighed. "I'm disappointed and concerned," said her mother as Dorina kept her eyes on the toes of her grass-stained boots, "but at the same time, I understand."

"What?" cried Evadne as Dorina looked up, feeling oddly hopeful. *"Mother!"*

"There was a girl, at school . . ." Mrs. Gray smiled vaguely. "Long before I met your father, of course," she explained, mostly to Evadne. "I never went so far as to . . . but if she had asked? Oh, who knows. It was only a phase, and in the end I grew out of it and turned out all right. At least, I like to think so."

Dorina kept her expression neutral. On one hand, she appreciated her mother's candor, especially as it seemed as though she would likely not be punished too terribly; on the other, her mother's equating of "all right" with "learning to like men" annoyed her deeply. This was no phase; Dorina could not think of a time when the male of the species had held any fascination for her whatsoever. Their arrogance did not attract her, the liberties they took did not astonish or titillate her, and their freedom to do what they liked did not impress her. Dorina discarded the lot of them—well, save for her father, and Uncle Basil. Even Freddie was rather limp; in spite of Evadne's obvious enthusiasm for the young would-be vicar, Dorina thought him unkind for stringing her sister along for so many years.

As far as Dorina could tell, that was the sort of thing boys did for fun.

No, she would not grow out of preferring women to men. But it was certainly in her best interest to pretend she might.

"Who cares if she gives up girls or not?" Evadne's question surprised Dorina. "The issue is whether she can be trusted in London, after demonstrating so perfectly that she cannot be trusted to come to tea on time. This is a serious matter, Mother. There should be consequences. She will represent not only herself, but our family name, and if she should besmirch it through wildness and—"

"Besmirch?"

"Girls!" They fell silent as their mother gracefully rose and walked over to her mahogany desk. For the first time since Dorina had entered, the girls exchanged a look not full of rancor. What, they asked one another with their eyes, could their mother be doing?

"There will be a consequence for your sister, Evadne, though it is not for you to tell me how to raise my daughter," said Mrs. Gray as she opened a drawer and retrieved a letter. She turned, looking severe. "Evadne is right, Dorina. You have betrayed my trust. I do not say this because you were with Juliana—I say this because a young woman cannot be too careful with her reputation, especially if she hopes to marry well. Therefore, I shall alter your London trip."

"Oh, but Mother—"

"I am not canceling it," said Mrs. Gray. "That would be cruel; I know how much you have longed to go. But I fear you will be too much for Basil to look after. Therefore, I have no choice but to command your sister go with you."

It was Evadne who cried "Mother!" this time.

Her sister was a character study in fury, her fists clenched at her sides, face red, back straighter than her silly swords. She would have made the perfect model for Isabella, before sticking her lover's head in a pot of basil, or Guinevere, standing over Lancelot and Elaine.

"I had a letter from your uncle a few days ago, asking if you would like to come along with your sister, Evadne; I hadn't thought to mention it, knowing your opinion of London. This seems a perfect compromise, however, as before your sister arrived all you could talk about was her need for supervision." Dorina shot her sister an indignant look; Evadne sniffed and turned her nose up. "Now *you* can supervise her." Evadne began to protest, but their mother held up her hand. "You claimed to have Dorina's best interests at heart when you told me everything, did you not?"

There was nothing Evadne could say to that; their mother had won. Dorina was elated, but was wise enough not to show it. She was still going to London—that was all that mattered!

"I suppose you'll need some new clothes, Evadne," said Mrs. Gray thoughtfully. "You can't possibly go to London wearing your" —she gazed at her elder daughter—"current fashions."

"My clothes are fine."

"Not for town. We'll go tomorrow. We've barely a fortnight to get everything ready for your journey, so—"

"Not tomorrow," said Evadne quickly. "It can't be tomorrow."

"Why ever not?"

"We're to go to dinner."

Mrs. Gray looked puzzled. "Really? Where?"

"Freddie's house." Evadne was blushing terribly. "Mrs. Thornton has invited us. To celebrate . . . his return."

A quiet descended upon the room in the wake of this announcement. The Thorntons, being of humbler means than the Grays, rarely invited them to dinner, and Dorina would have bet fifty pounds it meant Freddie had finally—*finally!*—proposed. Mrs. Gray also looked like she'd take that bet, too; she was staring at her daughter, trying not to smile too broadly. Dorina, however, did not hide her emotion.

"Evadne!" she exclaimed, moving to embrace her. "I'm so happy for you!"

"As am I," said their mother. "I'll send a servant to tell them we'll all be *delighted*."

Evadne did not look as pleased as she should, and she pushed Dorina away with more than necessary firmness. "There's nothing to be happy about," she said stiffly. "It's just dinner."

"Oh, Evadne. If Freddie hasn't proposed yet, surely he intends to," said their mother.

"No. Freddie is . . ." To her surprise, Dorina could see her sister struggling. "He's engaged. *She'll* be there too. He wants us to meet her, as we're friends of the family." She shrugged. "They've had an understanding for years."

Dorina's mouth fell open. All her ire toward her sister evaporated and condensed into outrage on her behalf. "Well I never! I can't believe he'd do that to you!"

Evadne tutted at her.

"He hasn't wronged me in any way," she said loftily, but Dorina could tell she was really quite upset.

"Yes he has!" declared Dorina, looking to their mother. Mrs. Gray did not look pleased. "Years! What are *years* to the devotion you've shown him for decades! The nerve of that . . . that rascal!"

"Freddie is blameless," said Evadne, but Dorina heard an ominous trembling in her voice. "He is following his heart, and I wish him joy."

Dorina couldn't believe what she was hearing. "His heart! His joy! What about your heart? Your—"

"Stop!" cried Evadne. "You're being a child about this! We're going—and we'll be polite!" With that, she fled the room, slamming the door behind her.

"Oh dear," said Mrs. Gray after Evadne's footsteps had retreated. "Perhaps this London trip will be good for you both. She will need a distraction. Poor Evadne. She's counted on him for so long!"

"You agree with me, don't you, Mother? That he treated her unjustly?"

"Whether I do or no, Evadne's feelings are the ones I'm most concerned with right now."

Dorina felt the rightness of her mother's admonishment. "Of course. I shall be polite. For her sake, not his, tomorrow."

"Good. And as for now, I forbid you from disturbing your sister. Let her feel her pain in private." Dorina nodded. "But, before you go . . ."

"Yes, Mother?"

"I do not wish you to think I am condoning your behavior with Juliana by allowing you to go to London. I seriously considered punishing you by canceling the trip, but I choose to believe you when you say this was a singular indiscretion." Dorina held her mother's gaze, even if privately she was cringing. "*Do not* betray my trust or insult Basil's generosity by behaving outrageously, do you understand me? Embarrassing yourself and this family while you are in London will have serious consequences for your later life. So keep away from girls like Juliana, with their novels, all right?"

"Yes, Mother."

"Don't you 'yes, Mother' me," said Mrs. Gray. "I know your ways, my dear, and you're not half so sincere as you pretend, while being twice as earnest as you'd like anyone to believe. Trust me when I say you court danger if you let your heart rule your head, especially at your age."

"I understand," said Dorina. "I do, really. I promise."

"Then go and occupy yourself in whatever way you find most intelligent," said her mother. "As for me, I shall go and reassure your father that everything is fine before writing to your uncle to let him know Evadne will be accepting his kind invitation."

Dorina kissed her mother on the cheek and walked calmly from the room, but once outside, she allowed herself a little jump of triumph. She was still going to London! Even with Evadne watching over her, she would have the grandest time, she just knew it.

3

Demons are present in the world of men even when no image of them can be found. Their presence is asserted as a suggestion, a manner. They can be sensed in the curve of a line, in a heady fragrance, in the subtleties of certain colors.

— On the Summoning of Demons

L OOKING EAGERLY AT THE LONDON streets beyond the cab window, with her nose and hands pressed against the glass and her feet tucked up under her bottom, Dorina looked much younger than her seventeen years. In spite of her annoyance at being in London, it brought a smile to Evadne's lips to see her sister so excited. She had been rather cross with Dorina for most of their journey — and most of the days leading up to it, truth be told — but in that moment she felt a surge of affection for her, remembering the family trip they'd all taken to Brighton over a decade ago.

Then, Dorina had clambered over their mother's lap, sitting in nearly the same posture to get her first look at the sea. How she had shrieked with joy to see the waves! Not Evadne, though — she had sat quietly, tall enough to see for herself, but unsure if she liked the gray, undulating expanse. Neither the strangeness nor the size of the water had impressed her.

She felt a similar sense of unease regarding London.

Dorina had been so different back then . . . The stunning young woman across from Evadne bore little resemblance to the little monster who had skinned her knee tumbling out of the coach

in her excitement. Her curly hair had stuck out at all angles before it matured into the cascade that tumbled down her back
when it wasn't pinned up; her nose had been round as a button
before lengthening into the straight sweep envied by all the girls
in Swadlincote; her arms had been chubby sausages, which time
had stretched and re-formed into the graceful limbs ending in the
slender — if ink-stained — palms and fingertips now on display for
London's passersby.

Dorina had changed in other ways, too. She used to think of
things other than herself and her own pleasure, for instance. Yet
even when Dorina had been less focused on herself, the two sisters
had never really gotten along. Like during that family trip to Brighton . . . Evadne's smile faded as she remembered the day Dorina had
nearly drowned — or so it had seemed to Evadne at the time.

Heedless of their mother's warnings, Dorina had swum out too
far only to panic when her feet no longer touched the sand. How
she had screamed! Believing her sister to be in real danger, Evadne
had shed her dress and struck out after her, thinking of nothing
but saving her, and quickly. Evadne remembered the taste of the
salt water, the cold against her bare skin, the shouts of her mother
and father. In the moment, she'd thought they were worried for the
safety of both their daughters; as it turned out, they had been calling to Evadne, telling her not to worry, that Dorina would be fine.
The area where the young children went swimming had been cor-
doned off by a net, guarding them against the capricious current.

Evadne had realized that when she reached Dorina, who by
then was happily clinging to a sturdy rope, and felt the embarrassment keenly after bringing her sister back to shore. Dripping
and exposed in her sodden shift, she'd shivered as Dorina gig-
gled in their mother's arms — in fact, every one at the beach had
laughed, even Evadne's parents. Only Evadne had found nothing
funny about the incident.

Over the years, Evadne had been forced to endure hearing the story told and retold. The laughter had continued, Dorina's theatrics always the star; Evadne's unnecessary rescue the punch line.

Turning away, Evadne caught sight of her own face reflected in the window. Dorina might have changed dramatically since their trip to Brighton, but Evadne looked much the same: broad of forehead and shoulder, grim of countenance, her hair never holding a style or her body a dress—not with any grace, at least, as evidenced by how she looked in her new and fashionable pearl-gray walking coat and skirt. The clothes were nice enough, save for the shoes, which still pinched, but the waist was narrower than Evadne liked, requiring more severe corseting, which in turn made her sit up straighter than she wanted to.

She had argued as hard as she could against the cut, but her mother hadn't listened to a word of it—Evadne must look presentable, even if she would not be appearing in proper London society. Her preferred loose jackets and skirts, casual shirtwaists, and boots, fine for tramping over hill and dale, were not appropriate for traipsing about town.

The worst part was, this outfit was one of the more reasonable of her new wardrobe. Her tea dress was not to be contemplated —with so much lace and pleating, she might as well be wearing a wedding cake. Well, she'd packed several pairs of tweed bloomers, too. Dorina would just have to deal with Evadne being comfortable every once in a while.

Evadne's smile almost returned as she contemplated what else she'd snuck into her trunk: her epee, fencing mask, and practice leathers. Her mother had seen them set out and protested their inclusion—when would Evadne find the time to fence?—but Evadne had secreted them in the bottom of her trunk the night before they left.

She had her reasons; she just didn't wish to discuss them with anyone.

Dinner with Freddie had been as mortifying as Evadne had

imagined it would be. Mr. and Mrs. Thornton had been excited and gracious; her parents and sister sober, their restraint bordering on disapproval. Of course Freddie had noticed, and it had made him tense. He'd fumbled over the grace he said before supper, and seemed overly anxious to champion his future bride to his old friends, especially after Dorina turned her nose up at the girl as if she were some despised dish at the table.

Evadne alone had treated Miss Bell with the respect she was due, shaking hands with her and drawing her into the conversation when it became obvious that half the guests were determined to ignore her. It hadn't been easy, but it had been the right thing to do, especially with her family being so stiff and unpleasant. But of course, that was Evadne's lot—she might be unfeminine in her appearance, but she could and would be a lady, even in the face of disappointment and heartbreak.

She had been rewarded for her forbearance, after a fashion. No, Freddie hadn't realized the error of his ways, leaping up to propose to Evadne as she made small talk with Miss Bell, but as the evening wore on, he'd taken Evadne out for a walk in the fresh air, just the two of them, when his fiancée entertained everyone else at the piano.

"So you are to go to London with your sister," he'd said, leading her down the garden path, her arm threaded through his.

Evadne had nodded in the starlit darkness. "I shall miss your wedding, I'm afraid."

"Oh, that's all right." Evadne had tried her best not to notice the obvious relief in his voice. "I know you wish me all the best."

"Of course."

"And I wish you all the best, too, Evadne," he'd said, patting her hand awkwardly. "I shall be gone once you return, and I don't know when I'll be visiting again. My parents have already declared we shall have Christmas in Middlesbrough, and after that, with any luck Miss Bell and I shall have a family to think of . . ."

Evadne had not known what to say, so she'd said nothing. She had not been particularly keen to join Freddie when he'd asked her, but he'd seemed so insistent, so full of purpose, that she had found herself unable to deny his request.

"You know, Evadne," he said after a pause, "were I not so in love with Miss Bell I would envy you."

"Oh? Why is that?"

"Because you are free to do what you like! London will be such an adventure."

"You think so?" Evadne had not been able to keep the incredulity from her voice.

"Yes!" Freddie had latched on to this. "I've taken the liberty of writing you a list of London activities you might enjoy . . . There are several good fencing supply shops you could explore, for example. And, well, you're always so attuned to what is proper, I'm not sure if you'd be interested, but . . ."

"But what?"

"Well, I wrote down the name and address of a friend of mine, George Cantrell." Evadne stared at Freddie, not quite understanding what he might possibly be suggesting. "George was a top-tier fencer when we were at Oxford together. And he was also a divinity student, which is why I knew him so well—why I've kept in touch, I mean. He lives in London now, and he teaches sport-fencing lessons at an academy, one of the best in London. Bit of a queer fish, but . . ."

"Queer how?"

"George always had a bit of a chip on his shoulder. Scholarship student, you know . . . didn't come from the same sort of family that many of us did. Seemed to always feel he had something to prove. It made him . . ." Freddie looked embarrassed, as well he might. "I realize I'm not making him seem appealing, am I?"

"No indeed." Evadne was, frankly, scandalized by Freddie's suggestion she might call on some stranger—some strange *man*—

just to enquire after fencing lessons, but she also knew Freddie was trying to be kind.

"At any rate," Freddie continued, "he's a good sort, George, and devilish talented."

"Thank you for the recommendation." Evadne was yearning for this interview to be concluded. She was just trying to think of a way to extricate herself when Freddie did it for her.

"I have it all written up already—the list, I mean, of things to do. And George's address. Shall we return to the house? I can pop upstairs and get it while you . . ." He sighed, then said, "Thank you for being so kind to Rose, Evadne."

"How could I not be? She's lovely."

"I'm so glad you approve."

What else could she do, really, other than reassure him? And though she was still so very disappointed, so very hurt, Evadne had done so—just as she had gone inside with a smile on her face, to rescue Miss Bell from the awkward conversation of her emotional sister and distant mother. Not only that, but she had made small talk until Freddie had returned and surreptitiously slipped his missive into the folds of her shawl. She'd thanked him with a smile, even though at the time she felt she could safely say she would *never* call on Mr. George Cantrell for fencing lessons.

But now that London was all around her, looming outside the windows of the cab, Evadne wasn't so certain. While she was as yet not inclined to seek out this Mr. Cantrell, it was comforting to know she had something secret, something private, something her own waiting for her if she should happen to change her mind.

At least Chelsea was quieter, greener, and far nicer than many of the areas they'd passed through since disembarking at St Pancras that morning. And as the coach slowed, it seemed her Uncle Basil's place was in easy walking distance of St Luke's . . . though, to be honest, she hadn't been quite as enthusiastic about attending services ever since it became obvious she'd never be a vicar's wife.

"We're getting close!" Dorina's enthusiasm was palpable; she shifted on the carriage seat, unable to sit still. "Oh, Evadne, I've never *been* so excited!"

Dorina did not ask Evadne's feelings on the matter. Either she did not care about her sister's state of mind, or she assumed—correctly—that Evadne was less than thrilled to be in London, where the tall buildings cast strange shadows, making her feel closed in and closed off from the world. The city odors seeping through the carriage door were so much less pleasant than grass and sun-warmed dirt, flowers, and fresh water. Evadne sighed, stretching as best she could in the confines of the cab. She did not wish to stumble out on half-asleep, tingling legs when greeting her uncle.

"I wonder if we'll visit a gallery today! Oh, I hope so!" gushed Dorina.

"Personally, I hope to visit a water closet, and then a table with a large luncheon upon it," said Evadne wryly. The train station had been busy; they'd had no time for personal matters, given the number of travelers and scarcity of cabs. It wasn't a long journey to Chelsea, but the bumps were making Evadne regret not insisting on a longer stop.

Dorina turned away from the window to give her sister a disgusted look. "Oh, *Evadne*. Where's your sense of adventure?"

"I had no room to pack it after you demanded I give you some of the space in my trunk for your absolutely essential collection of scarves, and eighth pair of boots."

"Oh, *ha ha*," said Dorina snottily. "Well, perhaps we can ask Mother to pack it up and send it along . . . I'm sure you'll enjoy your time in London much more with it close at hand."

"I'd rather not enjoy London at all, but I hadn't much choice in the matter."

"Think of how I feel. I shan't have nearly as good a time with you glowering at me the whole time."

"If you'd been more discreet or less wayward I wouldn't be here." Evadne knew well enough that she wouldn't be in London if she hadn't rushed off to tell their mother what she'd seen, but she pushed that thought away. She'd done what she thought was right, and she had to live with the consequences.

But had she really done what was right? Or, in a fit of pique, had she tried to ruin her sister's happiness in the wake of her own being dashed to pieces on a straw-strewn stable floor?

Whatever her motivations had been, the result was the same — and so was the truth of the matter. Dorina was impulsive, sneaky, untrustworthy, and selfish. She needed a chaperone, even an unwilling one.

The cab stopped on Cheyne Row, in front of a pretty little brick townhouse with white casements. Set back a bit from the road, shaded by magnolia trees, it was a far more pleasant home than Evadne had expected.

"Well," said Dorina, "I'm certain your unwavering attention will keep me out of trouble. To that end, why don't you get out first, and make sure there are no clods of dirt, turds, or refuse I might slip on my very first moment in London?"

"Don't say turds," said Evadne as the cab door swung open. She blushed when the driver, a roughly handsome young man, rewarded Evadne with a raised eyebrow as he helped her down.

"It's been a pleasure," he said, winking at Evadne as he helped Dorina out and then turned to begin unloading their trunks with the help of some footman or seneschal who had come sprinting out of Uncle Basil's doorway.

Uncle Basil himself was not far behind, but when he appeared, Evadne had to smother a gasp.

Basil Hallward was not a frequent guest at Swallowsroost, but he had come often enough for Evadne to immediately notice how ill and changed he was. Once robust, he looked withered. His thick black hair had gone thin and silver, and it seemed suffering had pooled in the hollows under his eyes. He did not stride out to meet them, but rather toddled along like a much older man.

"Uncle," said Dorina. From her tone, Evadne could tell that she, too, was shocked.

"Girls," he said, extending his hand. Dorina took it gently, barely shaking it. Evadne, too, treated him with delicacy. Had he lately survived some terrible illness? Even his voice lacked its former resonance. "How glad I am you've both arrived. Come inside, you must be famished. We held luncheon for you."

Dorina practically sprinted inside and made a show of cooing over the style and decoration of the entryway, especially the paintings. Evadne had other concerns.

"We?" she asked as she entered his townhouse. "Do you have company?"

"More like family," said Basil. "A dear friend of mine, Lady Henrietta Wotton."

"Wotton?" Dorina whirled. "Surely not *the* Lady Henrietta Wotton who writes for *The Ladies' Conversational Repository?*"

"The same," said Basil, his wracked face splitting into a delighted smile. He instantly looked much younger, Evadne noted. "I'm surprised you know her work—I thought your interests ran to the artistic rather than the botanical."

"A good critic should read broadly," said Dorina loftily.

Evadne was disinclined to discuss the nature of criticism—or critics—while standing in a foyer. "Before we meet your friend, I wonder if we might freshen up?" she asked. Dorina sighed, but Evadne ignored her.

"Of course, my dear niece! How inconsiderate of me. Hannah," he said, addressing a housemaid, "please show the young ladies to their rooms?"

Uncle Basil's townhouse was lovely; even Evadne noticed, though she was distracted by need and hunger. The stairs were wide and well lit, as were the corridors, and the rooms were airy, bright, and comfortably appointed. More pleased than she'd expected to be, Evadne generously told Dorina to choose which of the two chambers suited her more while she availed herself of the modern facilities. Evadne did not especially care for one over the other, their chief difference being the view and the color of the bed linens, but it did not displease her when she returned to find Dorina had decided on the street view, rather than the one that looked down on Basil's patio garden. The greenness of the space was a comfort to Evadne, as were the birds twittering in the shallow marble bath in the center; she would have a bit of nature and wildlife in this strange and dead-feeling city.

With a sigh, Evadne turned from the garden and went to seek her sister—and found that Dorina had already gone down. Annoyed though not particularly surprised, Evadne followed the enticing aromas of luncheon to a delightful little dining room.

Her sister was already deep in conversation with their uncle and a person who must be Lady Henrietta Wotton. Evadne was torn between feeling overjoyed by the sight of food and being completely scandalized by Basil's guest. She took an instant dislike to the woman—she was wearing a man's suit, for goodness' sake! Bloomers were one thing, as they modestly concealed a lady's leg while providing ease of motion, but a man's suit! Why, the woman's bottom was right there, for anyone to look at!

Evadne had expected she would be forced to mingle with Uncle Basil's louche friends, but not so soon after arriving.

"Ah, Evadne!" Basil motioned for her to come closer. "There you are. Come and meet Lady Henrietta—she's been ever so anxious to make your acquaintance."

"Is that so?" Evadne immediately gathered from Dorina's pained expression that she had not come off as particularly warm, but she could not for the life of her think of a single reason a strange woman might be "anxious" to meet her — *especially* a woman like Lady Henrietta Wotton.

"Yes, after everything Basil's told me, I've been quite curious," said Lady Henrietta, extending her hand. The sun shone through her fair hair, lending her a halo, a strange contrast to her rather sardonic smile and devil-may-care manners. "It's a pleasure. Please, call me Henry."

"Curiosity isn't a particularly polite reason to want to meet someone, Lady Henry," observed Evadne, accepting her hand rather hesitantly.

Lady Henry's palm was cool and dry, and she had a good, firm handshake, which Evadne appreciated; in fact, she warmed to Lady Henry considerably, approving of the strength of the woman's grip.

Yet when she let go, Evadne's opinion reversed. Once their hands parted, Evadne got the overwhelming sense that there was something deeply unappealing about the lady — no, something fundamentally *wrong* with her. Not wrong in the sense of moral wrongness or propriety — this went beyond Lady Henry's clothes or her manners. Evadne couldn't explain it, couldn't even put a name to her feeling, but it was alarming, disturbing, and she took back her hand feeling as if she would very much like to wipe it on her skirts. She resisted the urge.

Thankfully, Lady Henry didn't seem to notice anything amiss. "Curiosity is an uncouth way to put it," she admitted, "but Baz has told me you're a ferocious fencer, which is unusual. I take great delight in meeting unusual people."

Evadne bristled, her discomfort with some deeper, more esoteric issue than Lady Henry's manners forgotten. "I wouldn't say it's particularly polite to say I'm *unusual,* either, my lady . . ." She trailed off, staring, as the woman produced a snuffbox from her pocket and took a pinch in each nostril.

Only the faint and delicious odor of ginger reached Evadne's own nose, but she was appalled by this, and not at all impressed. Dorina, on the other hand, had drawn nearer, like a moth to a flame, and clearly wanted nothing more than to take a pinch herself. But before she could even hint at such, Lady Henry tucked the snuffbox away in the inner pocket of her suit jacket. Then she dug out a handkerchief and blew her nose loudly. It was the most horrifying thing Evadne had ever seen a woman do—even more so than wearing a man's suit and cravat to a luncheon with strangers.

Dorina, however, looked like a thirsty man who'd just been handed a large glass of cold lemonade. She was clearly very taken with Lady Henry.

"Shall we eat?" asked Basil, to cover the momentary awkwardness. "You girls must be hungry."

"Famished," said Evadne, grateful to have a reason to break off her conversation, such as it was, with Lady Henry.

"And while we eat, we can discuss what we'll do today!" said Dorina as she took a seat at the table. "I was thinking perhaps we could visit a gallery, and then—"

"Don't you want to take a day to recover from your journey?" Basil looked alarmed. "I had thought you would be exhausted!"

"I don't have *time* to be tired!" Dorina hadn't reached for a single dish; she was too excited. "I'll rest when I'm back in sleepy old Swadlincote with nothing to do but stare at the wallpaper. What's that, Evadne? Oh, thank you." Only with reluctance did Dorina accept the tureen of potatoes. Evadne, on the other hand, was already reaching for the cold ham.

"What are *you* hoping to see in London, Evadne?" asked Lady Henry, startling her—Evadne was used to being treated with as much regard as a decorative plant when Dorina was around. Then again, Lady Henry *was* a botanist . . .

"I hadn't thought about it," she said. "My journey here was so lately decided, I spent all my time preparing, and none planning."

"Well, I may be flattering myself, but I believe myself to be an excellent tour guide, and would love it if you would allow me to show you about? At the very least you must come and visit me in Curzon Street. I could show you my greenhouse! Being country girls, it might replace your bountiful nature for a few brief moments."

Evadne popped a potato into her mouth to give herself time to think of a way to politely decline the invitation. In spite of the tempting break from London her greenhouse offered, Evadne was not much interested in associating further with Lady Henry. Unfortunately, her pause gave Dorina exactly the opportunity she'd been looking for.

"I'd *love* to!" she exclaimed. "I'm very curious about your botanical researches, Lady Henry; I'd no notion I'd be so lucky as to meet you or I should have prepared questions in advance. Do you really cultivate a witch's garden, like you said in your article in the *Repository*?"

"Basil Hallward!" It was a relief to Evadne when Lady Henry's gaze slid to her uncle. "You didn't tell me Dorina was interested in horticulture!"

"I didn't know until today," he said, shrugging as he sawed at the ham.

"I'm interested in *everything*," said Dorina earnestly. "Really, I thought that article was one of the most interesting things I'd *ever* read. The idea of witches' gardens being a treasure-trove of specifically women's knowledge was remarkable! You're right, we do dismiss the idea of 'old wives' tales' but there's so much prejudice in that statement! While today we may go to a pharmacist, how many of their remedies are rooted—so to speak—in women's garden wisdom? If you'd be so kind as to let me see some of the plants you were discussing I'd absolutely love that."

"I say!" Lady Henry had scarcely sampled her luncheon, either. "And here I thought Evadne would be the one anxious to get her hands dirty while you'd be eager to run off and stare at pictures."

"Oh, I *am* eager—I am!—but so many painters are familiar with flower lore, and the significance of plants, that learning about it firsthand from someone as knowledgeable as *you* will help me become a better critic one day! After all, Uncle Basil frequently puts flowers in his paintings, so my monograph will only be enhanced if I can comment on the symbolism."

"I underestimated you, Dorina," said Lady Henry approvingly. "Basil said you wanted to write about art, but as you are so young I didn't take your ambition seriously enough. I apologize—and to make it up to you, I'd like to offer you the opportunity to come dig in the dirt with an old woman anytime you like . . . perhaps when you need a break from all those museums and galleries."

"Old! Why, you cannot be more than five and thirty!"

"Can I adopt her, Baz? Would her parents object, do you think?"

Looking from Lady Henry to Dorina, Evadne wondered if she should be concerned. They both seemed quite taken with the other, and Evadne did not see how Lady Henry could possibly be a good influence on her sister.

"I've never had a companion," mused Lady Henry, finally spearing a potato with her fork, "but these days it's so fashionable to keep some young, beautiful creature close at hand. Perhaps I ought to consider it."

"You should ask her mother before you propose such a thing," said Basil, to Evadne's dismay—surely he ought to shut down this particular notion *immediately*. Evadne was just about to say something to this effect when Lady Henry remembered she existed.

"You'll come too, won't you, Evadne?" The woman's smile was more polite than enthusiastic now that it was turned on her. "If you've no urge to look closely at root and leaf and stem while learning their lore, I assure you, there is no finer place in London to settle in with a good book."

"Oh, Evadne doesn't *read*," said Dorina dismissively, mortifying her sister without the slightest idea she'd done so—or maybe

she did know, and didn't care. "At least not anything you'd pe-
ruse in a fragrant bower. If you've some dog-eared fencing manual
you might tempt her; she cares only for swords and sticking them
into things." Dorina leaned in conspiratorially and said, "I tell you,
though, if we can but convince her that London is worth seeing,
she'll be our eager bodyguard. Her ferocious expression will deter
any pickpockets or murderers."

"I can't imagine anything more wonderful than a gallant knight
in petticoats," said Lady Henry, but Evadne, too embarrassed to
speak or look up from her ham and potatoes, would not meet the
lady's eyes. "Let's make this happen. Tomorrow morning why don't
you both come call on me in Curzon Street, and then after luncheon we'll go out and see some art."

Evadne thought it better to decline the invitation, but Dorina
was already nodding an enthusiastic yes—and after Uncle Basil declared that he was ever so pleased they were settling in so
quickly, Evadne couldn't bring herself to refuse.

As Evadne listened to Dorina and Lady Henry, she grew increasingly depressed about the weeks—the *months*—she would
be staying in London. She already felt so useless. Their mother
had commanded Evadne to be a good influence on her sister, but
at this rate, she would have to chain Dorina in the cellar to keep
her away from unsavory types, as they were clearly welcome to
come to lunch at their uncle's anytime they liked.

Yes, by the time they stood up from the table, Dorina and Lady
Henry had planned to meet not only the following day, but several
more times that same week, and it had been agreed that Evadne
would come, too, though they assumed rather than asked if she'd
be happy to join them. Evadne consoled herself with the thought
that they'd at least spend tonight in a quiet fashion, just family.

"Well, I must away," said Lady Henry, generating further ill
will from Evadne when she opened up a silver case to light up

an oddly spicy-smelling cigarette; at least she did not offer one to Dorina. "Meeting with my lawyer, what a bore! But it can't be helped."

"I can't wait to see your greenhouse tomorrow!" Dorina could scarcely stand still. "I think I shall *dream* of gardens, I'm so excited!"

"It's been a pleasure, Lady Henry," said Evadne. Dorina rolled her eyes. Enthusiasm trumped propriety when her sister dealt.

"It has been. And you know, they *do* say never to put off until tomorrow what you can do today," said Lady Henry. "I think they mean that to apply to work, but it ought to apply to pleasure, too. So, let's go to dinner tonight—what do you say, Basil? Shall we have a bite at the Criterion, say around nine?"

"Dine out!" exclaimed Evadne, astonished. "Three women, eating in a restaurant? Why, we shall be arrested! I never heard of such a thing in my life."

"Tosh," said Lady Henry. "They know me at the Criterion. London is a very modern city in its attitudes; we will see other women there, my dear, I assure you."

"I'd love to go. I mean, if Uncle Basil says we may," said Dorina.

Basil hesitated, looking from one sister to the other, but Evadne knew Dorina would win before he spoke.

"I suppose a celebration is in order, seeing as it's your first night in town," he said, turning to Evadne. "But you and I could always stay home if you'd rather get to bed early . . ."

Evadne shook her head. "Not at all," she said. "I'd be delighted." That wasn't the truth, but there was no way she would allow Dorina to eat in public without an appropriate chaperone.

For her part, Lady Henry seemed genuinely pleased they'd all go together. "Wonderful!" she said. "See you then!"

As Lady Henry shut the door behind her, Evadne finally felt how exhausted she was. The long journey had taken its toll on her, and even after a refreshing repast she was ready to put her feet up.

"May I see your studio now, Uncle Basil?" Dorina said, clearly ready for more excitement.

"If you like," said their uncle. "Evadne, would you like to ..."

"I'm going to go unpack," she said firmly.

Dorina blinked at her, astonished that someone might wish to unpack her things and settle in upon arriving in a new house.

"Don't have too much fun, Sister," she said.

"I never do," Evadne assured her.

4

Never let anyone tell you demons are unnatural things—
they are perpetual, like fragile flowers that blossom anew
each year, like the majestic pine that never goes brown.

— *On the Summoning of Demons*

T HEY HAD STARTED WITH OYSTERS and champagne
beneath the golden, vaulted ceiling of the Criterion, and
then moved on to salads and lamb dressed with mint and
summer peas. Evadne was impressed in spite of herself; the food
was as spectacular as their palatial surroundings—especially the
ices, and the spread of cheeses, fruits, and chocolates that arrived
at the end of their meal.

The quality of the dinner did not, however, make up for the fact
that despite Lady Henry's assurances, they were the only women
in the place. Just as Evadne had feared, Lady Henry had made
them a spectacle their very first night in town. Dorina wasn't even
out, and here she was, being gawked at in the heart of Piccadilly,
where likely every other diner was some personage of note who
could spread a story about the Gray sisters as easily as Evadne was
spreading butter across her bread. It was mortifying to be stared at
as if they were animals in some menagerie—the level of interest in
them was so great that Evadne wondered if any of the other diners
had ever seen a woman before, anywhere. In fact, it was difficult for
her to decide if she was more annoyed by their behavior, or Lady
Henry's lack of propriety in bringing them there in the first place.

Dorina, predictably, took no notice of the others who ate at the Criterion that night—she cared only for Lady Henry. Well, and the oysters. Evadne was pleased to see her sister eating more than she had at lunch, but there were few who could resist such a sumptuous repast, even someone like Dorina, who had once in all seriousness declared that "conversation was food for the soul." But, of course, to Dorina, the one presiding over the table was more interesting to her than anything laid upon it.

To be fair, Lady Henry was a considerate hostess. Perhaps it was the nap Evadne had taken that afternoon, but she enjoyed the woman's company far more during supper, even if she had made them yet more notorious by appearing in full men's evening dress, white scarf around her neck and top hat in hand. Still, she offered everyone choice bits of everything while making conversation so sparkling the champagne seemed flat, and most of the time she spoke not of herself, but of what they should do over the coming weeks and months.

Lady Henry also possessed the gift of holding her tongue as well as wagging it. She did not dominate the night—no, she seemed genuinely interested in Dorina's plans regarding her monograph. She tried her best to draw out Evadne, too.

"You know, Evadne, my brother used to fence when he was at Eton," she said. "He believed it as much an art as music, or painting. He favored the epee . . . well, most of the time."

"An epee fencer!" Evadne perked up now that the conversation had turned to something she was actually interested in. "Did you ever practice with him?"

"Oh no." Lady Henry shook her head. "He was terribly fast and aggressive. Watching him was rather like seeing lightning strike— too terrifying for me. No, I always stuck with the slow crawling of the earthworm, or the unfurling of a leaf."

"A fencer *must* be aggressive," said Evadne. "You must generate explosive power for the strikes, while remaining light enough to retreat quickly."

"You sound just like my brother," said Lady Henry, smiling. "I suppose it comes with the territory. Baz said you've been practicing for years. Do you compete?"

"I wouldn't, even if I could." Evadne blushed furiously at the thought. "I think I should die of embarrassment to show off in front of people! I've only ever practiced for my own pleasure."

"Is that so?" said Dorina, which made Evadne blush all the harder; she kept her eyes fixed on the remains of the cheeses, sensing what was coming next, and dreading it. "I always thought you practiced so you could beat Freddie when he came home for the holidays — not that he didn't deserve it."

"Freddie?" Lady Henry leaned in. "Who is Freddie?"

"A family friend," said Evadne firmly. "We have just congratulated him on his engagement to a lovely young woman."

"How delightful." Lady Henry earned a bit of Evadne's good will by not pursuing the enquiry any further. "Well, fencing for pleasure sounds like a fine way to keep fit. I know Oliver used to enjoy practicing more than competing; he only competed because he was expected to, being so good." Then she grinned across the table at Evadne. "Tomorrow when you come by, if you can *bear* to tear yourself away from my greenhouse, you should look over Oliver's fencing things. Who knows, there might be something you could use."

Evadne was delighted. "I'd love to, if it's all right with your brother. Uncle Basil! Are you all right?" The man sounded as if he had a piece of cheese stuck in his throat.

"Oliver passed away some months ago," said Lady Henry smoothly.

Evadne was mortified, but Lady Henry didn't seem upset; Basil, on the other hand, looked even worse — as if he might burst into tears.

Evadne glanced at Dorina, hoping for help, but her sister looked as though she might begin weeping herself. How ridiculous! She hadn't known the man even existed two moments before—hadn't known his sister before lunchtime today! Evadne stared down at her plate, feeling like the most awkward person ever born.

"You couldn't have known." Lady Henry's voice was composed and gentle. "I should have been clearer; the fault is entirely mine, Evadne. I didn't mean to embarrass you—I was just so very pleased to think that some of Oliver's old things might be used by someone who appreciated them."

Evadne nodded, still not looking up. She knew she ought to say something, accept Lady Henry's apology, but she felt humiliated, furious, and disinclined to be civil.

"Now, Dorina," said Lady Henry, obviously hoping to dispel the tension, "as you and I will be getting our hands dirty, you should plan on changing before we go out. For gardening, I suggest something loose-fitting, durable, and easily laundered."

"I'll just borrow something of Evadne's," said Dorina. "She has plenty of tweedy whatsits and cambric tents."

Evadne was not mollified by either the description of her wardrobe or Dorina's assumption that she could simply borrow whatever she liked without asking. Even so, she said nothing. Dorina would have her way; fighting it would only waste her breath and everyone's time.

"A cambric tent sounds perfect, and very similar to what I'll be wearing, but it will get very dirty. If you don't have anything of your own, I'll loan you something," said Lady Henry. Evadne finally looked up, but when Lady Henry winked at her, she pretended not to notice.

"I have a few old smocks that would likely work, too," said Basil.

"Perfect! Well, it sounds like we have a busy day ahead of us. Perhaps we should all head home to bed, though it's early."

She stood, and Evadne glanced at a clock—why, it was nearly midnight! To think, Lady Henry considered that early!

"Good idea," said Basil, dabbing at his lips a final time before tossing his napkin on the plate.

"You're the only artist I know who's in bed before eleven most nights," said Lady Henry. "You ought to keep later hours—it's more fashionable."

Evadne marveled at the woman. Given his wan appearance, Basil probably ought to have been in bed hours ago. What a thing to tease him about! At least her uncle seemed to perk up at this raillery.

"My duty is to create art, not be fashionable," he replied. "Anyway, didn't you say that getting to know me would cure Dorina of her ambition to be an art critic? I should be wronging her parents terribly if I let her go home thinking all artists are like they are in novels, lying about smoking opium half the day and drinking half the night. It makes one wonder when they have time to paint!"

It might have been the champagne, but Evadne felt a surge of affection for her fussy uncle. The look on Dorina's face after this speech was priceless.

It was scarcely half a mile to her home in Curzon Street, so Lady Henry elected to walk. As Evadne, Dorina, and Basil piled into a cab, Evadne looked over her shoulder at the lady's retreating figure. If she hadn't known better, she really would have mistaken her for a man.

"However did you meet such an extraordinary person?" she asked as Basil closed the door after them.

"Her brother and I were at school together," said Basil. "Oliver was a very good friend."

"I'm sorry for your loss," said Evadne. Her uncle was silent as he stared out the cab window. "Both of you."

"She's always been an odd one, Henry," he said after a moment, "but I don't know where I'd be without her. She looks after me, you know. Makes sure I'm eating properly, and sends my paintings to galleries."

"A good influence, then," said Dorina, looking pointedly at Evadne, as if proving a point.

Evadne said nothing. Even if the lady was a good influence on her uncle, she couldn't imagine the same would hold true for her sister.

"BELLADONNA WAS SAID TO OPEN the inner eye, but really it just causes hallucinations," said Lady Henry, pointing at some plant that to Evadne's eyes looked the same as all the rest of them —leafy, with some sort of berries or fruits on it. "And there you have monkshood, which apparently will help you become invisible, but I haven't tried it personally, as it's also poisonous."

Evadne stifled a yawn. She had come along to see Lady Henry's greenhouse, but while it was lovely, it was also warm and humid, which would have made her feel sleepy even if she'd been at all interested in the lecture. As it was . . .

"But, not everything in a witch's garden will kill you," said Lady Henry, leading them past a fountain where water splashed gaily from a nude nymph's amphora. "Witches need medicine, same as anyone, and a kitchen garden, too. See, here's parsley, thyme, coriander . . . Why, my dill is looking a bit limp." She squatted down, knees in the dirt, to inspect the great feathery bush.

"How fascinating this all is!" enthused Dorina, glancing upward at the bright panes of glass and ornate copper bracings, her arms over her head as she spun in place. She looked rather like a witch herself, with her hair tucked up, a smudge of dirt on her nose, and her curvy body making Basil's smock bulge and ripple in ways it certainly never had before. "It's like being in an enchanted forest, right in the heart of London. I'd never imagined anywhere this peaceful could exist here!"

For once, Evadne had to agree with her sister. Even though some of the glass panels had been propped open to allow in a cross breeze, she could not hear the city around her, even here in Mayfair. If only the paths were more open, she could happily practice her fencing footwork and forget where she was for a bit. But, space being at a premium, there was barely enough room for Dorina's spinning; if she wasn't careful, she'd end up scratched by a rosebush.

"An enchanted forest, and every other sort of place," said Lady Henry, brushing her hands on her workman's trousers as she stood. "A garden can take us anywhere we want to be. I have some desert plants over closer to the border, and of course more tropical varieties." She smiled. "My ginger collection is really quite extensive, even for a horticulturist."

"There's more than one kind of ginger?"

"Oh yes!" said Lady Henry. "Come and see!"

They peered down at what looked to Evadne like more bushes. She tried to see the difference, and all she could come up with was that these leaves were broader, and some were, what was the word? Variegated? Evadne decided she'd been more than polite, and this was probably the ideal time to make her escape.

"If we're heading out after luncheon, I was wondering . . ." she began.

"Oh, of course, you'll be wanting to look through Oliver's equipment," said Lady Henry.

"I'm afraid I'm the sort who appreciates nature as a whole," she said apologetically.

"I completely understand," said Lady Henry. "Dorina, please excuse me. I won't be more than a moment taking Evadne up to Oliver's room."

Evadne blushed. "His bedroom?"

"Yes, everything should still be in his closet," said Lady Henry. "I do hope that's all right?"

"I've just never been . . ." Evadne swallowed.

"Never been where? In a strange man's bedroom? No time like the present—you can't begin any younger, you know."

"I beg your pardon!" Evadne was shocked. The morning had been dull, but up until now she'd been feeling as if the visit had been going well enough. Now, she was ready to take Dorina straight back to their uncle's, no matter how her sister might cry and carry on.

"Forgive me." Lady Henry held up her hands. "I did not mean to offend. I forget sometimes that my sense of humor isn't as polite as it ought to be."

"Don't feel like you have to worry about *me*," said Dorina.

Evadne, seething, opened her mouth, but Lady Henry cut her off by saying, "Come along, my dear, and let's find you some pointy things to coo over."

Evadne really did not like Lady Henry—and very nearly said so—but she felt a bit better once she was out of the heat. The high ceilings and cooler air did much to revive her spirits.

"I'm sorry," said Lady Henry. "Really, I am. I've always been the sort of person to say the wrong thing, and it's getting worse now that I'm an old woman with an entire fortune instead of just half of one." Evadne said nothing, appalled—what sort of creature spoke of a sibling's death in such a callous manner? "See? There I go again, distressing you with my bad manners."

"It is not on my own behalf that I am distressed," said Evadne evenly. "My sister . . ."

"Forgive me, but your sister is far less alarmed by my behavior than you seem to be."

"She is young, and inclined to think less of her future than her present. Even if she does act like some wild thing from a circus, Dorina is a young lady and she ought to remember it. This trip to London . . ." Evadne realized she was speaking more freely than she ought to be. "I was sent along to keep watch over her," she continued, "for she is inclined to act thoughtlessly, and imitate those she finds amusing rather than respectable."

They had reached the second floor of the imposing townhouse and stood before a closed door. Lady Henry had her hand on the knob, but held it there. Now she was the one who appeared astonished, and Evadne realized just how rude she had been. How could she have said such a thing!

Lady Henry recovered her composure quickly. "One day, when you're older, you'll understand how delightful it is to be considered amusing by the young. This way."

As they entered Lord Oliver's bedroom, Evadne tried her best to think of some way to apologize, but her mind had suddenly gone blank. She felt cross and angry—at herself, but also at Lady Henry.

"We had some of his furniture cleared away to make use of it elsewhere," she said, her tone a bit cooler than before. "I'd say you'll have enough space to try on or try out whatever you like."

Evadne wished she could run off, or at least decline the lady's offer to look over the equipment, for she knew she was undeserving of any kindness after her little speech. She tried to find some excuse, any excuse not to pick out presents for herself after being so rude.

"The carpet," she said.

"What's that?"

"I shouldn't like to wear it out. Perhaps I'd better—"

"It's meant to be stepped on, isn't it?"

Evadne winced. "I suppose so."

"Anyway, here's everything," said Lady Henry. "The swords are here on the back of the door, hanging, and his outfits or whatever you call them are clean on the hangers."

"Thank you very much." Evadne sounded stiff, even to her own ears. "It's very kind of you to offer me the opportunity."

"It is, isn't it?" Lady Henry's smile seemed thinner. "Well, enjoy yourself."

Evadne nodded, smiling brightly, but after Lady Henry shut the door behind her, she collapsed into a chair and put her face in her hands. Why had she been so awful? Why was she *always* so awful?

She would just have to see this through, pick over a dead man's kit and accept *something*. To refuse everything would be rude. So she started rooting around, in the hopes of finding one or two items that weren't too expensive.

She quickly realized it was *all* expensive. His gloves were of the highest quality, and likely tailored exactly for him, but they worked well enough for her. She set them aside. His mask fit, too, but she put that back, liking her own better.

His jackets and trousers didn't work at all, being designed for a man, but the swords . . . oh, the swords! When she saw them, Evadne recalled her resolution to limit herself to something small; when she picked up the first one, she forgot it entirely. It was *perfect*—they were all perfect, from the sport-fencing epees to the martial weapons. Evadne desired them all. They were far nicer than hers, and hers were very nice indeed.

In the end, she settled on two epees and a real rapier, which was too heavy for her to do much with but was too beautifully balanced to resist. She looked at them, set out on the bed in a row, deliriously happy, until she remembered two things: *one,* she would have to talk to Lady Henry about what she had picked out, which meant talking to Lady Henry; and *two,* she had lost her only fencing partner. Certainly she could use this equipment to keep up on her drills, as she used to do when Freddie was away at school, but now he was never coming home again. He was gone—and so was she, for that matter.

Evadne sighed. Well, the second concern she couldn't do anything about; she would have to make the most of her situation, as she always had. As for the first, she would just have to eat her shame—swallow her pride—and apologize to Lady Henry.

Apologizing did not come easy to Evadne, though heaven knew she'd had enough practice at it over the years. Given that she stood upon her dignity, apologizing felt rather like having the carpet pulled out from under her feet and falling right on her bottom.

She glanced at the clock. It was not yet time for lunch; she didn't have to go back down yet. But how would she occupy herself? There was the entirety of Lord Oliver's room to look over . . . As embarrassed as she had been to enter a bachelor's bedroom, now that she was here, and alone, and there were no more swords to look at, she could explore to her heart's content.

Her focus had been Oliver's closet, but the room proper contained a dresser, a vanity, the bed upon which her finds now rested. In other words, it was perfectly ordinary, save for how exquisite everything was and the masculine flavor of it all. Even the combs and brushes and bottles of perfume and other toilet objects were ordinary. She unstoppered a phial at random and sniffed. The spiciness of the scent was intriguing, not only because it was bolder than any she would ever consider wearing, but also because it smelled rather like Lady Henry—or at least, her tobacco. Recalling the lady's enthusiasm for her ginger plants, Evadne wondered if that might be it. Evadne had only ever smelled ginger dried and powdered, but it was similar.

Curiously, the mirror before which Lord Oliver had once sat, applying this perfume, was also gingery, though not its odor. The frame in which it sat was made of ginger leaves wrought in metal. Evadne never would have noticed it before, not on her life, but now that she knew—now that she had been taught what to look for—she saw it. They were *variegated* ginger leaves, even.

The paintings were all of ginger plants, too, save for a large painting of Narcissus that was clearly her uncle's work. Evadne inspected all the various renditions of the plant, recognized the same spiky leaves, thick stalks, and conelike . . . *things* . . . with flowers on them. There were no fewer than twelve paintings, each with a distinct varietal; the walls were fairly covered in them. Curious to see if the motif repeated itself elsewhere, Evadne strolled about the room.

She had been avoiding looking at the bed too closely, for it seemed improper to pay too much attention to it beyond as a soft surface upon which she could place the swords — *her* swords, she thought with pleasure — but now that she had a quest, she inspected it. The coverlet was embroidered with a floral motif, though not distinctly gingery. But she only looked at it for a moment, for she noted that above it hung a sword so beautiful it made those on the bed look like the battered old practice epee Freddie had started her with.

The sword was not an English weapon, nor was it Italian or German. No, it was a double-edged Chinese blade, just like the one her uncle had brought back from his time in the military, but far lovelier. A long green tassel hung from the pommel, which, she noted, was shaped like a ginger blossom. And the leather wrapping the grip was tooled with a pattern of ginger leaves!

Evadne clambered onto the bed to get a better look at it. It was a gorgeous weapon, and gleamed as if it had been polished just that morning. Oh, how she wished it hung not here, but in his closet! She would have given up all the other weapons to keep this one. Epees she had, and rapiers were readily available, but a Chinese sword of this quality . . .

She looked again at the clock. Seeing she still had time, Evadne bit her lip — and reached for the pommel. She wanted to hold it, just for a moment, to test the balance, to see how it fit in her hand. Carefully — *gingerly,* even — she grasped it.

A shiver went through her, nose to toes, a physical and emotional experience of pure pleasure. It was a wonderful sword; no, it was a *perfect* sword. It fit her hand as if it had been forged for her use alone, and the balance was just right for her arm, for her strength, even.

Evadne leaped off the bed. Saluting the vanity, she performed several of her epee drills, though the thrusts and lunges weren't quite right for a sword of this type. Regardless, the feel of the blade was astonishing. Freddie had always told her that the best swordsmen treated their weapon as an extension of their arm — she had felt that, occasionally, during good practices. At least, she'd thought she had. This sword made her forget all that. It actually was an extension of her arm; it slashed, dipped, and parried according to her will. Its shape suggested how it ought to be wielded, and soon she felt she had its measure. Standing before Lord Oliver's mirror, she watched herself performing unexpectedly soft and graceful movements that would likely confound any sport-fencer, with devastating results.

It was glorious. She realized that prior to this moment she had only *thought* she enjoyed fencing. With this sword, it was a sensual experience. She could feel every muscle as it contracted, every tendon as it moved; she was keenly aware of her skin under her clothes, knew every drop of sweat as it emerged from her pores to run glorious ribbons down her body. She was supple as a reed, fluid as a swallow skimming the water, bold as a lion shaking its mane.

The clock struck one, and Evadne realized she'd be late to lunch if she didn't hurry; she needed to clean up now that she was all sweaty. But she couldn't resist doing one more sequence with the blade. It just felt so *good*.

"Miss Gray?"

Evadne squawked in alarm. Turning around, she saw a plump, elegantly attired, if not particularly handsome, young man perhaps five years her junior standing in the doorway. He was smiling at her in a way she could not exactly parse; there was amusement in his expression, but also — and more prominently — respect. He wasn't laughing at her. He was admiring her. It made her feel queer. She wasn't quite sure if he ought to be looking at her like that, especially as she could not quite determine what he was. His stance and his manners suggested he was some sort of superior servant, but his clothes were those of a gentleman.

"I beg your pardon," she said, tucking a sweaty lock of hair behind an equally sweaty ear. "I was just . . . just putting this away, as I ought to . . ." She had no wish to relate her need for a bathroom. "I beg your pardon, Mr. . . ."

"Jonas," he said.

"Well, Mr. Jonas—"

"My Christian name is Jonas, forgive me," he said. Evadne amended her judgment of his attractiveness, for his smile was nothing short of radiant. It illuminated his features and cast them into the best light possible, softening them, harmonizing them. "My name is Jonas Fuller, but I prefer to be called Jonas. I am . . . well, it's rather difficult to explain."

Evadne did not quite know what to say, so she turned and placed the sword on the bed. Strangely, as loath as she had been to put it down, she felt an odd abhorrence for the object after she did. It had felt so good in her hand, and yet now that it was out of it, she felt there was something odd about that sword, something she didn't like at all now that she wasn't touching it. Even looking at it unsettled her, so she turned, only to discover that the young man had been watching her backside. She blushed—as did he.

"Well, Jonas," she said, to cover the momentary awkwardness, "are you here to summon me to lunch?"

"I am," he said, recovering quickly. "Lady Henry and Miss Dorina thought you would be too occupied to note the time, but I see they misjudged you. You are a lady who clearly knows when she is wanted." He blushed again.

"Required, at any rate." Evadne ignored the eyebrow that leaped up at this. "The truth is, I got a bit caught up trying out Lord Oliver's excellent swords."

"Yes, Lady Henry said you were a fencer." He stepped into the room. "May I look over what you've selected?"

"Of course." Hope stirred in her breast. "Do you fence?"

"Alas, no," he said. Evadne was surprised to note the strength of her regret. "But, I always enjoyed watching Lord Oliver practice."

"If he was as good as his swords, he must have been magnificent."

"Perfection itself," said Jonas, gazing down upon the bounty on the bed, "and I have always admired perfection—or rather the pursuit of it." He straightened, and looking her in the eye, said, "So few of us ever try to be perfect at anything that I can't help but hold the attempt in high regard, even if it proves ultimately futile."

Evadne wondered if all of her uncle's friends were of such an esoteric turn of mind. If so, she feared that this whole trip she would feel rather like a ham sandwich set out among dishes of caviar and calipash.

"I really couldn't say," she replied.

"No?" Jonas favored her with another smile. "Judging from your interest—and your selections—I feel comfortable saying you've a keen eye for quality as well as a thirst for the sort of variety that does not distract, but rather promotes true excellence. And, if you would allow me to be so bold, I'd note that your, ah, current appearance indicates you drive yourself very hard; even an impromptu practice leaves you . . ."

"Shall I take that as a hint?" Evadne smiled; Jonas's delightful conversation had her feeling less embarrassed about her sweaty state. In fact, Jonas was the first person she'd felt comfortable around since she'd arrived in London. "I confess I had rather hoped to freshen up."

"Then let me show you to where you might do so. Meanwhile, I'll see all your selections packaged up and sent straightaway to Mr. Hallward's," he said, before further confounding her by offering her his arm.

Evadne hesitated, then shook her head. "I'm afraid I must decline," she said. "I don't wish to sully your suit."

"As you like," he said. "I certainly don't mind if you sully me, but I'm happy to respect your wishes."

Evadne approved of Jonas—even his admittedly risqué banter—and his company was not unwelcome as he led her to the nicest bathroom she'd ever seen. After providing her with directions to the dining room, and the information that he would be joining them for luncheon, he left her there.

A cool damp towel to the forehead and back of the neck left her feeling refreshed, and for the first time Evadne felt enthusiastic about the rest of her day. Perhaps Jonas would not only join them for lunch, but come with them to wherever they were going. It was reasonable to assume he might, regardless of whether he was a servant or a guest or a relative. And if he did come, he might talk to her in his pretty, warm manner. She would hardly be bothered by Lady Henry and Dorina prattling on about things she did not care about if she had someone so pleasant by her side.

Evadne did not linger over her toilet. After applying a bit of water here and there and hastily replaiting her hair, she almost skipped down the stairs. But just as she was about to turn the corner into the dining room, she heard her name—and paused.

She knew it was in no way respectable to eavesdrop, but it was Jonas speaking, and she was curious to hear what he would say.

"—will be down presently. She needed a moment to herself first."

"Worked herself into a fine lather, I hope." That was Dorina. "She looked as if she needed it. If Evadne doesn't sweat half a gallon a week she gets this sort of *haunted* look."

"She did not look haunted when I approached her," replied Jonas. "She looked bright and invigorated . . . if in need of a comb, basin, and a bit of soapy water."

Evadne blushed, ashamed she had only given herself a cursory going-over; she ought to have spent more time making herself presentable. It hadn't occurred to her that Lady Henry's friends would prefer to wait for a more elegant companion than appreciate a less polished one who appeared on time. Evadne leaned back against the wall, unsure if she should go back or soldier on.

"I do hope your sister is having a good time," said Lady Henry. "I would do anything in my power to assure it, but I do not seem to be able to put her at ease."

"Oh, I'm certain Evadne is having as good a time as she's able," said Dorina. "She didn't want to come, you know; she's annoyed to be away from Swallowsroost. Well, it's her own fault."

"For coming?" asked Jonas.

"For being sent." Evadne was surprised when Dorina hesitated; surely the girl was eager to convey to strangers every single fact she possibly could about their family and its private discussions. "She expressed to our mother that she did not believe I could be trusted to behave in London. Not without a chaperone."

"Was she correct?" Lady Henry sounded amused.

"Oh, *absolutely*," purred Dorina.

Evadne could listen no longer, but she did not want to barge in, not when they'd all been speaking of her so candidly, and not when she was so furious over being caricatured behind her back. Thankfully, Jonas intervened by changing the subject—and yet, Evadne could not feel wholly grateful to someone who had allowed such a disreputable conversation to go on for so long.

"And here I thought your goal was not to scandalize London society, but to visit galleries and museums," he said.

"Oh, it is, it is!" Dorina said. "I care nothing for London society; I see myself as a sponge, and what I want to do is soak up culture, absorb it into myself!"

"What happens when someone *squeezes* you, I wonder?" asked Lady Henry.

"I shall squeeze myself, thank you—spill everything onto the page via my pen."

Evadne decided to enter then, as they were past her person as a subject. She found them sitting around a small table in a bright and lovely room, sipping something golden from glasses—all of them, even Jonas. So he was not a servant . . . Perhaps he was a cousin?

"Forgive me," she said. "I did not mean to take so long."

"No forgiveness necessary," said Lady Henry, rising with Jonas. "Did you have a good time?"

She enquired so warmly that Evadne almost replied in turn, but then she recalled this woman had let a seventeen-year-old girl blackguard her own sister—had been amused by such a spectacle, had not done anything to guide her or curb her bad behavior. Lady Henry might say she wished she could put Evadne at ease, but it was easy to speak, and another thing entirely to act respectably. Evadne wasn't sure she wished to be in her debt, even now. In spite of her earlier decision to accept Lady Henry's offer, she resolved to decline it.

"I did," said Evadne stiffly. "I thank you."

Oddly, Jonas did not sit back down as Evadne took a chair; rather, to her disappointment, he shimmered out of the room.

"And did you find anything to your taste?"

"All of it," she said. "Unfortunately, I don't think I ought to take home anything. Really, it wouldn't be . . . you know . . ."

"Oh, don't be silly!" cried Lady Henry. "Really, Evadne, it would make me so happy to know Oliver's things were being used for some purpose. I insist on you taking as much of it as you like."

"I cannot." Evadne was very firm, though momentarily distracted by the sight of Jonas when he re-entered, bearing a large bowl of some sort of salad. "Thank you, but I have enough swords at home, and I cannot think where I would store them while I am in town."

"But Miss Gray, I've already given orders to have them packaged up and sent to Mr. Hallward's," he said as he set the dish on the table. "Don't tell me you've changed your mind?"

"Oh. Well . . ."

"What has changed?" Lady Henry looked keenly at Evadne.

"Nothing," she replied, abashed. Desperate to save face, she stammered, "I-I'm delighted to have them. Thank you, they are superb. I shall just have to find some way to repay you."

"Repay me by enjoying them, that is all I ask," said Lady Henry as she dished out salad onto their plates. "Now, as for this afternoon! Dorina's dying to dive into the art scene, and we've decided there's really no better place to start a tour of London's masterpieces than the National Gallery. We can see Raphael's *Ansidei Madonna*!"

"And Miss Gray might enjoy some of the depictions of swords," said Jonas eagerly. "One is featured rather prominently in Van Dyck's portrait of Charles the First."

Evadne did not ask if Jonas would be coming with them; she just said, "How delightful," and made other appropriate noises when needed. Soon enough, Lady Henry and Dorina went back to only acknowledging her in passing, which, if it didn't exactly suit her, was at least to be expected.

5

Men, in our madness, have separated the harmony of soul and body, making our realities vulgar, and our ideality void. When a demon is conjured, some subtle influence of consonance passes from it into us, and for the first time we may see what we have always looked for, and always missed.

— *On the Summoning of Demons*

Tears started in Dorina's eyes as the grand entrance of the National Gallery came into view beyond the wide expanse of Trafalgar Square. Craning her neck to see better out of the coach window, past the lions and pillars and fountain and people, Dorina thought it was ever so fitting that the museum should look like a Greek temple. It was a place of divine worship, after all, but to gods more real to her than any she'd ever found in church — the gods of Art and Culture and Beauty and Truth.

Her stomach fluttered; she was nervous. So long had she anticipated this moment!

"The lovely thing about the National Gallery is that the architecture of the building is almost as beautiful as what it contains," said Lady Henry, before taking a pinch of her spicy-smelling snuff. "The newer Barry Rooms are delightful, and would be worth a look even if they didn't have Italian and British masterpieces covering up the walls. And the mosaic floors are also not to be overlooked."

Dorina eyed the filigreed snuffbox with greed, but as usual, Lady Henry did not offer it to her. Jonas took a pinch; the two of them sniffled and blew their noses as they jolted the final few yards over the cobblestones.

Evadne sniffed, too—out of disgust. Her sister looked as distraught as Waterhouse's *Lady of Shalott*, with her mouth hanging open slightly, and her hands braced on either side of her on the seat.

Dorina kept back a sigh only with effort. It pained her to see Evadne so unhappy. She had hoped that once they arrived in London and all the journeying was over her sister would relax and let herself have a good time. So far, that had not been the case. It was vexing, especially when Lady Henry was clearly doing everything she could to make their trip pleasant and more exciting than it would have been if Uncle Basil had been in charge of them. Dorina loved and admired her uncle, but he was a bit of a homebody —which made sense, him being a working artist and all.

True, she needed to watch him work to write her monograph . . . But she had plenty of time for that. She needed experience and context before she could say anything valuable about her uncle's place in the canon, and that's exactly what she was getting. Being shown around London by an expert would only help.

Help *her*, at least . . . Dorina looked back to her unhappy sister. Perhaps Evadne just needed more time. It was only their first full day, after all. Surely the glories of the National Gallery would make Evadne see that spending time in London was worthwhile, even if she wasn't sweating all over herself in a lonely garden.

"And here we are!" said Lady Henry. They had, at last, arrived, and once the driver opened the door, the older woman hopped out to hand Dorina down, gallant as any beau in an Andreotti painting. Though they connected but for a moment, her touch made Dorina's stomach flutter a second time, but with a different sort of anticipation.

Lady Henry was the most fascinating person Dorina had ever met in her life. Her manners were so free and easy, and she was so intelligent—so unaffected. She was utterly unlike the simple country girls Dorina had wooed back in Swadlincote, or the older women she had watched and admired as they drank tea and verbally dissected everything from the news of the day to one another. Lady Henry was an aesthete, a sensualist who appreciated everything from the feeling of dirt between her fingers to the art of the masters.

Not only that, but she was breathtakingly handsome, with her pale hair and ageless face. Dorina had never been involved with anyone more than a few months older than herself, and she had already contemplated what it would be like to kiss Lady Henry's mouth, which was only distinguished by the fine wrinkles around it, to unbutton her outrageous waistcoats and men's shirts and see what the body beneath them was like. Was all her hair going gray?

And yet, Dorina had no idea if she would ever get to find out. Lady Henry seemed like she should be game for a tumble, but Dorina had no idea how to suggest such a thing. Not to someone with a title, at least.

Evadne declined Lady Henry's assistance when disembarking from the coach, and stood on the curb, looking awkward and out of place while the people cutting through Trafalgar Square surged around her. Dorina walked over to her, threaded her arm through her sister's, and squeezed the impressive bicep there.

"I'm *so* glad you're here," she whispered in Evadne's ear.

Evadne looked genuinely astonished. "Are you?" Her eyes flickered to where Lady Henry was giving instructions to her driver.

Dorina squeezed again, which redirected Evadne's attention. "Of course! You've had to endure listening to me talk in the abstract about all these great works of art—and now we shall experience them together! Isn't that fun?"

"I suppose that depends."

"On what?"

"Whether you'll keep talking about them while we're *experiencing* them."

Evadne was almost smiling when she said this.

"You made a joke!" exclaimed Dorina, delighted.

"A joke!" Lady Henry was there, Jonas hovering just behind her. "Can I hear it?"

Evadne snapped shut like an oyster. "It wasn't really a joke," she said, to Dorina's dismay.

"Oh," said Lady Henry. "Well, I'm sorry to have missed the moment! Shall we go in?"

Evadne nodded once, brusquely, like one of those comical counting horses, and took off for the entrance. The somewhat portly Jonas trotted to catch up with her, puffing a bit. Dorina watched them intently, curious to see if this young man might succeed where the lady had failed, and indeed, Evadne slowed her pace when he called to her.

That was good. Dorina suspected Jonas might have taken a liking to her sister, which was adorable, but it also meant it was Lady Henry who was devastating her sister's mood. Why that was, Dorina couldn't begin to conceive. All she had done was be pleasant and personable! Evadne usually took her time warming up to everyone, but still . . .

"They seem to get on well." To Lady Henry's credit, she did not mention Evadne's coldness toward her.

"Jonas is delightful," said Dorina. "But I'm curious. Is he . . ."

Lady Henry seemed to understand. "Jonas was my brother's valet," she said. "Now, he is mine, when I have need of one. It's awful of me, retaining him I mean, being a woman and all. As far as I'm concerned he's the best valet in the world, so I know I'm depriving some worthy person of his skill. But Jonas is also my friend, and keeping him to myself means I can be certain he's as well taken care of as he takes care of others."

In spite of herself, Dorina was surprised. Living with a man, even one who was in part a servant, was rather more louche than she'd expected even from Lady Henry. Evadne would be scandalized when she found out.

If she found out . . .

"Well, my dear, what are you most eager to see?" said Lady Henry, distracting her from such thoughts. "Foreign masters, or domestic geniuses?"

"Don't force me to choose!" cried Dorina, clasping her hands to her breast. "It is like asking me which of your delightful plants I was most excited to meet."

"If you want to be a critic, you'll have to start choosing," said Lady Henry as they ascended the stone steps. "You must declare some pieces better than others; you must decide what is good and what is rubbish, just like as a gardener I must decide which growing things are weeds to be pulled out and discarded, and which are shoots to be nurtured and encouraged until they blossom. But this is an imperfect analogy, for your job does not stop with recognition, nor does it begin with nurturing. No, it is your task to help those with less discernment develop some, and you must do that by taking a stance and declaring why you're correct in a way everyone can understand. Your job is to wield a pen like a meat cleaver."

"A meat cleaver!" Doubt crept into Dorina's heart for the first time. A cleaver was as much a weapon as a tool, and all Dorina wanted to do was draw with words what painters did with brushes and oil, to carve with ink as sculptors did with chisels. "How can that be?"

"A butcher knows what ought to be trimmed—and what's a choice cut. Critics cannot love uncritically."

"Of course." Dorina fell silent, a bit in awe of her companion. She had never in her life thought about art criticism that way, though of course she had read plenty of scathing reviews of gallery exhibitions. She, however, had always wanted to share her love, not her disdain, with the world. Perhaps that was childish . . .

"You seem troubled," said Lady Henry, pausing before the grand doors, in the cooler shade behind the thick Corinthian columns. People were everywhere around them, but Dorina saw only Lady Henry.

"Perhaps I am," said Dorina, happy to hesitate before stepping inside the National Gallery, even if the reason was an awkward conversation. She'd anticipated this moment for so long that to charge right in like a dog after a squirrel seemed anticlimactic. "It's just, I have never been to a gallery or museum. I'm more eager to see and absorb than judge and dismiss . . . but what, then, does that make me? Not a critic . . ."

"Forgive me," said Lady Henry, tenderly sweeping an escaped lock of Dorina's hair away from her eyes. "You know so much about art I completely forgot it was all theoretical. How important a moment this must be for you! It was rude of me to lecture you on what you ought to be, when you are trying to find out who you are. One cannot train a plant until it has sprouted—I of all people should know that. Let us go in, then, and see and feel and breathe and *be*. How does that sound?"

Dorina fought the urge to grab the lady's hand and kiss the palm; the impulse, or the resisting of it perhaps, gave her strength. "I'd like to go in," she said, conquering her nerves. "I think."

"You think?"

Under any other circumstances Dorina would have been perfectly content to remain where she was, gazing at Lady Henry, taking in every part of her. But they were standing before the National Gallery, and people of all sorts were going in and coming out, and Dorina could scarcely remember a time when she hadn't wanted to be one of them. She looked in past the doors, and saw the shadowed interior full of . . . *everything*.

She wanted to say yes, but her throat had closed up tight, and her tears had risen again. Lady Henry seemed to understand. She took Dorina's hand, and like Saint Peter at the gates, led her inside.

DORINA HAD YIELDED TO LADY Henry's wisdom regarding visiting the National Gallery first because she respected the woman's knowledge, but also because she knew it was often a good idea to give in to those one had a mind to win over. She hadn't really expected to enjoy the paintings of the old masters as much as those modern artists she idolized.

Almost immediately she realized her error. Standing before the rich pigments and elegant brushstrokes of so many Italian, Dutch, and English painters humbled her . . . It felt like an awakening, as arousing as a lover's touch, but as soothing as a cup of tea.

The four of them made their way slowly from room to room. They didn't always look at the same paintings at the same time, but when they came together, their conversations were always interesting—at least, they were to Dorina, who had never had the pleasure of hearing what other people felt about art. Critics she could quote, but as for those who had no pretension to expertise, their observations were wholly new to her, and therefore fascinating.

Evadne was one who had no such pretensions, and perhaps because of that she had been having a difficult time. At first, Dorina had thought her sister might be a good sport about the visit, as she had bought them all museum guides out of her pocket money, but several rather acid remarks had escaped her mouth as they wandered, the most amusing of which had been her dismissal of what she deemed "an entire art movement dedicated to painting cow-eyed Dutch women standing beside breadboards." Neither was she impressed by the narrative-heavy, classical scenes of the Renaissance, such as Titian's astonishing *Bacchus and Ariadne,* but Dorina could not tear herself away from the enormous painting, glorying in the deep blue of the heavens, the rose-pink of the god's mantle, the rich browns and golds.

Evadne stood beside her, her arms folded over her chest, lips pursed, guide crinkled up in her hand.

"What do you think?" asked Dorina.

"It's very beautiful."

"You like it?"

"I'm not sure if I *like* it. I didn't say that." She squinted at it. "I know who Bacchus is, but what is he supposed to be doing here, exactly?"

Dorina was only too delighted to have this conversation with her sister. "That woman is the abandoned princess Ariadne, left on Naxos by Theseus—the fellow who defeated the minotaur."

"Why did he abandon her?"

"Accounts vary," said Dorina. "But, it's agreed upon that she was discovered by Bacchus, who fell in love with her, and made her his queen. She gave him many sons, and her wedding crown was set into the heavens to honor her—that's her constellation up there, you see?"

"He's in love with her? It looks like he's attacking her." Evadne's head was canted to the side rather like a dog puzzling out an unfamiliar command. "She looks terrified."

"Ariadne *is* terrified by Bacchus's approach with his followers, but he's not attacking her. He's leaping from his chariot to reassure her that he means her no harm."

"I can see why she'd need reassuring!" Evadne wasn't convinced by Dorina's interpretation—Dorina could see that plain as day. "If he doesn't mean to be terrifying, why on earth is he showing her his ... affair ... and gadding about with two leopards, a man covered in snakes, and loose women with tambourines?"

"Well, male nudity was more common in ancient Greece, and Bacchus is typically depicted with an entourage," said Dorina, trying not to let her amusement show—her sister was extremely sensitive about being taken seriously. "They flock to him rather like children to the Pied Piper. His followers, the satyrs and maenads, adore him and help him spread his message."

"One has a torn-off cow's leg in his hand."

"Bacchus's rites imbue his followers, male and female alike, with great strength as well as great joy," said Dorina. "In some stories about Bacchus, women become so enthralled that they gain the power to tear a man to pieces with their bare hands."

"That's horrible!"

"Well, their most famous victim really was a bit of a clot," said Lady Henry, who had come up behind them. She was by herself; Jonas was off somewhere. "And the others who were spying on the maenads were doing it to gawk at them, thinking they'd catch a peek of a bunch of women off in the woods together being drunk and wanton."

"And they weren't?" Evadne still looked skeptical as she eyed Titian's sultry, half-clothed females.

"Bacchus is the god of wine and religious ecstasy," said Dorina, "but also, in a more general sense, the uncontrollable—he represents that which exists outside of societal norms, but cannot be denied. Sexual ecstasy isn't necessarily a part of it, though it can be. That said, the maenads were possessed by the spirit of the god, so their activities were legitimately holy."

"Why, Dorina, I'm impressed," said Lady Henry, to Dorina's pleasure. "It's rare for young ladies to be so knowledgeable about the rites of the Bacchae."

"Possessed . . ." said Evadne, who did not look particularly impressed. "That's an interesting word, isn't it."

"How so?" asked Dorina.

"It makes you wonder . . . perhaps these so-called gods of the old world *did* exist. They might have been something akin to demons, preying on the weakness of man."

"Demons!" exclaimed Lady Henry. Her surprise seemed genuine.

"What?" snapped Evadne, already red-faced and defensive.

"I just never imagined both of Baz's nieces turning out to be amateur scholars. You're not the first to suggest such a theory."

Now Evadne looked surprised. "All I mean is that our village priest used to talk about demons, and temptation. Bacchus is certainly tempting her in every possible way."

"Only if she likes cats," said Lady Henry lightly. "If Ariadne had proven allergic, theirs might not have been a particularly enjoyable alliance, demonic or otherwise."

"I don't care to speculate on whether demonic possession might be *enjoyable*," said Evadne, prim again.

"Why else would anyone agree to traffic with such a being?" asked Lady Henry. "Surely no one would if it were boring, or annoying, or unpleasant."

"This conversation is unseemly, and I regret beginning it," said Evadne. "I was simply trying to think of something to say about the picture, as the two of you always seem to have some quip or pithy remark at hand." And after throwing a very sharp look at Lady Henry, she stalked off.

"Oh, Evadne," murmured Dorina, not sure if she was more appalled by her sister's behavior, or that she might believe in poppycock like *demons*. Of the two of them, Evadne was certainly the more devout, but still.

"You don't believe?"

Dorina startled at the question. "Believe? Believe in what?"

"Demons."

She laughed. "Of course not!"

"Is it an 'of course'?" Lady Henry's smile was a challenge. "Your sister just said you've heard—or at least *endured*—sermons about resisting demonic temptation ..."

"And eschewing those who use witchcraft. Our vicar might well be the oldest man in England." She shrugged. "Demons are just a supernatural excuse for that which we cannot yet explain with science."

This was not at all a conversation she'd expected to have—not in front of Titian's *Bacchus and Ariadne*, not in the National Gallery, not at all. But even more surprising was Lady Henry's response.

"They might be the latter without being the former," she said, her eyes upon Bacchus as he sprang from his chariot.

As someone who scarcely ever even prayed—why, when she never got an answer?—the idea that *demons* might really be out there, scheming and corrupting the souls of the innocent, was too bizarre. Yet even more bizarre was that *Lady Henry* would be the one defending their existence, when that morning, while showing Dorina her Scripture Garden, she had confessed it had been three years since she'd set foot in a church, even for Christmas or Easter service!

"Ah, but this is hardly the place for such a conversation. Your sister has wandered off, and I see dear Jonas looking for her. Shall we go searching?"

"All right," said Dorina, still uneasy.

They found Evadne looking even more skeptical of Peter Paul Rubens's *The Judgement of Paris* than the Titian they had just admired.

"Rubens has never been quite to my taste," said Dorina as they joined her sister, "but I must say, the original is exquisite in person."

"If you like bare bodies," said Evadne. "I suppose the benefit of being an artist with a classical education is that you always have an excuse to paint bottoms."

Dorina felt a surge of affection for her sister at this remark, but it was Jonas who laughed the hardest.

"He's given Paris a tough job, to be sure," opined the young man, with a sly look at Evadne that cemented Dorina's suspicion that he fancied her. That, and he'd scarcely opened his museum guide

—he was holding it like it was the most precious thing in the entire gallery. "Three goddesses, all so beautiful! Why, I have three women here, none of which could smite me if I displeased them, and I doubt I could choose among them." He looked from Dorina to Lady Henry to Evadne, on whom he noticeably lingered the longest—until she flushed and turned away. "Then again, perhaps I'm wrong . . . I *do* have three goddesses here, though I rather doubt any of you three would be silly enough to be turned against one another by an apple, golden or otherwise."

"Oh *stop*," said Lady Henry, with a roll of her pale eyes. "There's no Goddess Henrietta."

"No, but there is a Hera, and you'd make for a passable one," said Jonas, looking her up and down appraisingly. "True, you're a bit gamey for Zeus's taste, if Rubens's, ah, *bottoms* are any indication, but I rather doubt you'd lose much sleep over trying to please *him*."

"No indeed," said Lady Henry.

"Now, Miss Dorina I think would make an elegant love goddess, a modern Aphrodite," he continued, disappointing Dorina terribly. She loved compliments, but if Jonas liked Evadne, what was he about? He ought to be crowning her sister the Queen of Love! "Those waving tresses . . . those pouting lips! Who could fail to believe her capable of charming Adonis himself?"

"Though why I would wish to is another matter entirely," she said, with a toss of said waving tresses.

"Now, as for Miss Gray . . ." He turned once again to Dorina's sister, who was looking even more sour than usual. In fact, she looked downright annoyed. Could Evadne possibly return Jonas's interest? Already? As far as Dorina knew, Evadne had never loved anyone other than Freddie. She hoped Jonas's next statement would mollify her sister. "In Miss Gray we have a *perfect* Athena. Her strength, her integrity, her proficiency in the martial arts! She is a warrior, and—"

"You're wrong," said Evadne, who had gone red, then white. Dorina could see that something was wrong; what, she couldn't imagine. A more flattering description of her sister, or one more likely to please, she had never heard in her life. But it had not pleased her for some unfathomable reason. "I'm no Athena. I'd *never* want be her. I'd rather — rather be *anyone* but her!"

"Miss Gray!" Jonas looked shocked. "I apologize; I did not mean to offend."

"Athena is the most unnatural goddess of them all," she said, voice low and hard. "Born from a man, doomed to be alone — forever consulted, but never cherished, neither bride nor mother. What woman would be pleased to be compared to her?"

"I meant only to compliment you, Miss Gray," said Jonas, looking forlorn.

"I have no interest in being complimented," Evadne said haughtily. "I believe we ought to spend our time here more rationally — for why else have we come?"

"Let's leave the classical world, shall we?" said Lady Henry. "I tire of the ancients."

"I'd love to take a longer look at some of those triptychs we passed," admitted Dorina. "Jonas . . . do you have any preference? Evadne?"

"Anything is fine by me," said Jonas as Evadne shrugged.

"Onward, then," said Lady Henry. "Let us go and bask before stern glances, so we may repent our sins."

Dorina shot her a wry glance as Evadne, more somber than any saint, took off in the direction Lady Henry pointed.

THE REST OF THEIR AFTERNOON at the National Gallery passed quietly, and in something of a haze. Dorina tried to listen attentively to all Lady Henry had to say about this picture or that, but the entire time, she was preoccupied by her sullen sister and her new friend's assertion that demons might be real.

Really real, too — not metaphors, not moral lessons, but beings that lived in the same world as men and beasts.

She was so distracted that afterward, when Evadne requested they go home to Uncle Basil's rather than joining Lady Henry and Jonas for dinner, Dorina didn't argue. Indeed, she felt a quiet night in might be just what she needed to cool her heated mind. Lady Henry seemed surprised, but did not press the issue; she merely bid her coachman to drive to Chelsea rather than Curzon Street. There, they said their goodnights, and it was decided they should meet again tomorrow, if the weather proved fair, to go to the Royal Botanic Gardens.

Uncle Basil was working when they arrived home, and he tended not to eat when he was thus occupied, according to his housekeeper. Dorina had no desire to dine at a big table with only her sister for company, for Evadne's countenance had darkened with the evening, so she asked if something might be sent to their rooms in a few hours. In the meantime she stripped off her clothes, took a long bath, and tried to relax.

And yet, she found she could not. *Demons!* Of all the strange things for such a rational creature like Lady Henry to believe in! Dorina thought back to old folk tales she'd heard as a girl. Her great aunt had once delighted her with a yarn about a man who made a deal with a demon, and it gave him power over unmarried girls. The man collected one hundred of them in a castle, but one of the hundred had a sister, a young wife, who disguised herself and defeated him with a cross of willow wood tied together with her wedding garter. She plunged it straight through his heart, saving her sister and the rest.

And then there had been the tale of the poor scholar who so longed to travel that he spent years finding the name of a demon who could show him the world. He denied Christ and made a bargain with it, but his wording wasn't quite right, and it betrayed him by turning him into the wind.

Ridiculous, of course—as ridiculous as a wolf in a wig fooling Red Riding Hood, or a cat tricking an entire countryside into believing his master was the Marquis of Carabas.

Or was it?

She tried her best to reason it through. She wouldn't be disturbed or bemused to find out a new acquaintance believed—*really* believed—in God. Why did a belief in demons seem so much more peculiar? People believed they had seen evidence of the existence of God, or the Devil, even if she herself had never experienced anything that indicated either existed.

She chuckled to herself, shaking her head. If her mother—if most people—heard that she doubted the existence of God, they would surely be just as appalled as she was by Lady Henry's suggestion that something far less benevolent might be real!

Dorina was famished by the time her supper arrived. But when she summoned her sister with a knock on Evadne's door, there was no reply. Dorina knocked a second time, and the light spilling out onto the hall carpet went out suddenly. Taking the hint, Dorina returned to her own chambers to pick at her meal. After, she fought the urge to go knock on Evadne's door again, to see if she could discover what was troubling her sister so much. If Evadne wanted to be alone . . .

Dorina slept but ill that night, plagued by nightmares inspired by her day at the National Gallery. In one, she and her sister squabbled jealously over something bright and beautiful, the shape of which she could not remember when she gasped herself awake. When at last she fell asleep again, Dorina dreamed she was Ariadne, terrified of a deity that bounded toward her on long golden legs. She ran from it, but it caught her in its paws. While its touch was gentle, she smelled its hot spicy breath as it breathed down her neck; its claws pressed into her flesh; she was powerless to stop its teeth from sinking into her throat. And yet, this violation gave her only pleasure. She moaned at its touch, even as the blood ran down her neck, over her breasts, through her pubic hair.

Dorina awoke, her eyes sandy, her back aching. Evadne somehow looked even worse when she finally stumbled down to breakfast; her hair did not appear to be thoroughly brushed, and her skin looked a bit gray. Dorina was just spreading marmalade on her toast when her sister lurched into a chair to fumble for the teapot.

"Did you girls have a nice time yesterday?" Uncle Basil, who for once seemed the healthiest of their little family, was totally oblivious to anything save what he was immediately concentrating upon: in this case, taking the top off his egg. "How was your first gallery visit?"

"Lovely," Dorina mumbled, after swallowing a bite of her toast.

Evadne snorted, not looking up from her tea. Maybe it was her poor night's sleep, or maybe it was her mounting frustration with her sister, but the sound piqued Dorina's ire. She was in no mood to put up with Evadne's constant disdain for everyone and everything.

"What was that, Evadne?" asked Basil.

"Hmm?"

"He heard you," answered Dorina.

"Heard me what?"

"Heard you snort derisively when I said we'd had a lovely time."

"I did nothing of the sort!"

"Of course you did!"

"My goodness!" exclaimed Basil, turning from one to the other. "Evadne, did you not enjoy yourself?"

"Of course I didn't!" Evadne seemed astonished Basil could have ever imagined otherwise. "What interest have I in galleries? What people call *art* seems to me to be merely a bunch of naked bodies clustered together."

"Nude, not naked," corrected Dorina.

Evadne ignored her. "People like looking at them, and claim they're actually allegories with some moral worth to excuse what's really just—just voyeurism!"

"You don't really believe that!" cried Dorina.

"How would you know?" snapped Evadne. "You've never asked —never cared!"

"That's not true!"

"Isn't it?" Evadne set down her teacup. "What have we done since arriving but humor *your* whims? You haven't asked me once what I might like to do! Why, you made plans to go to some stupid garden today without seeing if I've any interest in such a thing!"

"Why should I?" Dorina shot back, furious. "This was supposed to be *my* trip to London—*you* inserted yourself where you weren't wanted, so you can either go along with what I want to do, or go occupy yourself in some way you find more pleasing!"

Evadne seemed to swell as Dorina spoke. Dorina thrust her chin in the air defiantly. Let her sister puff herself up with righteous indignation; she'd have a difficult time denying *anything* Dorina had said. It might have been rude, but it had all been true.

"Not wanted!" said Evadne. "Just yesterday you said you were glad I'd come along!"

"That was before you spent more time making yourself unpleasant than doing anything else!" Dorina was in high dudgeon now; she had keenly felt Evadne's barb regarding not asking what her sister might like to do—Evadne was, of course, correct—but as she had felt concern over her sister's lack of enjoyment, the allegation of selfishness made her savage. "You're so determined to *hate* everything, even me, that already I'm sick to death of you! All you do is stomp around looking like you're sucking on a lemon, and you take no pleasure in anything that doesn't involve ruining other people's fun! You huff and smack and sniff at everything you see, including me, because nothing lives up to your personal standards! Like poor Jonas! You were downright cruel to him! And for what—the crime of paying you a compliment?"

"It wasn't a compliment I appreciated!" But Dorina could see from Evadne's expression that she knew very well what she'd done.

"Still pining after Freddie? Do you only like boys who aren't actually interested in you? I suppose that would disqualify Jonas!"

"Jonas isn't *interested* in me!"

"Girls!" Uncle Basil stood, hands on the table, looking more ferocious than Dorina would have thought possible, given his frail state. "I must insist you cease this bickering!"

Dorina crossed her arms under her bosom. Evadne sniffed haughtily again, but realizing she had, turned crimson.

"You're such a spoiled little child," said Evadne. "Silly of me to expect you might appreciate anything as pedestrian as a sister's sincere concern for your future."

Basil looked alarmed, and Dorina suddenly realized she was in grave danger of getting herself disinvited without a week in London having passed.

"You may think I'm a spoiled child," she said, "but I'm perfectly capable of looking after myself. Why, I haven't even considered going out without a chaperone!"

"Your chaperone ..." Evadne, after glancing at Uncle Basil, who was now looking lost rather than annoyed, continued, "doesn't know how much she's bitten off." It was obviously not what she'd meant to say, but Dorina let it be, given Basil was staring at them as if they were monstrosities in a zoo. "Much luck to the both of you. As by your own admission you're sick of me, I *shall* go off on my own and do what I please—beyond stomping around looking like I'm sucking on a lemon, I mean."

"Evadne," said Dorina, regretting at least some of her harsh words, but her sister had already pushed her chair back from the table. She did not look back as she strode from the room.

"Do sisters always fight?" Basil mopped his forehead with a

handkerchief. "I confess, when I invited you both, I didn't think there would be a row!"

"We won't let it happen again," she promised. "I'm sorry, Uncle."

"Oh, it's all right," he said, turning back to his now-cold egg. "I was thinking I would have to write to your mother about it, but if you're sorry . . . just can't stand the noise. Bad for my nerves, you know."

Dorina longed to ask what his nerves had to do with anything—if they, perhaps, were the source of his strange change.

"Please excuse me," she said. "Lady Henry will be here soon, and I should get ready."

"Have fun," said her uncle, already absorbed in his paper. He looked small again, wasted and washed out, poor thing. What could have happened to him?

Evadne's door wasn't just shut—it was locked. Dorina knew because after there was yet again no response to her knocking, she tried the handle. Her anger returned at this snub, and she flounced across to her own room. Let her sister skip all her meals and sulk in her room if that's what she wanted!

She calmed down after almost yanking out her hair while brushing it, but she dressed herself more calmly, forcing herself to go slowly. By the time she finished it all, she heard the bell ring, and she descended with dignity to find Lady Henry in the hall, looking dashing in a natty pinstripe morning suit.

"Ah, Dorina," she said. "You're looking much better. You were not yourself last night."

"No," she agreed. "I apologize."

"No apology necessary," said Lady Henry. "I was concerned, that's all. Well! The weather is very fine. Shall we go to Kew? Or would you prefer some other sojourn?"

Dorina thought of Evadne, alone in her room, and almost suggested that they consult her to see what she might like. Then she remembered that door, locked against her, and tossed her hair defiantly.

"The Royal Gardens sound *lovely*," she said.

"Fantastic! There are several interesting arrangements I think you would enjoy seeing, if your appreciation of my humble greenhouse is any indication. But where is your sister? Will she be joining us?"

"No," said Dorina, and dissolved into tears.

6

Becoming a diabolist is not by any means an easy process. There are only two ways by which man can attain it. One is by being cultured; the other, by being corrupt.

— *On the Summoning of Demons*

L ADY HENRY DID NOT TAKE Dorina deeper inside Basil Hallward's house to comfort her; instead, she gave Dorina her handkerchief, which was scented with a delicate ginger perfume, and led her outside to the waiting coach. It was a decent drive to Kew, so they would have time to talk over whatever could be the matter before they need face the public, and anyway, she did not like the idea that Evadne might walk in on them. She sensed that Dorina would speak of her sister quite freely before she'd cried herself out.

"She's *always* been like this," gasped Dorina. "All my life, she's *hated* me."

"Surely not," said Henry mildly. *This* was why she had been so certain that Evadne would be the more interesting of the two girls: young women of eight and twenty did not often dramatically declare that their siblings *"hated"* them while weeping and carrying on. They tended to be more temperate in their views; their life experience helped them reason through their emotions.

Then again, she had been wrong about Dorina to begin with; perhaps the sisters did have deeper troubles. Evadne was hardly the most pleasant person she'd ever met in her life, it was true.

If only all siblings could be as happy as she and Oliver had been!

The thought of Oliver caused the presence in her mind to stir and shiver, like a cat stretches during a nap without fully awakening. Henry fought the urge to take a pinch of snuff to enhance her appreciation and understanding of the situation, at least aesthetically speaking, but eventually she gave in and sent a puff up either nostril.

Dorina became yet more beautiful; her grief, more elegant as the demon woke, drinking the girl in as Henry did. Its admiration was palpable, like a pleasant pressure in her mind.

"She *does* hate me," said Dorina. "She's *always* resented me."

Goodness. "Why do you think that?" asked Henry patiently.

"I don't know! She hates everything!"

The girl might be a prodigy, but she was in danger of becoming tiresome. "Not *everything*," Henry corrected her. "She loves fencing, and swords, and—"

"Bother her swords! She'd stick one into *me* if she could."

"That seems rather unfair, don't you think?"

Dorina sighed. "Perhaps. But Lady Henry—"

"Why don't you just call me Henry? I've been remiss in calling you *Miss* Dorina, after all, and there's no reason we shouldn't treat one another as equals."

This calmed the girl substantially; Henry was pleased to have said the right thing.

She was such a queer creature, Dorina—so awfully predictable in some ways; so delightfully surprising in others. She was wise but innocent, fresh but savvy. Henry liked her very much, but couldn't help but feel she ought to be reserved around her. The way Dorina looked at her made her worry that the girl might be interested in initiating something more than friendship—more than what passed between mentor and pupil.

This was, of course, impossible. Even if there hadn't been a shocking difference in their ages, there was another, and more substantial barrier to them becoming any closer.

Again, the presence in her mind stirred, more agitated this time. It thought of itself as an enhancement, an improvement, not a barrier!

"Well, *Henry* . . ." said Dorina, suddenly shy, "I just mean that Evadne has never really seemed to think anything I cared about, anything I liked, was particularly meritorious. She's been very discouraging over the years, regarding my . . . interests."

"Art, you mean? There are some who will never concede that art is worthwhile."

"She always seemed to think it would be a bad influence on me."

"Ah, well, those who find ugliness in beauty are the ones who are truly corrupt."

"I have other interests, besides art," said Dorina, "and she's never cared for those, either."

Henry sensed Dorina was trying to tell her something—something she already knew, or had at least guessed. Still, better to let the girl take the lead.

"Oh? What sort of interests?"

"Do you promise not to be angry?" she said. "I believe I can tell *you* about myself without worrying that you'll be cross with me for being who I am . . . but I have been surprised before."

"You don't kill people, do you? Or steal, or—" Henry smiled to see Dorina look so appalled. "I didn't think so. I'm a very perceptive person, and I believe what you are about to say will come as absolutely no surprise to me."

"What do you mean?" Dorina looked less at ease, rather than more.

"I mean that I'm a rather good judge of character, given what my brother was . . . and what I am too."

"What you—oh!" Realization and relief dawned together.

Henry smiled, nodded. "When did you know you were different?"

"I think I always have." Dorina looked out the coach window

at the sun-drenched street beyond, seemingly embarrassed for the first time.

"I chewed my way through so many nice young men before I figured out that it wasn't their fault that I wished I was with their sisters every moment they were romancing me."

"Really!" Dorina seemed intrigued. "I never even tried. My first conquests were women. I've never met a boy I cared to get to know better. I mean, your Jonas is a delight, really he is, but . . ."

"Oh, I know. I appreciate Jonas on many levels, but he's safe from me, even living in my house."

Dorina was much more relaxed now that this was no longer between them. "You know, Evadne made some snide remark today, when we had our row, about you influencing my opinions. It seems she was right."

"Oh, don't say that! I prefer to think of myself as helping you find yourself. Influencing someone is terribly immoral."

"How so?"

"It's difficult to explain, but when you influence someone, you risk replacing their soul with yours. An influenced person ceases to think her own thoughts or chase her own passions. Her virtues are no longer her own, and her sins—if there is such a thing as sin—are borrowed. She becomes rather like an echo, or perhaps an actor reading lines. If the purpose of life is developing one's self—if we are all artists whose canvas is our person—we must strive to realize ourselves as we wish ultimately to be. What would be the purpose of becoming someone else?"

"I suppose I never thought of it that way." Dorina looked rather startled by Lady Henry's suggestion; well, she was at that age where young people wanted nothing more than to be wholly themselves . . . and also everyone they found interesting.

"It will help you in life, my dear, if you seek to be only who *you* want to be."

"And yet, we say artists have influences, don't we?"

Henry smiled. "Of course, but that's not quite the same meaning of the word. If an artist sees something she admires in another, and chooses to treat it as a lesson, that is wholly different from someone seeking specifically to change someone on a whim, isn't it?"

Dorina nodded.

"I think it is especially reprehensible to seek to influence someone because we are all so afraid of ourselves these days, even the bravest of us. If we were to live our lives fully, completely, and give in to our impulses, the world would be better for it. But we squash our impulses, we strangle them . . . and yet, they cannot be wholly suppressed. When denied, these impulses begin to poison us from within. We brood over what we forbid ourselves, whether or not we admit it. I think the only way to know one's self is to yield to those urges, to not fear them. I had no idea, before I met you, that one as young as yourself would be courageous enough to give in to that which is considered reprehensible rather than suppressing or fearing what is within you—that which makes you *you*. I certainly wasn't so confident at your age."

"I'm not so sure I'm *so* confident," said Dorina.

"No?"

"Actually, I was thrown for a loop yesterday . . ."

"By what?"

"Well . . . our conversation. The one we had before the painting of Bacchus."

The demon was amused; Henry felt its mirth as keenly as her own stirrings of panic. It had been very foolish of her to challenge Dorina over the issue of demons. She had just been so surprised by Evadne's remarks, and entertained by Dorina's dismay. She did not wish to get the girl interested in the subject. Henry had, after all, vowed never to recruit another. Not after what happened with Oliver.

The demon let her know its displeasure at this, but she ignored it. Their relationship was one of equals; she was its host, not its servant. She had no obligation to obey.

"Oh, that," said Henry, with as much nonchalance as she could. "You mean about the gods of the ancient world being . . ."

The girl blushed. "Well, *yes*. I thought about it quite a lot last night."

"Don't give it too much mind."

"How could I not?" Dorina's eyes were so very wide.

"I'm sorry," said Henry. "I meant to tease your sister, not you. It was just an intellectual exercise." The demon scolded her for lying. Knowing she was being disrespectful toward Dorina by telling her half-truths, Henry tried to walk a middle path.

"Might there be some merit to the idea? Who can say! You believe there is a scientific explanation for what appears to be supernatural. But what if what we believed was supernatural was just natural? The paranormal, normal?"

Dorina laughed a little, dispelling the tension that had gathered like steam in the carriage—and even better, they had arrived at the Royal Gardens. Before Dorina could say anything further on the subject, the door opened, letting in bright light and the cries of the peacocks. The girl gasped with pleasure, and almost leaped out to get a better look.

Henry was thankful for the distraction, grateful to leave off with *that* particular conversation. Dorina was too quick—she would have to really watch her tongue.

For now, it was a fine, hot day, summer sun beating upon them as they sifted in among the other visitors, and the air smelled even greener than everything looked. The shade of the trees and shrubs and the little ponds and lakes lent the air a coolness that was pleasant when the wind gusted. Dorina leaned into the smell, inhaling deeply, her face glowing with pleasure.

The presence in Henry's mind reasserted itself when she lit a ginger-scented cigarette as they strolled along the gravel paths. The blooms on the flowers seemed to open before her eyes; the color of their leaves deepened as their stems became more graceful; the grass appeared more perfectly manicured. Henry felt unalloyed joy to see it all; it was so very *beautiful,* and her appreciation knew no beginning and no end.

Dorina cozied up to her just as she was finishing her cigarette, the younger woman snaking her arm around the older's waist, leaning her head on her shoulder.

"It's magnificent here. I can see why you wanted to show me. It's as if I were walking through an Impressionist painting! See that woman over there? Standing as she does, in the breeze, she looks just like *Woman with a Parasol.* The people are but tongue lickings, strips of color and motion, unless one stops and stares impolitely . . . Henry?"

Henry had pulled away, too aware of her own response to Dorina's touch, too cognizant that the invisible thing that lived in her mind and body had also responded positively—*eagerly,* even. It was not often that she and the presence in her mind disagreed; they were usually in perfect harmony with one another, but they had both been so electrified by the girl's sudden intimacy it was as if Dorina had struck some secret chord neither of them had ever heard before.

Dorina was watching her, smiling. Why, the little minx knew exactly the impression her touch had produced. She was *flirting* with her!

The nerve of the creature, thinking that she, Lady Henry Wotton, would ever be interested in such a young, unformed, innocent as Dorina Gray! It was insulting, the insinuation that she could be tempted by such a liaison . . .

And yet, she *was* tempted. Dorina was delightful, physically and mentally. Henry had been denying it to herself, but the demon knew. It reminded her that she had just given Dorina a lecture about the virtue of yielding to impulses—but theory was just that, and she made a mental note to qualify her earlier statement to Dorina at some point. She did not want the girl thinking *she* had been flirting with *her* . . . even if perhaps she had been. At least a little.

Henry withdrew a cigarette and lit it to cover the awkwardness of having jerked away from Dorina.

"Can I have one?" Dorina asked boldly. "They smell delicious, and you just said I shouldn't deny myself things I want."

Oh, Henry had dug herself an interesting hole!

"You may *not* have one," she answered, tucking away the case. "They are not for beautiful young girls. The smoke toughens the skin as well as making your throat raspy."

"You think I'm beautiful?"

"Of course," said Henry. "You *are* beautiful, and you are young, and for me to do anything that would jeopardize either would be a terrible crime. Beauty is useless . . . but appreciating it is the highest calling we can answer."

Dorina looked around. "We are answering it now, I think."

"Yes. Through gardening, I have truly learned to appreciate beauty. I know it lasts but a short time . . . Flowers wither, no matter what you do, and while they blossom again, they are never the same blooms. You may regret the loss of some and forget others, but they are gone just the same. People are similar . . . Youth is a flower, one that will never return. Joy diminishes as we age. Our bodies betray us, and we become hideous, haunted creatures."

You still fear that? asked the presence in her mind, not in words, but in a sense of surprise that was close enough to speech after all the years she had hearkened to it.

For others, she replied, looking at Dorina. They had wandered by a fountain, and the girl was lifting her face as the spray dotted her skin and dappled her shirtwaist.

She need not wither. She could—

"No," said Lady Henry aloud, surprising Dorina.

"No what?" she asked, turning. The droplets of water across the bridge of her nose, clinging to her hair, sparkled like diamonds in the sunshine.

"No telling what's around the next bend here," she said quickly. "They plan the gardens so pleasantly—every new sight is delightful, don't you think?" She ambled away from the fountain; Dorina followed.

"You know . . ." The girl caught up to her, looking thoughtful. "Even though I find I agree with nearly everything we've spoken of since the very moment we met, I can't help but disagree with you on a point."

"Oh?"

"I would *love* to be influenced by you. You're the most interesting person I've ever met, and while I can't imagine you'd inspire some sort of passion for trousers in me, I believe you'd encourage me to . . . do better. I'm already trying to think of art in a different way."

Henry felt a pang. "Pray don't! You should be your own person, my dearest Dorina, because the person you are is *delightful*. And you've known me far too short a time to know if I ought to be influencing you."

"You sound like Evadne," said Dorina, making a little moue.

"Maybe I do, and maybe I don't. I think your sister worries about you changing in a certain way—I'm concerned that you should change at all." The demon chided her, and this time she acknowledged it was correct. "Then again . . . everything is always changing. Nothing can remain static and exist in this world." Dorina looked perplexed, hurt almost, and Henry felt another swell of affection for the child. "Oh, you darling girl, this is why I hardly ever make friends with young women. When a woman reaches a certain age, she is more or less formed. But at your age, you are in a constant state of flux. You tell me you want to be influenced by me, but in a fortnight you may find me as tiresome as any other old woman. *Shh*—I know of what I speak, trust me. And I know from experience it will be *my* heart that breaks, not yours."

"Do not speak of heartbreak," said Dorina. "It is a beautiful day, and we are together, and nothing will change, ever."

"You cannot promise that. No one can," said Henry. "As for me, I hardly ever promise anything. But, perhaps you will stay the same —perhaps your desires will not change, and you will grow straight and tall, in the same direction you are growing now."

Dorina looked a bit overwhelmed, so Henry took her hand and squeezed it. The presence in her mind approved—very much so. She tried to ignore it, but she could feel it. It had appetites like any living creature, and desires and loves and needs. But she would not let it have Dorina. Not if she could help it.

No one knew better just how much was at stake . . .

"You're right," Henry continued. "It's a beautiful day, and I want ice cream. Let us leave off with this topic—or at least, leave it for another day. But I would beg you: if you remember one thing from this conversation, remember this . . . trusting someone too quickly is a very dangerous thing for a young woman to do."

"There's ice cream?" asked Dorina.

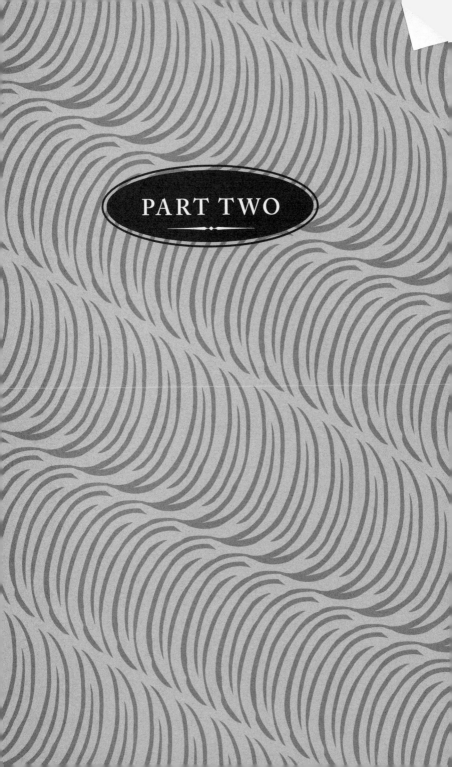

PART TWO

1

Demons do not understand what friendship is — or what resentment is, for that matter. They simultaneously like and are indifferent to everyone . . . except their enemies.

— *On the Summoning of Demons*

THE FENCING SCHOOL WAS FAIRLY close to Lady Henry's house, just across St James's Park. Evadne noticed the familiar streets as she rode in the cab by herself. She hadn't told anyone where she was going — had only told her uncle she was going out for a few hours. He'd seemed supremely unconcerned by this, for he was already in his studio, though he didn't seem to be working. Just sitting, staring at, or perhaps meditating upon, some painting or other.

While she was glad on some level that Basil did not seem inclined to enquire where she might be going, it surprised her; she'd assumed that as their guardian in the city, he would care more about such matters. Evadne felt momentarily glad she'd come along on this trip, given that their uncle did not seem interested in keeping an eye on Dorina, before recalling how quickly she'd cracked and left Dorina to her own devices.

Her annoyance returned with a vengeance as she again recalled their visit to Brighton. Her urge to protect Dorina was just that day at the seaside all over again.

Evadne paid the cabman and shouldered the canvas bag that held all her practice foils — the ones she had brought from Swadlincote. She had not opened the package bearing Lady Henry's address; her feeling on the matter was that she would return it, unopened, at the end of their stay. That way, she could leave London with nothing between them—no obligations, and no awkwardness.

No obligations or awkwardness . . . Evadne sighed. That sounded so nice, as she already needed to apologize to Lady Henry. And to Jonas . . . She had been rude to the former and cruel to the latter.

Evadne knew Jonas couldn't have known that being compared to Athena was a bit of a sore spot with her. Regardless, he kept company with Lady Henry. She was fairly certain she would never be comfortable around someone who was in the thrall of that woman . . . even if he was the only young man who had ever looked at her like she was some rare beauty. And when she was sweaty, no less.

A miniature epee depended from the sign hanging above the Westminster Fencing Academy. It glinted in the sunlight when Evadne glanced up at it. She swallowed. The fire of her anger had burned itself out during the drive; now, she mostly felt nervous. It seemed terribly improper for her to be here; she'd never been inside a fencing school, and it wasn't as if she'd been *invited*. If this George Cantrell person wasn't in, what would she do? Why, she didn't know if they even taught women here! It would be so embarrassing to be laughed at, or punted out the door.

She'd come this far. She might as well take the risk. If they wouldn't teach her, that was on them. If they did . . . well, it would mean she could do more than sit around the house moping, or being dragged along to where she wasn't wanted. In a rush she strode up to the door, knocked, and let herself in.

The sound of steel scraping steel hit her ears, putting her at ease, as did the smell of sweaty practice leathers. Evadne made her way through the entryway and peeked around the corner to find a young man with a sparse blond mustache scribbling away behind a desk.

"Hello?" she said.

The fellow registered momentary surprise, then stood to greet her cordially. "Welcome to the Westminster Fencing Academy," he said, coming around the side to shake her left hand. When she did so without hesitation, he smiled approvingly at her; Evadne silently thanked Freddie for teaching her fencing etiquette along with swordplay. "What can I help you with today?"

"Is Mr. Cantrell in?" she asked.

"Why yes," he said, looking intrigued, "but he's teaching a lesson now. Would you care to wait?"

"Ah, yes, thank you," said Evadne, relaxing a bit. At least she hadn't been laughed out the door.

"So you've heard of our Mr. Cantrell?" asked the young man. Evadne realized he was fighting a losing battle against his curiosity.

"A good friend recommended I take lessons from him when he heard I would be staying in London for the summer."

"I see! Forgive me, I don't mean to pry. It's just that we don't get many young women in here."

"Oh?" Her stomach clenched—nerves again. "Why is that? Are the men very rough?"

"Some of the young ones are . . . enthusiastic," he said diplomatically, "but not the instructors. Certainly not Cantrell! He's known as *Saint George,* and for more than just having attended divinity school." Evadne smiled, in spite of herself. "That said, we are competition-oriented."

"Competition is the furthest thing from my mind," Evadne assured him.

"So you fence for . . ."

"Personal pleasure."

The young man brightened. "What a wonderful thing to hear! So many of our students want to win ribbons—which is fine, of course, for them and for us. But, at the end of the day, fencing is really about keeping fit. That's a rare and precious thing in this modern world, where it seems that fewer of us every year must depend on the strength of our arm or the swiftness of our feet to survive." He grinned. "I must beg your pardon a second time — I don't mean to go on! It's only, it's delightful to meet you, ah . . ."

"Evadne Gray."

"A pleasure, Miss Gray! And I am Burton, Burton Trawless. I apologize for not introducing myself sooner."

"That's quite all right."

"I see you already have weapons . . ."

"I have everything."

"Delightful!" said Trawless, and she could see he was trying his best not to look too surprised. "Ah . . . then would you fancy a tour while you wait?"

"I would love one," she replied, feeling genuinely happy for the first time in . . . she didn't know how long. The friendly Trawless had put her at ease. Evadne rather liked the way he was trying his best to not make her feel like an anomaly.

Her doubts had left her. She was certain she'd done the right thing by coming.

Trawless had her leave her bag in the changing room, though he took it inside for her as there were young men within. Evadne caught sight of several bare, glistening torsos before she realized where they were going, and turned away, blushing furiously. Trawless apologized — he was not accustomed to giving tours to women — but after that, everything was simply lovely.

The corridor between the practice floor and the changing facilities had several doors that led to "school offices," and a small kitchen; in between the doors were shelves lining the walls, all full of brightly polished trophies, plates, and other awards. Trawless pointed a few out, mostly international events where the students had overcome Germans and Italians and even, surprisingly, a Japanese prodigy who had traveled all the way from Kyoto just to compete.

The practice floor was a wooden expanse marked with lines of tape. It could have accommodated twelve pair, but only four were out. Evadne watched for a few minutes, Trawless by her side. Only one couple used swords; the others were doing a technique exercise involving pressing fencing gloves between their palms and stepping forward and backwards — anticipating the other's movements, if Evadne had to guess.

As for the pair with swords, Evadne felt certain the large man in the darker leathers was the instructor. His footwork was immaculate and his strikes were terrifyingly accurate. And yet, even so, Evadne got the distinct impression he was holding back.

"That's Cantrell there," said Trawless, confirming her suspicion by nodding at the big man. "He's not the lead instructor, that's Mr. Perkins, but Perkins isn't here right now. He doesn't teach beginners, just the senior students, so he's only around in the evenings, or by appointment."

"I see," said Evadne, only half listening. She was too mesmerized by the lesson. If the student Mr. Cantrell was teaching was a beginner, she would have quite a bit of catching up to do!

"Mr. Perkins founded the academy," continued Trawless. "Best damn fencer I ever — oh, I *do* beg your pardon!"

"I don't mind," said Evadne warmly. "Please, go on."

Trawless was blushing under his mustache. "What I ought to have said was that Perkins learned from Henry William, who was one of Angelo's children. Angelo was — oh, I see you know him!"

"Yes, of course. I actually have a copy of *The School of Fencing* in my kit. I've read it many times."

Trawless looked extremely impressed. "You'll fit right in here, Miss Gray."

"Do you think so?"

"I do. And I see you thriving, especially if you've come for Cantrell. Perkins is a fantastic teacher as well as a swordsman, but Cantrell there . . . I've never met anyone who can teach like him. He brings out the best in everyone. He'd tell you himself that he's a better teacher than a fencer, so I'm not insulting him by saying that —after all, as you can see, he's an astonishing fencer."

"Yes, he is," said Evadne. Mr. Cantrell had just fumbled a move, but it was clearly a ruse to draw in his opponent—who did not see the feint for what it was, and got himself jabbed in the thigh for his foolishness.

"That's ten!" said Cantrell, taking off his mask, and revealing a sandy-haired, ruggedly handsome man of perhaps five and thirty; he gave off such an aura of vibrancy and health it was difficult for Evadne to guess his exact age. A dueling scar marked his cheek, but to her mind that just lent him an air of danger and sophistication.

The two men shook hands, and the loser scuttled off; the victor wiped his brow, and seeing Trawless gesture at him, came over.

"Who's this?" He eyed Evadne with open curiosity, but she approved of how he stood a respectful distance back so he would not loom over her. He was really very tall, and was possessed of a piercing stare that made her uncomfortable. She got the impression he was looking into her very soul; it took her breath away. She would not break his gaze, however; she lifted her chin defiantly, and she sensed his approval.

"This is Miss Evadne Gray. She's come to have lessons."

"Lessons!" Cantrell exclaimed. "How unusual!"

"Is it?" said Evadne, deciding to answer his surprise with a challenge. "My friend who recommended I do so didn't seem to think there would be anything *unusual* about it—and he's a very proper sort of man, respectful of my feelings as a woman."

Mr. Cantrell sobered immediately. "You were recommended to me? By whom?"

"Freddie Thornton."

"Freddie Thornton!" Cantrell's broad, tanned face split into a winning grin. "There's a name I didn't expect to hear today. Freddie and I were at Oxford together," he explained to Trawless, who looked mystified. "Good student, and a good fencer, too. Why, of course!" Mr. Cantrell, abashed, smacked his left palm against his forehead. "Miss Gray! I've heard of you, you know." He turned back to Trawless. "We all marveled how old Thorny didn't get as badly out of practice as the rest of us over the hols. We always teased him about it, and eventually he revealed his secret—he had a *girl* at home, fiercer than any opponent we faced at school. Apparently Miss Gray set up the most remarkable gauntlet for herself, to compensate for having no one to practice with."

"What sort of gauntlet?" Trawless asked.

"I don't know if I'd call it a *gauntlet*," said Evadne, feeling a bit exposed. She couldn't quite tell if they were laughing at her. "I attached a ball to an indiarubber cord, for example, and would try to poke it as it bounced," she said, "and I had a few other dummies I'd use for various purposes."

"Don't be so modest," said Cantrell. Of course, his command just made Evadne blush, but at the same time she enjoyed his frank approval. "Thorny told us about you getting your village blacksmith to hammer an epee point to a heavy spring so you could fence it! Just think of it, Trawless, it would bounce back to center every time!"

"It almost took my eye out the first time I used it. I didn't anticipate needing a mask to fence with a dummy, but I was wrong."

"Genius!" said Trawless. "Why, no reason we couldn't get a few of those for the academy. We'd have to run it by Perkins first, but seems like a good idea, especially as we have their inventor here with us now." Evadne blushed. She'd never had the pleasure of hearing herself casually included as part of a group. "That is, if the lady will agree to giving us the secrets of her success."

"They're not secrets," she said. "I'd be happy to help."

"Good, good!" said Cantrell. "But the two of you'd better propose it to Perkins. He's still sore at me." Mr. Cantrell did not elaborate, and instead asked, "Did Thorny practice with your dummies, too, Miss Gray?"

"Sometimes ... when I would let him." Cantrell's eyebrow quirked up, and Evadne clarified, "I so rarely had anyone to fence with, I made him practice with me when he was home from school."

"Good for you. He needed it, poor boy."

Evadne would have strongly protested that statement just a month before; now, not so much. But, feeling some residual stirrings of loyalty, she replied, "Mr. Thornton made me the fencer I am, rather than the reverse."

"Shall we put that to the test?"

"I beg your pardon?"

"I fenced often enough with Thorny that I'll be able to tell if you helped him or not," he said. "We can lend you some gear, and—"

"Oh, she brought everything she'll need," said Trawless. "What do you say, Miss Gray? You came prepared!"

Evadne had never fenced anyone but Freddie; the idea of going a few rounds with such a physically imposing man—a man whom Trawless had also described as the best teacher in the school—was more than a little intimidating. Especially as he'd obviously heard so many overinflated tales of her prowess.

"I came for a lesson, not a match," she protested.

"Oh come now!" urged Cantrell. "I've been curious about you for *years,* Miss Gray. We were all so intrigued by Thorny's stories. Trawless, go chase all those lazy boys out of the changing room so Miss Gray can slip on her gear, and then we'll have some fun. If, of course, the lady will oblige me."

Evadne felt herself nod. "I won't be but a minute."

She thanked her lucky stars she'd worn one of her more reasonable ensembles that day; she had relatively little trouble shimmying out of her shirtwaist and skirts, and she'd laced her corset as loosely as she could.

Her hands were shaking as she stripped down. She was very nervous. Well, all her life she'd wanted for partners. Now was her chance.

Her hands steadied once she got on her practice gear: her bloomers and skirt, thick socks, and the special shoes with india-rubber soles she'd ordered through a catalogue; her shirt, leather breastplate, plastron, padded jacket, and gloves. She hadn't put it all on for far too long, and it was delightful to be back in her comfortable, worn-in clothes. She felt fantastic—and eager to face Mr. Cantrell to show him what she could do.

She grabbed two epees and her mask and headed to the floor. Mr. Cantrell was drinking a cup of water, but when he saw her, he set it down and came over to shake hands.

"Very fetching," he said, which made her frown, rather than the reverse. He instantly bowed. "My apologies, Miss Gray. Of course, a serious fencer like you will not be looking for compliments on style, but rather skill. It's only that I see ladies' fencing gear so rarely, it caught me rather off guard how well it suited you."

"Thank you," she said firmly, pleased by his apology—and his compliments, if she was honest with herself. She pushed that thought out of her mind. "What shall we do? Best of ten?"

"Anything you like."

"Ten, then," she replied, trying not to let her eyes slip to his broad shoulders, powerful arms, or where his chest tapered pleasingly to a narrow waist.

"I'll judge," offered Trawless.

Evadne saluted Mr. Cantrell, then put on her mask. She swallowed, her mouth suddenly dry, and she wished she'd thought to ask for some water before they began.

"En garde," said Trawless. "*Allez!*"

Mr. Cantrell came at her like a charging bull and scored a point on her chest before she had a chance to think. She resisted the urge to rub at the spot; it smarted even through her armor, but she didn't want to appear weak.

Trawless called it in Mr. Cantrell's favor. She thought about what she'd seen as she reset—he had a strong attack, naturally, but his poor footwork had simply been him trying to trick her, like he had with his student. Next time Trawless called *allez!* she tested this hypothesis, challenging him with a tricky maneuver she'd practiced endlessly with her dummy, and managed to confound him into backing up. Unfortunately, her days off had made her slow on her feet, and he scored on her bicep.

When she felt the impact, she resolved she would not be given a lesson—not like this. Their next fight was far more ferocious, and lasted much longer; by the time she tagged him on the thigh—a good one, too—Evadne was sweating. She had won the point, but only barely. It had taken a toll on her physically to mentally shift herself away from her love of technique and into essentially a point-delivery engine.

She narrowed her focus to Mr. Cantrell's feet and glove; she would not allow herself to look at his other hand, his eyes, or anything beyond of the line of their fencing. Even the sounds of the school receded, save for Trawless's voice. She tried to see Mr. Cantrell as her dummy, as a bouncing ball, as anything other than a large, strong man with surprising grace and devastating nimbleness, as well as much more experience than she when it came to fencing actual opponents.

It worked fairly well, actually. She scored several more touches in quick succession, and felt Mr. Cantrell's surprise radiating from him like heat from a fireplace in spite of his earlier statements that she would likely prove to be some sort of protégé.

As she became more aggressive, so did he, and they were both breathing heavily at eight and nine when they scored a double, bringing Mr. Cantrell the win. He tore off his mask as Trawless announced it. His face was red as a strawberry, and his jacket was soaked several inches down his neck.

She was pleased it hadn't been easy for him. In fact, she was almost certain she was less winded than he as she removed her mask and stepped forward to shake hands, which he did with enthusiasm.

Only then did she realize how loudly the other students were shouting and clapping . . . although they did not seem to be cheering their teacher, but rather the match itself.

"You're a brutal little monster, aren't you?" Cantrell panted. "I've never had anyone come in off the street and put me through my paces like that."

"It wasn't a sure thing at all," said Trawless, taking their masks. "Good show, Miss Gray. You really had him going."

"So it would seem," said Evadne. "I was worried you were going easy on me, but I can see you treated me fairly."

Mr. Cantrell smiled at her incredulously, and even though he was smiling down at her, she felt as if the distance between them was shrinking. "Why, of course I treated you fairly. How else could I assess your skill?"

The other students had wandered off; only Trawless remained. "And how do you assess it?" she asked.

"Remarkable, given your training. I can't imagine how dangerous you'll be after a few lessons. You're devilish strong . . . strong enough I'd say we should put a real rapier in your hand and see how you do with that."

"George," said Trawless, in a warning tone that surprised Evadne.

"What's the harm?" said Cantrell.

"You know what Perkins would say."

"Perkins isn't here," said Cantrell, winking at Evadne. "What do you say, Miss Gray? Want to try something new?"

She looked from the frowning Trawless to the smiling Mr. Cantrell, and though she was usually a stickler for rules she found she couldn't resist the chance to try out a real rapier.

She shrugged. "Why not?"

"I'll be back," said Cantrell, and left her with Trawless.

"Am I to understand this is forbidden?" she said. She'd rather know.

"Not *forbidden* . . . not exactly. Mr. Perkins doesn't want West-minster Academy students learning how to duel, only to sport fence," said Trawless. "He feels using real rapiers will encourage recklessness among our students. One of his best students was once involved in a real sword fight, and though he won it, he did not escape . . . *unscathed.*"

Mr. Cantrell returned, and Evadne noticed that against his still-flushed face his white dueling scar stood out. She told herself not to jump to any conclusions; Mr. Perkins would have had hundreds of students over the years. Mr. Cantrell could not be the only one with a scar.

"I think this will be about the right length for you," he said, handing her a weapon with a ball on the tip, secured with some kind of sticky tape. She eyed the elaborate basket hilt suspiciously, but it felt good in her hand, even if the grip was a bit thick for her liking.

"Let's just do some basic drills," said Cantrell, "to get your arm used to the weight. How about just a step and strike exercise? That way you can see how your footwork might change with a heavier weapon in your hand."

"All right."

"Masks, Trawless," said Cantrell. Trawless reluctantly handed them over, and Evadne slipped hers over her face. She shivered a bit as the clammy neck guard brushed her flesh.

The blunted rapier might not feel so much heavier just hold-ing it in her hand, but after a few minutes of drilling, Evadne was positively soaked with sweat and her arm was trembling. Perhaps, she thought, she would actually use some of Lord Oliver's swords to train—or just get her own with her pocket money. If she did her exercises with a heavier blade, surely it would help her endur-ance with her epee.

"What the deuce is going on here!"

Evadne almost dropped her rapier; she had been concentrating so completely that she hadn't noticed anyone come into the academy, but barreling across the practice floor was a short but ferocious-looking older man with close-cropped white hair and a bristly mustache. He looked extremely annoyed.

"George! How dare you—teaching dueling! At my academy!"

Cantrell's mask was off in a moment. "Mr. Perkins, I—"

"Thought you'd do it while I wasn't here, eh? Thought you could just carry on covertly without me knowing? I may look old, but my mind is still sharp."

"I wasn't teaching dueling," protested Cantrell. "I was just showing our newest student the virtues of—"

"A new student, on his first day, using a real rapier! Can't you see how that would affect the mentality of someone new to the sport?"

"But she's not new to it, Mr. Perkins." Mr. Cantrell, who had seemed so bright and sparkling with joy and health, seemed to be shrinking under the berating of his master. "She's fenced for years. I only barely beat her when I was testing her, and she had me panting like a greyhound at the end of it."

"She!" Astonished, Mr. Perkins looked at Evadne. She dutifully removed her mask, and clutching it under her arm, moved to shake his hand. He seemed surprised, but took it. His grip was cool and dry, in spite of his anger.

"My name is Evadne Gray. A friend of mine recommended I train here while I was staying in London."

"Here? Why didn't he send you to one of the ladies' fencing clubs? They're more common than ever; lots of girls these days do it to keep fit."

"I assume he sent me here because you are the best." It was the right thing to say; her compliment calmed him substantially. Plenty of time later for him to find out that Mr. Cantrell and Freddie had been old school friends.

Perkins stroked his mustache. "I don't know if we're the *best*, but he's not wrong that we are a quality institution—no matter what you may have seen today."

"Mr. Cantrell wanted to show me how training with a heavier weapon might improve my endurance," she said, taking a risk—she knew that hadn't really been Mr. Cantrell's intent, nor was it wholly polite to contradict a master, but at the same time, she would pour oil on these troubled waters if she could. She felt some responsibility for Mr. Cantrell's public dressing-down. "I will need to increase my upper body strength, especially fencing *here*."

"Well, well," said Perkins, who to her pleasure seemed further mollified, "there are indeed good reasons to put a heavier weapon in someone's hand . . . but on day one! I'm not sure if it's appropriate for any student of any level, and that's leaving aside the risk of falling into *old habits*." He gave Mr. Cantrell a rather hard look. "But, I've said my piece. Welcome, Miss Gray—and I mean that, you are very welcome. You nearly beat George, eh?"

"Nine-ten, and the last was a double," supplied Cantrell. "You should have seen me after; I was in a right state." He smiled at Evadne warmly, and she was glad to see he didn't seem miffed that she'd interceded on his behalf; in her experience, some men were sensitive about such things.

"Not bad, not bad," said Perkins, looking Evadne up and down. "There's always room for improvement. My feeling on the matter is that the goal of quality instruction isn't to make a student the best fencer in the world, but rather the best fencer they can be."

"That's what I want," said Evadne. In spite of his brusque manners, she liked Perkins very much. "After all, I shan't be competing."

"Competitions are well and good, but fencing ought to build one's character first and foremost," said Perkins. "Ah, well, I've already blathered on long enough! Go, practice, have a good time. I'll be in my office." And with that, he ambled away down the hall.

"Whew," said Cantrell. He looked pale. "Sorry about that, Miss Gray, I wasn't expecting . . ."

"It's my fault," she said.

"No, it's not. I should have known better, as Trawless said." Cantrell wiped a thin sheen of sweat from his forehead. He looked unwell; the encounter with Perkins must have shaken him worse than Evadne had realized. "Here, come — let's have a cup of tea. I'm parched."

Evadne wasn't sure. Her eyes flickered over to Trawless, who nodded encouragingly before mouthing the words *"Saint George."*

"I'd be delighted," she said, smiling.

In the kitchen Mr. Cantrell filled a kettle and then set it to boil over a little gas burner.

"So, how is Thorny?" he asked, sitting down at the table.

"Very well," said Evadne as neutrally as possible. "He's engaged to a young woman, Miss Bell."

"Oh, he finally popped the question, did he?" Cantrell chuckled. "Good! As pious as he pretended to be, I'm fairly certain he was thinking of her when we were supposed to be praying. Used to sneak out to meet her, too, after Sunday service. I very much disapproved of *that;* I mean, really, how unseemly for a future shepherd of souls to . . . well, it's not important, is it?" he amended after glancing at her face. Evadne sat up straighter, mindful of Dorina's remark that she always looked like she was sucking on a lemon.

"I'm very happy for him," she said hastily. "He's got himself a living, up in the north, and I think they shall be very happy together."

"Perhaps so. To each his own . . . What I mean to say is, London may be a den of thieves, but at least there's something to do other than cut wood or argue with one's neighbors about sheep breeds."

Evadne surprised herself with a laugh. "You might be right. I couldn't say. I haven't enjoyed London so far, but I've not been here long. At least now I know there's somewhere I can go where sensible people act sensibly."

"I agree with you," said Cantrell. "People these days, they think it's mad—fencing, I mean—but I say you never know when it'll come in handy." He unconsciously ran a finger along the white scar on his cheek. "Ah, there's the kettle."

He fussed over the tea for a few minutes, and Evadne made herself useful finding the sugar and milk. Eventually they met again at the table, mugs in hand.

"There we are," he said, adding milk, but he did not take sugar from the bowl. Instead, he dropped in a little pastille, something just as white from a little tin he took from his pocket. Evadne hadn't meant to stare—it was just so queer; when he noticed her looking, she blushed.

"Problems with my digestion," he confided. "I'm supposed to take it with liquid."

"I beg your pardon, I didn't mean to pry," said Evadne.

"You didn't." He sipped his tea. "*Ahh*, that's better. Nothing like a cup of tea to revive a chap . . . or a lady," he amended, with a nod of his head. "Well, Miss Gray, what do you think? Are you satisfied with the facilities? Do you think you'd like to become a student?" He quirked an eyebrow at her. "*My* student?"

"Absolutely!" She blushed. "I mean . . . yes, I'd very much like to."

"Miss Gray. If you become my student, I must insist you stop doing that." Evadne was lost until he added, "You are a spirited fencer, a spirited person. There's no reason why you should be ashamed of your enthusiasm."

Usually, such impertinence would have sent Evadne right to the door. Instead, she smiled, albeit shyly, and nodded. "All right."

"Let's schedule you some lessons, then, before you go—but you should attend as many of the open clinics as you can. We need to get you practicing with different people at all levels. Oh, don't worry. I'm sure the fellows won't hassle you too much. Probably most of them will fall in love with you."

Evadne hadn't been concerned about being harassed or fallen in love with; she had been contemplating what it would mean to be so very social, with so many different people. "I hope none of them fall in love with me," she said, alarmed. "I did not come here to earn an MRS in fencing."

"Of course you didn't. I was only teasing . . . but a serious young woman like yourself will not like being teased. Forgive me."

Evadne stared at him, astonished that this man could so quickly intuit something about her that her family never had, not in twenty-eight years of knowing her. He was so perceptive . . . which was probably why Mr. Cantrell was such a fantastic teacher. Oh, she was so glad she'd decided to come to the Westminster Fencing Academy! She couldn't explain it, but she was supremely confident in his ability to improve her. The way he looked at her—focused on her.

No one had ever looked at her like that.

Evadne drained her tea and stood so hastily she almost upended her chair.

"I should go. They will wonder what's kept me for so long," she said, knowing it was entirely possible—no, *probable*—that her family had failed to notice she'd been gone at all.

"They is who?"

"My sister, Dorina, and my uncle, Basil Hallward."

"Really?"

Something about the way he said it made Evadne think they might be acquainted. "Do you know him?"

He hesitated, then nodded. "He was the friend of a former student here, Oliver Wotton."

Evadne hadn't realized Oliver Wotton had fenced *here*. Her expression must have betrayed her surprise.

"You knew him?"

"No, but I've met his sister."

Mr. Cantrell stood, and Evadne took a step back; it seemed the proper thing to do. "Funny old thing, isn't she? I don't know her well—she rarely ever came by. Mr. Hallward, however, used to come round to watch quite a bit. Sketched a few of us once—he's supposed to be a fine artist."

"My sister thinks so . . . She's here to write a monograph on him. She wants to be an art critic."

"And what do *you* want to be, Miss Gray?"

Evadne shrugged. "For now, a better fencer."

"Touché!" He smiled down at her. "I'm glad you decided to join us."

He extended his hand. She hesitated—before, when they'd shaken hands, he'd been wearing gloves. Touching his skin seemed an intimate act. Then again, she'd shaken hands with Trawless.

She grasped his hand and shook it firmly.

"I am too," she said as he released her, more certain than ever that she'd made the right choice in coming here. She felt wonderful—better than she'd felt . . . well, maybe ever in her life. There was something about him—something about the idea of being under his supervision—that made her feel safe and warm.

And *happy.*

The way he was looking at her made Evadne quite confident that he understood. She smiled back at him, noting how much better he looked after his cup of tea and their brief conversation. If there had been a mirror in the kitchen, she guessed she would look just as invigorated.

2

Every work that is done with feeling, be it artistic or political or violent or diabolic, is done in the honor of its creator, not its subject. It is not the subject that is revealed by the creator; it is rather the creator who reveals himself.

— *On the Summoning of Demons*

A FTER HER ILLUMINATING conversation with Henry regarding her queer statements about demons — *of course* she didn't actually believe in them, she was only an open-minded sort of person — it was only her fight with Evadne that hung like a cloud over Dorina's otherwise glorious day. She thought of her sister often as they toured the gardens, as they ate lovely ice creams, and even after they finished at the gardens, as they lingered over a lovely tea at the Savoy.

Dorina had been unfair to Evadne. She could admit it. She had said some things she did not really mean, and wanted to talk over the incident with her sister. Soon.

"Shall we do something tomorrow?" asked Henry as she polished off the last cress sandwich. "I dragged you all over the gardens today; I thought our next outing could be to the Victoria and Albert Museum."

"Perhaps," said Dorina. When Henry cocked an eyebrow at her, she sighed. "I should see if my sister has anything in mind. Now that I'm not so angry, I can see why she would be rather cross. She was sent to London because Mother decided I needed a chaperone, and I was so *annoyed* with her . . . but I really ought to have thought about how resentful she must feel about not only being in the city, but having to go to places she cares nothing about."

"Where do you think she'd like to go?" There was no edge to Henry's voice—she genuinely seemed to want to find something to do that interested both sisters. "Does she like shopping? We could walk down Regent Street and see the department stores."

"Not really," said Dorina. She felt a bit sheepish; apart from fencing, she couldn't quite say what Evadne liked. "We should let her choose . . . Then again, it couldn't hurt to offer a few ideas of our own?"

As they headed home, Dorina and Henry discussed the possibility of taking Evadne on a tour of London's best chip shops, the Zoological Gardens, or perhaps Madame Tussaud's waxworks. But, Lady Henry cautioned, they would have to finish their fun by five o'clock; she was having friends over that evening.

"Oh?" asked Dorina. Something about Henry's tone made her very curious.

"Yes, just a little society I host at my home, nothing special," she said, not quite meeting Dorina's eyes.

This prevarication only made Dorina keener, of course. "I'm sure it's lovely. What sort of society is it?"

Henry smiled. "A small group of like-minded individuals who appreciate the finer things."

"What sort of finer things? Are you gourmands? Art critics? Theater aficionados?" Henry was not forthcoming, so Dorina prompted her further. "Horse racing? What do you do?"

"We . . . *appreciate*, that's all," said Henry. "But! Even if I'm busy tomorrow evening, that doesn't mean we can't do something in the late morning or early afternoon, so do ask your sister, and then send word to me."

Dorina knew she would sound like a child if she tried to wrangle herself an invitation, when Henry was quite obviously avoiding taking her hints, but just the same, she was deeply intrigued. A society based around *appreciation* was just the sort of society she had dreamed of joining back in Swadlincote after determining that the life of a London intellectual was the life she wanted.

She decided to play it cool—for now. She had already been feeling Henry out all day: touching her to see her response, begging for cigarettes, so on and so forth. She would leave this for another day.

But before she left London, one way or another, she vowed she would find out what this little appreciation society was all about.

The coach turned the final corner before it reached Uncle Basil's townhouse, and Dorina reached up and plunged her hands into her vast mass of curls, shaking out her mane while shimmying her shoulders in that way that girls always seemed to like. To her delight, Lady Henry watched her, and while her expression was skeptical, there was a hint of a smile that indicated she was enjoying the view. Dorina decided to take this as a good sign. She liked the older woman tremendously, and thought she was gorgeous . . . but she *also* sensed it would be easier to get an invite to her society if they were to become more than friends.

"That's better," she said, leaving off with her preening. "What a lovely day! I knew I would love London, but your attention has made this trip truly special."

"I'm happy to give it," said Henry, "and I confess I've enjoyed seeing London through your eyes. *Fresh* eyes. It's been delightful."

"Well, I'm determined to keep delighting you," said Dorina playfully as they came to a halt. "I'll send you a message soon. Bye!"

And she hopped out of the carriage without waiting for a reply, feeling very pleased with herself indeed. Henry was the sort of person who liked to have the last word, and who was very rarely frustrated; in Dorina's experience with people like that, denying them only served to intrigue them.

She'd intended to speak with her sister directly, but to Dorina's surprise, Evadne wasn't home, and all the housekeeper could say was that Miss Gray was "out." Her uncle was also unavailable—working, or at least, he was in his studio.

Feeling a bit annoyed that she'd ended her day early only to find herself alone, Dorina went up to her room, washed her face and hands, put on a more comfortable dress, and took down pen and paper so she could write their mother. The day they'd come in, Evadne had dashed off something to her about them being safely arrived, but Dorina had promised frequent and full accounts of their adventures. She ought to make good on the promise.

She hadn't written more than a few paragraphs when Evadne returned. Dorina heard her at the door, and jumped up to greet her sister, only to stop short when she saw the state she was in.

Evadne had clearly been active in some way. It was a lovely hot day, and Dorina had taken many breaks in the shade while touring the pools and shady grottos of the Royal Gardens in order to avoid getting sweaty. Evadne, on the other hand, looked—and *smelled*—as if she'd gotten soaked through. Her hair lay plastered across her forehead and over her neck. She was wearing her bizarre fencing trouser-and-skirt combination, and had the grotesquely damp strap of her kit slung over her shoulder. A button on the bag had come undone, and to Dorina's horror, she saw a scrap of one of Evadne's new walking suits poking through—she had just balled it up in there! Why, the maid would never be able get the wrinkles out!

But she was looking happier than Dorina had seen her in a very long time.

"You've been fencing," she said, and even to her own ears it sounded like an accusation.

"No, I went to the Seventh Annual All-London Lemon-Sucking Competition. I won a prize! But, as you can see, the competition was quite fierce, so I ought to go and change clothes before supper."

"Don't be ridiculous!"

"Then don't be nosy."

Opening her mouth to retort, Dorina caught herself. She had wanted to apologize, not antagonize.

"I'm glad you had a good time," she said.

"I did, rather."

Dorina chased after Evadne, who had headed upstairs. "I'm sorry I said those things," she said. "They weren't kind."

"Perhaps not," said Evadne, over her shoulder, "but you were right."

"I was?"

"Yes. I *do* stomp around, ruining your fun. So I won't anymore. Go off—be your own person. Expose yourself all over London in whatever ways seem most entertaining to you. I shan't try to stop you anymore."

They had reached her door. Evadne let herself inside, and would have shut out her sister, but Dorina stepped inside before Evadne could manage it.

Dorina resisted rising to the bait of replying to that remark about exposing herself. "I don't *just* want to go off on my own," she said. "Really, I don't. In fact, I came home early today, just so see you."

This brought Evadne up short. "Why?"

"To say I'm sorry," said Dorina, "and to ask you what you'd like to do tomorrow." Evadne had stopped in the middle of her room. The light from the windows behind her gave her a kind of halo. "So . . . is there anything you'd like to do?"

"I have an appointment in the afternoon . . ."

"Doing what?"

"Fencing class," said Evadne absently.

"There are fencing classes?"

"Yes, at the academy."

"The academy?"

"The one I've just joined, yes. Every afternoon except Sunday there's a clinic—tomorrow's is on strike accuracy."

"Oh." Dorina was disappointed, but just as she was about to say that Evadne should do as she liked, her sister spoke.

"Why?"

"I just thought we might do something . . . together."

Evadne's face lit up. "I don't have to go," she said. "I'd love to do something with you."

"Name it!"

"Promise you won't laugh?"

"Why would I laugh?"

"It's not very exciting," said Evadne a bit shyly, "but I'd love to walk across London Bridge."

"Of course!" said Dorina. "It's something they say you simply *must* do while you're in town."

"Then let's do it!"

"And let's go in the morning," said Dorina, eager to further mollify her sister, "that way, we can be back in time for you to go to your class."

Evadne looked sincerely touched by this. "That would be perfect."

"It's settled, then," said Dorina. She resisted the urge to embrace her sister; Evadne had only grown gamier as they spoke. "Well! I'll let you change. I don't know if Uncle will join us for dinner tonight . . . especially after our row this morning. But, I don't mind a quiet supper."

"Neither do I," said Evadne, and Dorina left feeling better than she had since before they'd come to London, really.

Dorina couldn't quite put her finger on when she and her sister had begun to grow apart. Perhaps they never had; perhaps they'd been born at cats and dogs with one another. Certainly they'd had good times together over the years, but something always seemed to ruin their peace. Dorina had always blamed Evadne for it, as her sister's obvious disapproval and tendency to scold made Dorina childishly eager to act yet more outrageously. But really, she ought to amend her own behavior, and stop wishing for Evadne to change.

Dorina set aside the letter to her mother in order to write Henry of their plans. After, she was too antsy to settle in and finish her missive, so she wandered down to Basil's studio to see if he was painting. He was, though he assured her he would join them for dinner.

"May I watch?" she asked as he daubed at the canvas.

"Of course," he said absently. "Harry's always hanging about, staring at me, so I'm used to it."

His work in progress had been covered with a cloth when she'd entered his studio the last time. Dorina was surprised to find the picture was rather macabre, quite unlike his earlier jewel-bright works they had hanging on the walls at Swallowsroost, or that she'd seen printed in journals. No classical motif or medieval allusion greeted her: the subject was a bored-looking woman with long, waving blue-black hair. While the flesh of her face was young and healthy, a skeletal arm emerged from her off-the-shoulder gown, and one of her legs was mere bone, as well. She sat lounging upon a throne of peacocks—though it was obvious from the studio's setup that a pile of cushions substituted for the live birds when the model was posing. The girl was no beauty, but in the painting she had a regal bearing that was somehow more impressive than beauty. She looked familiar, almost . . .

"Is that the scullery maid?"

"Yes, Bonnie. She sat most wonderfully for this; I think I shall use her again." Basil added, "If she can pose in this heat, with that wig on her head, she can do anything."

Dorina watched him for a bit longer, then wandered about, looking at the other paintings. Before Lady Henry had burst into her life so unexpectedly, Dorina had assumed she would spend many hours studying her uncle as he worked in this room: watching him paint, learning from his methods, writing it all down. Her vision for her article was to do it on his entire body of work, from his juvenilia to his current masterpieces. But, given the apparent tone of his more modern works, where youth and beauty partnered with death and madness, she felt she ought to consider focusing on the recent shift in his subject matter . . .

She felt a sudden and burning desire to begin her research. The studio was filled with golden light filtered through the green leaves and plentiful blossoms of the garden beyond, and it cast a sort of glamour over everything, making it seem divine. The gilt frames of the paintings glowed, and the pictures within, scattered amongst his own works—a smudgy, writhing Delacroix; a jewel-bright Millais; a portrait of a stony-faced young woman that could only be a Cassatt, and a delirious de Morgan—were a curated selection of some of the best masters working today.

And yet, it was her uncle's work that drew her eye most often. She lingered before a nightscape diptych. In the first panel, dancing corpses coupled with maidens with swelling bosoms on a windswept mountaintop; in the second, two youths of vibrant beauty sat in a dark room, the moon beyond, one cutting the finger off the hand of the other where it rested on a silver platter, the former ravenous, the latter ecstatic.

Dorina shuddered, and turned away to find a work more akin to what she'd been expecting to see: a simple portrait of a slight, handsome, rather dashing young gentleman who bore a striking resemblance to Henry. His hair was a little lighter than hers, but they shared a smile, a nose, even a sense of style. In fact, looking closer, Dorina was certain she'd seen Henry wearing his exact suit, and she too had a tendency to pose in that fashion.

He *must* be her brother—her twin, the fencer, Lord Oliver. Henry had not spoken of him, except in passing; Dorina had no notion of how he had died. He certainly looked healthy, at least in this portrait . . . and as Henry didn't look much older, his death must have been relatively recent.

Dorina wished she had known this man, which was not a sensation she was accustomed to feeling—not with men, at any rate.

But if the painting were true to life, she felt he might have been neither bore nor boor. He had the look of someone who would make even fencing seem interesting. His eyes held the most extraordinary expression, a vibrancy she had only ever seen in one other person: Lady Henry, when she was speaking passionately about one thing or another. Dorina found she was unable to look away from the man's gaze, even to admire the crook of his lip or the cant of his cheekbone, the pattern of his waistcoat or the angles of his fingers as he held a cigarette just away from his lips. He was captivating, even in oils, even in death, and the longer she looked, the longer she wanted to look. She almost felt as if she could hear him whispering to her, speaking of—

"I think I'll leave off," said Basil, startling Dorina. She had been squinting at the portrait in the dimming light for she knew not how long. "I ought to wash the paint off before—I say, Dorina, are you quite all right?"

She nodded, even though that was not at all the case. "Is this Lady Henry's brother?" she asked, indicating the portrait. She felt she knew the answer, but making small talk would hopefully alleviate Basil's concern.

"Yes." Basil did not look at the painting; he kept his eyes firmly on his brushes and paints. "I painted that after he . . ."

"How—" Dorina realized it was a rather rude question. "Lady Henry has never spoken of how he passed."

Basil didn't say anything for a moment, but then he said, "It is a painful subject, as it was a surprise. No one suspected he was ill. He always seemed so *healthy* . . . and then when I realized something was wrong, *really* wrong, Henry didn't do anything to— well, whether she *could* have, at that point, who can say . . ."

It wasn't an answer, but Dorina elected not to press the matter. Basil seemed distraught, and given his fragile state she was anxious about doing anything that would upset him further, especially after the spectacle she and Evadne had made of themselves at breakfast.

"Forgive me for asking, Uncle," she said softly.

"No, no. Of course you would be curious . . ." His eyes finally focused on her — only her — for perhaps the first time since she'd arrived in his house. "You've been spending a lot of time with Harry, haven't you? I know you've only been here a few days, but it seems as if you've been with her every moment."

"Not *every* moment," said Dorina defensively. "Last night we dined in, but you were busy."

"Oh. Was I?"

"You were in your studio."

"I suppose I was," he said vaguely. "But in general you have been. I wonder . . . has she asked you to do anything?"

"We went to the Royal Gardens today on her suggestion."

"No, I mean . . ." He swallowed. "Henry, she has a way of influencing people."

"She'd deny that," said Dorina, recalling their earlier conversation. "She thinks it's a disgrace to influence anyone. She believes people ought to discover themselves for themselves."

"What Henry says and what Henry does can be two very different things. She has a good heart; I would never say otherwise. It's only, I have known her to act without thinking, producing results that no one could have guessed."

"You could say that about anybody, couldn't you?" Dorina was confused — she wished her uncle would just speak plainly, and said so. "What has Henry done that makes you feel you ought to warn me about her?"

Basil frowned, casting aside the rag on which he had been wiping his hands for some minutes. "I'm not *warning* you," he said firmly. "I wouldn't have introduced you to Harry if I didn't think she would be a good friend to you. I just didn't expect you to become so close so quickly. It seems like she has already taken you into many of her confidences — as well as sharing her personal philosophies with a girl who is not yet eighteen years old." He smiled.

"Ah, but look at your face—you do not like being reminded of your youth, do not like to consider the idea that you might not be ready to make certain decisions that will affect your future." He sighed. "Perhaps I'm just an old man speaking nonsense. All I will say is, *be careful*. And with that, I must go to dress for dinner."

He patted her awkwardly on the shoulder and then headed for the door. Dorina watched him go, confounded and annoyed. Basil was Henry's friend—and by his own admission he had introduced them thinking they would like one another. Did he know something concerning about Henry?

"Uncle," she called, as something occurred to her. "Are you going to her party tomorrow?"

"No," he said, and his tone told her that it was his final word on that matter.

IN SPITE OF HER AWKWARD conversation with her uncle, and the earlier unpleasantness with her mercurial sister, supper that evening was pleasant—and afterward, they spent a friendly if quiet evening together, listening to the light thunder and rain that had begun to fall as they dined. Evadne was reading the only book Dorina had ever seen her truly absorbed in, *The School of Fencing*, while Dorina asked Basil questions about the current London art scene, his upcoming shows, and his artistic process, all the while taking notes.

Then, around nine o'clock, there was a knock at the door, and a damp gentleman by the name of Cyril Manning came in, dressed for an evening out. As it turned out, Mr. Manning owned a gallery, and he had come by to beg Basil to come out with him to their club in order to discuss some upcoming show of the former Hogarth Club's collection of Pre-Raphaelite canvases. Basil was reluctant and kept making excuses about needing to look after his nieces, but in the end Dorina and Manning managed to convince him it was important that he go and talk over a few things.

"If you're sure," he said doubtfully, looking from Dorina to Evadne. "This is our first real evening together since you've arrived, and I feel it's terribly rude to just go out . . . and in this weather, too . . ."

"You *must* go," insisted Dorina. "You would, if we weren't here."

"Don't be so sure," said Manning, with a wink at Dorina. "Prying Basil away from his studio or his sitting room is a task Hercules might shrink from."

"The Augean Uncle, eh?" said Dorina.

"It is so boring, putting on evening dress," muttered Basil, who had "dressed for dinner" by taking off his smock and putting on a clean shirt. "Then, when you have the damned clothes on, they are horrible."

"Oh, Basil," said Manning, disgusted.

"I'll probably turn in soon anyhow," said Evadne as the clock struck half nine. "The sound of the rain is making me yawn."

"Me too," said Dorina, "Evadne and I are going out early tomorrow if this clears off, so I ought to get my rest." In all likelihood, she would actually be up for hours, reading, or writing, or sneaking into Basil's studio to look more at his collection, but it was the right thing to say—Evadne beamed at her.

"Oh, fine. I can't kick against these goads," said Basil. "I won't be but a moment—in the meantime, Cyril, why don't you tell Dorina about your gallery? I'm sure she'd love to hear all about it. Tell her about that *Women of Impressionism* show, she'll like that."

"An entire exhibition on lady Impressionists?" she exclaimed, totally enthralled by this. "Did you include Marie Bracquemond? I know people look down on her for being self-taught, but I think she's marvelous."

"Of course. But you mustn't give me any compliments, I allowed the Society of Lady Artists to arrange most of the exhibit. Lady Henry suggested it, when I was musing on how I wanted something fresh and new."

"Did she now!" There was nothing Dorina heard about Henry that didn't make her admire her more. "Oh, what a shame it's closed. I would have loved to look at them all individually, up close."

"And together, I'm sure," he said playfully. "We managed to obtain both Eva Gonzalès's *A Loge at the Theatre des Italiens* as well as Renoir's *La Loge* so—"

"Oh! I've never even seen a *print* of Gonzalès's, but I heard it described . . . Is it true it bears more in common with Manet than—"

"By Jove, Basil!" cried Manning, interrupting her as her uncle came back into the room, wearing crumpled but acceptable evening dress. "Dorina has thought more about art than any of my employees! Do you think her parents would let me rent her for a bit?"

"Cyril, if you wish to offer my niece *employment*, you are welcome to do so, but let us never again suggest the possibility of you *renting* a girl under my care."

"We'll discuss it later," said Manning, with a wave of his hand. "For now, let's get to the club and talk over the show."

Evadne did not sit back down after the gentlemen took their leave—instead, she collected her book, and said she would go up to bed.

"I'm worn out from fencing," she confessed, "and I want to be fresh for tomorrow."

"Of course." Dorina stood. "I shall turn in as well, I think . . . let the servants go to bed. You go on ahead; I want a cup of tea." She actually felt inspired to write a bit about her uncle.

"Dorina . . ." Evadne hesitated before departing. "I was really impressed by the way you spoke to Mr. Manning. It's very admirable, how you can talk so intelligently about your passion. I'm sorry I never acknowledged how serious you were about this. I won't make that mistake again."

Dorina was genuinely touched. "Thank you," she said. "That really means a lot to me."

"Anyway . . . good night," said Evadne, suddenly awkward again. Dorina felt another swell of affection for her sister.

"Sleep well, Evadne," she said. "I hope this rain lets up by tomorrow, but if it doesn't, we'll find something to do together."

Evadne nodded, and departed; Dorina followed her sister after asking for a cup of tea to be sent up, and spent a few pleasant moments collecting and then arranging her notebooks, pens, and ink. She wasn't ready yet to try to assign a structure to her monograph, not after such a brief interview with her uncle; she just wanted to scribble out a few thoughts. The skeleton-armed girl had made her think. She wrote:

> They say that painting from life is one of the most important skills for an artist to develop, but what concerns me more is painting from experience. While drawing a model can teach someone how the human figure moves and doesn't move, if an artist has no ideas to express in the drawing of that human body, what exactly is the point of drawing it at all? Simply to perfectly reproduce what exists? We have photography for that. Yes, nature will teach us how something ought to look, but artists must find a way to express their feelings, their unique vision, in order to see how it ought to behave, how it ought to relate to the other elements we pair it with, those becoming and unbecoming conjunctions that create visual interest. Only then can we produce thoroughly good art, for good art overtakes convention and rote learning; it transcends it . . .

A knock at the door startled Dorina, but she welcomed the cup of tea. After thanking the maid and telling her she'd require nothing else that night, Dorina sipped thoughtfully, and wandered to the casement to look out at the quiet street beyond, and the old, rather romantic house across the way. The rain and the gaslights together lent a magical glamour to the view—the trees looked softer; the rare passersby, more intimate in their conversations under their umbrellas.

She tried to see the scene as her uncle would, but it was no good. She wasn't one for penny dreadfuls or sensation novels; the fiction in *Lippincott's* was quite horrific enough for her taste. Why, Mr. Conan Doyle's *The Sign of the Four* had very nearly sent her into fits when she got to that bit about the poisoned dart. Likely her uncle would imagine that gentleman there with a cadaver's head. The thought of seeing such an apparition made Dorina shudder.

For some reason, that thought put her in mind of the picture of Oliver Wotton. What a curious thing it was—how beautiful, how lifelike. How it had transfixed her like no other painting had ever done! The memory of the sensation instantly reignited her curiosity; she resolved to look at it again now that she was at her leisure, without the risk of anyone interrupting her.

She threw a shawl over her shoulders, and after lighting a candle she ventured into the darkened corridor. The sound of the rain almost disappeared as she trod the heavy carpet of the hallway—she thought perhaps the deluge had slaked, but that was not the case; if anything, the storm was worse, rain and wind lashing the windowpanes. Thankfully, Basil's studio was snug; her candle did not so much as gutter, for which she was grateful. The thought of a man with a skull's face was still in the back of her mind, and she did not want to be alone in the dismal room without a light.

As she approached the portrait she held up the candle to look again on the visage of her friend's twin. They were even more alike by the dim light, when she could not see their fine differences; this only obsessed her further.

At first, she avoided Lord Oliver's eyes, instead focusing on anything, everything else . . . but eventually, his gaze claimed her. It seemed more intense, more captivating, more beautiful than before. She knew not how long she stood staring into his eyes, feeling them pierce her very soul. She felt as if he might be speaking to her, *somehow*, a fancy that seemed even more real in the darkness of the chamber, late in the evening, with the drum of the unceasing rain in her ears. But try as she might, she could not understand the low whispers at the back of her mind.

The sound of the front door slamming and what could only be her uncle's footsteps pulled Dorina from her reverie. She panicked, sensing she should not be here, should not be staring at this strange picture, not alone, not with a candle, not in her dressing gown. Not at this hour. For reasons she could not explain she felt as if she had been discovered in the middle of an intimate act —she felt more bashful about this than even when Evadne had found her with poor, forgotten Juliana. She blew out the light and quickly retreated into the shadows behind an easel, drawing an enormous fern on castors a bit in front of herself for good measure.

Her hope that Basil would not come into the studio was dashed when she heard the door creak on its hinges and then heavy footsteps. Basil was mumbling to himself—she couldn't quite hear what he was saying, but soon his intentions were clear.

Dorina and her uncle were of one mind, for he, too, approached the painting.

She drew back farther into the gloaming, smelling spirits. Her uncle was drunk! He had been at his club; still, it didn't seem like him. The times he had visited Swallowsroost he rarely had more than a glass or two of wine, perhaps an after-dinner sip of port or brandy, but he was stumbling about like a sot. He would put his foot through a painting or plant if he wasn't careful!

"Oliver," he said, the first coherent word she'd heard from him. "My dearest Oliver! Why?"

This was worse than anything Dorina could have imagined. Long had she suspected that she and her uncle were of a kind, so to speak, but for him to tell her unknowingly, while intoxicated, speaking to a painting . . . it was embarrassing beyond anything. If she could have escaped, she would have, but as it stood she had to listen. She might startle him into doing something foolish if she revealed her presence now.

Her uncle ungracefully dragged a chair over before the portrait; he almost fell into it, and then she heard a hollow pop. He had uncorked a bottle with his teeth! Spitting away the stopper, he drank deeply.

"Oliver," he breathed, beholding his portrait, "I could have understood, in time, if there had been another . . . but there wasn't, at least, not another *man*. Or woman. Even *that* I could have borne, just not you leaving me alone like . . . like *this* . . ."

Basil sighed deeply, and drank more. She heard him retch a little.

"Ugh," he said, wiping his mouth with his hand, dropping the bottle; its contents spilled over the floor. Basil scarcely seemed to notice. "Oliver . . ." he muttered. "Oh, *Oliver*, I've never despised someone for possessing ideals, but . . ." The sound of sick gurgled in his throat again. Dorina felt the tea she'd drunk rolling around in her own stomach. There was really nothing more disgusting than listening to someone vomit. "I always told you, your ideals were a dead end, a disaster. Moderation was never your strong point. If only I could damn your sister for what she did, what she did to you, what she showed you . . . but I can't. It made you happy . . . happier than *I* made you . . . than I ever could have made you, not in ten thousand years as your hierophant. I understand, of course . . . I know what it's like. I know what it does, how it bewitches you, makes you *see* . . . but just the same, Oliver, *it* couldn't hold you . . . couldn't sleep beside you . . ."

Thank goodness his mumbling became incoherent after that, and finally a snore told Dorina her uncle had fallen asleep in his chair. She waited for a few moments, then cautiously moved aside the potted fern, slipped from her hiding place—and fled.

She knew it would be a kindness to alert someone to her uncle's situation, but how could she? To do so would be to admit she had seen him, which meant admitting she had been in his studio. She had no desire to let him know that she had heard his drunken ramblings!

And yet . . . curiosity made her question her decision. Pausing outside his studio door, Dorina contemplated getting him up, getting him to bed. Then she could ask him what he had meant by it all. What had Henry shown her brother that had damned him, but made him happy? What had bewitched him? What had made him see? It—whatever *it* was—had claimed Oliver, according to her uncle, but Basil knew, and both he and Henry were alive . . .

A sound from Basil's studio made her decision for her. Over the sound of the rain, she heard that her uncle had woken, and was now sobbing his heart out.

"Oliver," he cried, but Dorina would stay and hear no more. Yes, she wanted answers, but not enough to listen to a grown man weeping for his dead lover. Lightly she fled, down the hall, up the stairs, through the dark house, for she had left her candle in the studio. Hopefully he wouldn't notice it before the servants cleared it away.

It wasn't until she was back in her room that Dorina let herself breathe, gasping for several seconds, her back against the shut door. What a strange night! She felt desperately sorry for her unhappy uncle, but though it pained her to admit it, she felt sorry for herself, too. She couldn't think of a single way she could ask Henry about what she had heard her uncle saying without admitting she had eavesdropped—or admitting that at least in part, Basil blamed her for the death of her twin brother.

3

To give one's self to a demon is to be cherished without risk of abandonment. The risk is, rather, that they will *never* grow tired of you—and if they agree to release you, it will be only with the strongest reluctance. Other men will never understand that sort of commitment; their lives change too often.

— *On the Summoning of Demons*

THE RAIN WOKE DORINA late the next morning. Her eyes were sandy and her mouth dry; she coughed as she rose, and groped blindly for the water glass she always kept on her bedside table. A few swallows and she felt much better, but remembering what she had done last night, and how she had left her uncle, she collapsed back against the pillows.

A soft knock brought her back to herself. When Evadne let herself in, her hair already combed and dressed in an almost pretty morning gown, Dorina sat up.

"Forgive me," she said, "the rain kept me asleep."

"There was no reason for you to rise," said Evadne, coming to sit on the foot of her bed. "I don't think we'll be traversing London Bridge—at least, not today."

"Perhaps not," admitted Dorina. "But, we shall find *something* to do, to wile away the hours until you go to your fencing clinic."

"Fencing clinic!" Evadne rose, and went to stand before the rain-splashed windows. Whatever she saw on the street below made her shake her head and turn away again. "I don't know if I shall go. It seems rather, well, wet."

"Oh, but you *must* go!" cried Dorina. "You were so looking forward to it."

Evadne looked surprised, as if she had not expected Dorina to understand this. "True, but I have no wish to catch my death getting damp and chilled."

"Surely the exercise will keep you warm, and then once you're back, have Hannah draw you a bath. Trust me, you'll feel ever so much better if you get out for a bit."

"Are you going out?"

Dorina frowned, thinking of Henry's refusal to invite her to her party. "Probably not, but who can say what the day will hold?"

Evadne patted Dorina's foot under the coverlet. "Come down to breakfast," she said. "You'll feel better with a bit of toast in you."

"What do you mean?" It was Dorina's turn to be surprised.

"You didn't leap out of bed at first light to tell everyone how they're failing to appreciate the glories of the dawn. Something *must* be troubling you."

Dorina smiled fondly at her sister. "You're right . . . tea and toast will be just the thing."

"So you *are* troubled?" Evadne's concern was sincere, but Dorina did not feel she could confide in her sister without making Evadne further doubt the fitness of their guardian. She shook her head.

"Not really," she said, "just disappointed. I had very much wanted to go out with you."

"Oh, it's all right," said Evadne, blushing slightly. "It's my fault. If I were more interested in the sorts of things you like, our plans need not have changed at all, eh? But, as the thought of spending another moment of my life gazing at Sabine women or doubting Thomases makes me want to scream . . ." She shrugged.

"Well, we can't have you screaming," said Dorina, throwing her bedcovers over her sister's head. As Evadne struggled to get free, protesting loudly, Dorina got out of bed and grabbed her brush and let down her hair. She was suddenly ravenous, and therefore eager to make herself presentable. "Hmm," she said, "and I'll warrant your fencing class is during high tea."

"See you downstairs," said Evadne, straightening her hair with her fingers—but she was smiling.

Dorina rushed through her ablutions, and came down just as Evadne had started on the sausages. Dorina took a bit of everything.

"No sign of Uncle Basil," remarked Evadne. "I wonder if he had a late night at his club?"

"Mmph," said Dorina, taking an enormous bite of marmalade-slathered toast to avoid replying.

As they had nothing to do and nowhere to go, they lingered over their meal, each drinking several more cups of tea than they were accustomed to, which resulted in them becoming even more jittery and dissatisfied with staying in. They asked a maid to bring in a guidebook to the city and were just in the final stages of deciding whether they should bother visiting the Crystal Palace when Basil finally came downstairs, ashen-faced and a little unsteady on his feet.

"Uncle," said Evadne, who to Dorina's relief seemed amused rather than appalled, "did you have a good time last night?"

"I had a fine time," he assured her weakly. "Thank you." He winced as he sat down, suppressing a belch. To Dorina's amazement, Evadne seemed actually cheerful to see her uncle in a bad way; then again, she was the sort of person to take delight in the consequences of someone else's excess. "But, what about you?" he managed after a moment. "A dull evening in, and now I fear for a dull day."

"Not at all," said Evadne heartily. "Dorina and I have resolved to enjoy ourselves no matter what."

The doorbell rang, and Dorina jumped—a quick glance at the clock revealed it was the hour that Henry was to have come for them. She felt suddenly apprehensive, fearing her friend's presence would upset the pleasant peace. Likely not even Basil's distress would counterbalance Lady Henry Wotton at ten in the morning.

"I wonder who that could be?" asked Evadne, turning back to the guidebook.

"Henry, I wouldn't doubt," muttered Basil. Dorina detected a hint of sourness; apparently, his thoughts of last night were still on his mind. "Probably she doesn't have anything better to do than lord over me in my weakness."

Evadne had looked up sharply when Basil mentioned Henry's name, and Dorina couldn't quite meet her sister's gaze when Basil was proven right and the lady strode in, Jonas in her wake. Dorina did not need visual confirmation to know the storm had come indoors.

Henry looked dashing in a morning coat and trousers the same color as the sky outside, but a waistcoat of egg-yolk yellow with blue beadwork as bright as any sunny summer's day. Jonas, while attired far more plainly in a well-cut dark suit, looked just as tidy —tidier than usual, actually, which was saying something. He kept turning to Evadne, eager for her to acknowledge him. The extra grooming had clearly been for her sake. Poor man! Evadne was the last person in the world who would pick up on it. Dorina tried to think of something, anything, to say to get Evadne to look up from her plate, but her uncle beat her to it, as Jonas had the day's papers under his arm.

"Good of you to bring those broadsheets," he said, reaching for them.

"Ah, Dorina—I don't think we'll be taking that walk across the bridge," said Henry, by way of hello over the rustling of newsprint. "Sorry, girls, but it's coming down sideways; even an umbrella won't do us much good."

"We had already decided against it," said Evadne, looking annoyed as Henry sat down beside Dorina. "We have enough sense to stay in when it's wet."

Demonstrating the very patience of Job, Henry actually smiled as she poured herself a cup of tea. Jonas hovered behind Basil—he had been moving to take a chair beside Evadne, but her chilliness was making him uncertain. Dorina caught his eye and nodded; he blushed, and went for it. Unfortunately, Evadne gave him a look that would wither an oak tree and turned away from him, nose in the air. Dorina's heart went out to the young man—he looked so disappointed.

"Plenty to do indoors," he said anxiously, his desire for her attention so obvious it was almost painful. "Ah, and I see you have a recent Baedeker's, what were you considering?"

"I think I heard the Crystal Palace mentioned," said Basil, who had just helped himself to dry toast.

"I'm afraid it would take too much time," buzzed Evadne waspishly. "I have an afternoon appointment."

"Oh?" Henry reached for a croissant. "What will you be doing?"

"Evadne's taking fencing lessons," said Dorina quickly, before Evadne could tell the woman to mind her own business.

"Really!" cried Jonas, with genuine enthusiasm. "How wonderful, Miss Gray! There are so many good schools in the area. When you said you weren't planning on attending any lessons I was disappointed, but I didn't like to second-guess a lady . . . Still, I confess it seemed a shame to fail to take advantage of what London has to offer while you're here. I think it's a fantastic idea!"

Evadne looked a bit less like an ice sculpture by the end of this pretty speech, but when Henry spoke, she froze over again.

"I do wish you'd told us before signing up," Henry said, unaware of the chill—or choosing to ignore it. "I could have told you the name of Oliver's old school. It was called the *something* Academy . . ."

"The Westminster Fencing Academy," supplied Jonas. "The head teacher, Mr. Perkins, is supposed to be the best in the city. We could very easily introduce you if you like . . ."

Evadne, oddly enough, seemed displeased. "I need no introduction. That's where I'm going," she said stiffly. "A friend recommended the school to me, actually. They remember your brother, Lady Henry, and speak very highly of him."

"Independent confirmations of superiority often speak to something's merit," said Basil. "If one of my paintings received such universal praise from the critics, I feel I'd be justified in considering myself a genius."

"I should hope not," said Dorina, hoping to divert the conversation; Evadne looked ready to bolt. "It's when the critics disagree that an artist knows he's doing what he ought."

"I'm not sure if the same applies to fencing schools," said Henry, amused. "What did you think of the academy, Evadne? Oliver always thought the world of Perkins."

"Mr. Perkins seems very experienced," she said, now glacial. "I believe I shall improve under his tutelage."

"Yesterday you seemed *thrilled* with the place!" cried Dorina, by way of protesting her sister's coolness. But Evadne was like Rapunzel in the story; she had let down her hair for a few moments, only to pull it back up and hide in her tower, presenting no opportunity for anyone to join her in her isolation.

"Don't worry, Evadne," said Henry kindly. "I never fenced, nor do I plan to begin; my relationship with the academy ended with my brother's death. I doubt they'd even know me there if I showed up . . . Well, maybe in these clothes—we *were* twins after all— but barring that, I can't imagine . . . Evadne?"

But Evadne had excused herself, and disregarding the entreaties of her sister, her uncle, and Jonas, did not return.

"You know, Dorina, I don't think your sister cares for my company," said Henry. She said it in the manner of someone commenting upon the weather, but Dorina could tell she was annoyed. And why shouldn't she be? She'd tried to be friendly, talked to Evadne about her interests, given her presents . . . but just the same, Dorina felt guilty. It occurred to her that she hadn't mentioned to Evadne that she'd invited Henry along, and perhaps she should have.

No, she *certainly* should have. Evadne must have believed they would be going alone to the bridge, and had been taken by surprise, which she never liked.

"Evadne takes her time coming around to people," said Dorina. "This I fear was my fault—I hadn't mentioned you would be coming with us."

"I see," said Henry gravely. "Well, that just means I'm correct in my assumption—if I'm not a pleasant surprise, then I'm an unpleasant one."

"It might have been me," said Jonas, eyes flickering to the door Evadne had gone through. "Miss Gray and I didn't part on the best of terms after our afternoon at the National Gallery."

"She was in such a good mood yesterday." Dorina sighed. "I'm a fool—I'd hoped the two of us would do something together today."

"Should we leave?"

"No," said Dorina firmly. "Or rather, I should say, it is not for me to turn you out of my uncle's house, or for Evadne to make you unwelcome. Please excuse me. I shall be down shortly, either way."

"Don't," said Evadne, when Dorina found her changing into her practice clothing even though it was hours before she'd said she'd be going to her lesson. "Just *don't.* I should have known you wouldn't be interested in . . . well, it doesn't matter."

There it was. Evadne had wanted to do something just the two of them.

"Evadne," she said, pleading with her sister. "Henry and I had talked about doing something today, but we both agreed it ought to be what *you* wanted to do."

"So, I'm not interesting enough on my own," growled her sister. "I understand."

"That's not it at all!"

"No?" Evadne advanced on her sister like they were about to do battle; Dorina took a step backwards involuntarily. "You mean you wanted to spend time with me *without* your ghastly friend and her bizarre associate?" She sniffed.

"Jonas was Lord Oliver's valet," said Dorina, annoyed. "Now he helps Henry, but really they're just friends."

Evadne was completely taken aback by this intelligence. "He's a servant?"

"Oh, don't be such a snob!"

This brought her sister up short. "I'm not a *snob*," she said, sounding wounded. "I just . . . I didn't . . ."

"Who cares what he is? He's a perfectly lovely person—and he likes you!"

"He does not!"

"Yes, he does—and trust me, I'm very good at spotting such things."

"I don't care to be liked by him," she said haughtily, deflecting the flow of the conversation. "It has nothing to do with *what* he is, Dorina, but *who* he is. What he said to me in that museum!"

Dorina was astonished. "He was teasing you, you goose! He thought you'd enjoy being compared to a warrior goddess—he didn't mean all that about her being a virgin or whatever. I can assure you, if your virginity was on his mind, it was . . . ah . . ."

That had absolutely been the wrong thing to say, given Evadne's tight mouth and high color, but realizing her own error, Dorina finally became angry. Why did she always have to walk on eggshells around her sister? Why couldn't they just be friends—laugh, talk about romance and friendship?

"You're impossible," she snapped. "It's not just him you don't 'care' to be liked by, though, it's everybody! What care you for friendship, when you can storm up to your room and—"

"You've already made clear your true sentiments about me," said Evadne, "and more truthfully, I think, than your protestations regarding your desire for my company."

Dorina did not like to be called a liar. She tossed her hair. *"Fine,"* she said, now advancing on her sister. "Stay in your room in your awful smelly clothes until it's time for you to go to your stupid class — you'll have more fun sulking by yourself than you would laughing with those who care for you and desire your companionship."

"Ha!"

"Believe what you like," said Dorina, "for I shan't trouble myself about you *ever again!*" And with that, she turned on her heel, and left her sister alone, just like she obviously wanted.

Their exchange had shaken her. Dorina had wanted so much for things to be easy between them, and yet here they were again, angry at one another, having said more unkind things. Dorina sat down on the top stair, suddenly exhausted.

Perhaps she was selfish, but Evadne was impossible! At least she, Dorina, could admit when she was wrong — and she would let something go! Evadne would hold on to every slight until the end of time.

Let her. Dorina resolved to not trouble herself about her sister; moping alone was doing the exact opposite of that. No reason she shouldn't enjoy herself just because Evadne had decided she never would.

Her uncle and his guests had repaired to his studio. Dorina was happy to see the servants had cleaned up the mess from last night; neither the spilled wine nor Dorina's abandoned candlestick were in evidence, and the fern's misplacement was not noticeable as Henry and Jonas had created a sort of bower with the various potted plants. They were seated on an Oriental carpet and cushions in the center of the grove, just lounging; Jonas looked up eagerly at the sound of Dorina's footsteps, but seeing she was alone, his face fell. He amended the error in an instant; Dorina shot him a sympathetic smile to show she understood.

"Basil is going to draw us," announced Henry, gesturing at where her uncle mixed paints. "Isn't that a splendid way to spend a rainy day?"

"We shall have a memorial of our pleasant morning," said Jonas wryly, helping himself to a cigarette from Henry's case.

"At least we shall have a story to tell when it's exhibited — or at least, part of one," said Henry, noting Dorina's frown. "No confidences regarding lapses in temper will be betrayed, naturally. Anyway, there's no way we shall be ourselves. We'll all have the heads of pigs, or mouths for eyes. No longer can we count on being a pleasure party with Lancelot or what have you. We'll be ... *symbolic* of something."

"Wonderful." Dorina knew she sounded as sour as her sister. Realizing this, she said more brightly, "But how shall we behave if we don't know what we're to become?"

"Oh, for now he just wants us to drape ourselves artfully, so he can sketch," said Jonas. "Come and join us! And we brought enough cushions for four ..."

"Then the three of us will be extra comfortable," said Dorina. She sighed. "I'll join you in a moment. I just ..."

"Take your time," said Basil idly as he did things with pigments and oils.

Dorina wandered up behind him to see what he was doing, but she was in no mood to make keen observations about the ways of artists. Instead, she wandered the perimeter of the studio, weaving in among the various plants, the patter of the rain on the windows a more fitting accompaniment to her mood than any sonata.

She passed listlessly in front of the picture of Lord Oliver Wotton and turned toward it. Henry joined her, and out of the corner of her eye, Dorina saw the older woman's cheeks flush from pleasure as she gazed upon it. Oh, Henry was so lovely, *too* lovely even; her profile was immaculate, her cheek was as delicate and vibrant as any peony in a Japanese woodcut. She was luminous, like a cloud bank turned pink from the sun. Dorina longed to turn, to make Henry acknowledge her glance, her desire, to kiss that mouth and . . .

She became dimly aware that her uncle was speaking to them, but she hadn't caught what he was saying. She had never seen a beauty like Henry before. She was wholly intoxicating; her aroma, heady, and her flaws — as the simple-minded might call the faint wrinkles around her eyes and lips — just made her more interesting to look at. Dorina had never been vain about her youth. In fact, she had always longed to be older than she was, and looking at Henry she desired more than ever a few silver hairs of her own, little character lines. And not only that, if she were older, perhaps Henry would consider returning her longing. But their ages were always to be a set number of years apart. She would always be too young; she felt the pain of it like a knife, and her eyes filled with tears.

"Don't you like it?" asked her uncle. "You were staring at it long enough yesterday."

"Of course she likes it," said Henry, with a smile that told Dorina she knew exactly what the younger woman had been thinking. "Who wouldn't like it? It's your masterpiece. One need not have known Oliver to appreciate its genius."

"I wish you would take it, if you admire it so much," said Basil. There was a tone in his voice that surprised Dorina, a simmering . . . *something*, not quite anger, not quite frustration. "I painted it for you."

"I thought you were painting it for yourself, with all your talk of never exhibiting it."

"I've changed my mind."

"It's yours. I insist; you must keep it."

"You've damned me, then," said Basil, quite seriously. "How sad, to live every day with it hanging there, haunting me. Oliver will always remain as he is—beautiful, in his prime—while I grow old and gray and frail. He will always be laughing as I lose my sight, always be straight as my spine curves, always remain firm as I begin to shake and—"

"Baz," said Henry gently.

Basil shook his head. "I'm sorry. I'm not accustomed to loving my own art," he said. Dorina made a mental note of that—it had never occurred to her that artists might not love the things they created, but she filed it away for later pondering. The present was currently far too interesting for her to be ruminating on what she might write in the future. "I've certainly never loved my art more than a person. And I still don't. But now that Oliver is—is *gone*, I can't love him as a person. I can only love him like an ivory Hermes or a silver faun . . ."

"You are not yourself," said Henry. "Don't talk like this."

"Why shouldn't I?" The house was full of tension that morning; Basil was angry now. "Oliver was finer than any material thing, and now he is *only* a material thing. I would have cherished the opportunity to see him grow old and die, but now he will stay the same forever. Maybe I could live with that *thing* if the picture could change, could grow as foul as I shall . . . bah!" Basil tore his eyes from the golden portrait, which almost seemed to glow, and stalked away back to his work table. Henry followed him. Dorina did not; feeling weak in her legs, she joined Jonas on the sprawling carpet. She looked at him nervously, but he shrugged—this conversation had clearly happened before. She nodded in return, and he patted the back of her hand with his palm, a familiar gesture from a servant, no doubt, but Dorina didn't mind. *She* was no snob.

"I should never have painted that picture," said Basil. "You're right—it is my masterpiece, the finest piece of work I've ever done, and I hate it. I think I shall destroy it if you don't take it away."

"Have a cigarette," said Henry, opening her case, "and relax, look at it again, and—"

"Don't you dare offer me one of those things ever again," said Basil, whirling around so quickly that if Henry hadn't stepped back, he surely would have knocked it from her hand. "And don't you dare offer one to my niece, either!"

"I haven't," said Henry, sounding wounded. "You know I wouldn't . . ." She glanced at Dorina. "I've already told her no several times, if you must know."

"But you smoke them around her just the same, and take your bloody snuff, and whatever else . . . You make it look so . . . so *delightful*, as you'd say."

"I'm right here," said Dorina, appalled.

Basil passed a hand over his eyes. "For now," she thought she heard him murmur.

"I think I shall go," said Henry, all dignity. "I don't believe I'm of a mood to sit quietly and be sketched."

Dorina sprang to her feet. "Don't go," she implored her. "I shall see nothing of you tonight, you've already said so . . ." Henry looked so serious, Dorina went to her and took the older woman's hands in her own. "If you go, today shall have even less sunshine in it, and it needs all it can get. If you go, I shall cry so much that the house will surely flood. If you go—"

"Oh, just invite her to your bloody meeting," snapped Basil. "She's yours already, completely—or if she isn't already, she will be. You won't be easy until you've taken her under your wing, shown her what Oliver showed me . . . what you showed Oliver. Don't worry—look at us, we're all doing just fine!"

Henry extracted her hands from Dorina's. "I told her no, Baz. She's not coming."

"Not tonight. But in a week? In a fortnight?"

"I told her no," repeated Henry. "What more do you want? She's a person, with her own thoughts and feelings and interests."

"I'm not in the mood to paint," muttered Basil. "I'm going upstairs, and I don't wish to be disturbed." He stalked from the room.

"Oh dear," said Dorina. She sat back down again. She felt awful. "Now *everyone* is cross with me in this house . . . and I don't feel as if I'd done anything—well, not much—to deserve it." She sighed. "You'd better go, Henry. Perhaps I can figure out how best to apologize to my uncle and my sister." Tears of frustration began to roll down her cheeks. "I think they both want me to be someone other than who I am . . . Well, maybe they're right, and I am a selfish beast, and a—"

"Don't say that!" Henry was beside her, had her arm around her. "Don't ever wish to be anyone but who you are!"

"I want . . . I want to be older. I want to be old enough that you'll let me be like you . . . come to your society, learn to appreciate the world instead of just seeing it. I want to be like you said, a critic with a meat cleaver; I want . . . I want to be anyone in the world less prosaic than myself."

"You're not prosaic!"

"No? And yet you treat me like I'm a stupid little country girl!"

Henry looked helplessly at Jonas, who shrugged.

"Let her come," he said.

"But . . ."

"We can make arrangements for her, like any other junior member."

What this might mean, Dorina could not say, but she did not pry; she did not wish to press her luck. Her tears of frustration had been sincere, but they dried quickly upon hearing that she might be invited to Henry's appreciation society.

Ah, well. Perhaps she was still a child!

"All right," said Henry at last.

"Are you sure?"

"Baz was right . . . I would have relented, sooner or later. I'm only human, and you're very persuasive." Henry smiled sadly. "Jonas, let's help her pack. She'll need something suitable for tonight, and you'll know even better than I what she should wear."

"Something white and sacrificial?" suggested Dorina. She'd meant it as a joke, but it only made Henry look more somber.

"Let's put you in as many colors as we can, in good taste," said Jonas, nervously looking at Henry.

"She'll be just as tempting, whatever we do," said Henry.

4

If demons have taught us anything, it is that the senses
and the soul must be treated with equal consideration.

— *On the Summoning of Demons*

DORINA LEFT HER UNCLE'S HOUSE without telling her
sister where she was going. Basil knew where she'd be, so
it wasn't as if she was ducking out without anyone knowing where she could be found.

She also wanted to protect her own happiness. Evadne had
a way of making people feel bad about things they were excited
about, and Dorina was *very* excited. She didn't want any clouds
hanging over this triumph — there were enough in the sky already.

Henry had a few little errands, and Dorina could think of literally nothing she'd rather do than come along. Not only was she
curious, but she also needed to find some way to manage her nervous enthusiasm. She didn't want to seem like an overeager puppy.

They headed to the Borough Market, in Southwark, where
could be found Henry's favorite florist in all of London. Henry's
greenhouse would provide the more exotic blooms for the table
and the meeting rooms, but she could not produce the needed volume for all the arrangements.

The young woman who ran the shop was as genteel a shop-
keeper as Dorina had ever met, an absolutely delightful young
woman who seemed to be intimately acquainted with Henry. So
intimately that Dorina felt a twinge of envy over the way they

laughed and joked with one another about the young woman enjoying the bouquets "in person." After they got back in the carriage, perhaps sensing Dorina's discomfort, Henry told her that the girl would be not only bringing the arrangements, but staying for the gathering.

They then went on to tour the rest of the market to look for a few ingredients Henry's cook had forgotten, and pick up a few extras, as well. They purchased some lovely asparagus, mushrooms, and strawberries from the greengrocer's, as well as a variety of orange Dorina had never tasted before; from a patissier they bought delicate almond-cream tarts and from a baker, beautiful fresh breads.

Given that Jonas was kind enough to carry their parcels for them, they used their umbrellas to shield him from the downpour as they walked to meet Henry's carriage. They got soaked in the process, but it was tremendous fun. Dorina was certain she saw Henry's eyes flickering her way as they laughed and scurried through the deluge, and later, in the cab, when Dorina artfully complained of her clammy bodice.

When they got back to Henry's, they all three called for baths, and after shedding a few outer garments sat shivering, wrapped up in blankets in Henry's warm kitchen with a pot of steaming-hot ginger-scented tea to stave off any ill effects of going out in such weather.

"I really can't recall the last time I had such a good time," said Dorina, freshening Henry and Jonas's cups.

"Ah, to be young again," said Henry. "There was a time when running through the rain and getting wet feet would have charmed me too."

"Tosh," said Dorina. "You loved it."

"Good company makes just about anything better," said Jonas.

"Lady Henry, your bath," said one of her servants, poking her head in, and then withdrawing.

"Oh, you take it," said Henry to Dorina.

"Let's take it together," suggested Dorina. "It'll be less work for the servants, and after all, we're both *girls*."

"The tub isn't big enough," said Henry smoothly as Jonas grinned into his cup.

Dorina tried not to show her disappointment. "All right," she said lightly. "But I don't know the way to your room."

"I'm sure Beth is waiting outside the door to help whoever emerges. Go on, Dorina."

Henry's bedroom was large and lavishly appointed, though — unsurprisingly — not as feminine a space as Dorina might have chosen for herself. The furniture was of rather plain, dark wood, though the linens and wallpaper were both delightfully floral, giving the room a rather jungle-like feel. A canopied four-poster was the most ostentatious piece in the room. It was so tall there was a little step to get into it.

Dorina did not waste any time. The steam emerging from the attached bath was too tempting, and anyway, Beth was already helping her out of her underclothes. She had shed her dress earlier, but still had to remove her camisole, corset, knickers, and so on before she could step into the tantalizingly hot, scented water. The help was much appreciated.

The tub, she noted, could absolutely have held the two of them.

She wasn't *too* disappointed. She hadn't yet met a nut she couldn't crack, given enough time. And pressure.

"Ginger," she remarked as she identified the unusual odor of the steam. "Always ginger!"

"I thought it would be the lady who would be bathing first," said Beth. "Does it not suit you, miss?"

"It's perfectly lovely," she assured the girl. "Thank you."

"Let me help you with your hair, miss," said Beth shyly. "It's so long, and I know the difficulty of managing it all."

A glorious half-hour later, Dorina was swaddled in fluffy golden-yellow towels and a thick slub-silk robe, her cheeks pink, her hair clean and drying before the fire in Lady Henry's room. Beth filled the bath again, and after turning off the taps, went to fetch her mistress. Though Beth hinted that Dorina could situate herself in a guest room, Dorina lingered in her comfortable chair until Henry appeared.

"Ah! For a moment, I thought perhaps Jonas had picked out some charming new statue for my chambers," she said.

"A statue would be nude," said Dorina, loosening the neck of her robe. To her surprise, this actually drew a blush from the un-flappable Henry, who then elected to undress with the bathroom door shut—and locked. Dorina took this as a hint, and when Beth re-emerged with Henry's trousers and shirt over her arm, she ac-knowledged it was time she moved to another room.

The guests were expected at eight o'clock; by the time Dorina's hair had dried it was only six, so with Beth's help she changed into a light cotton robe Henry called a *yukata*. Henry wore one, too. They were very convenient; the sleeves were short enough that they could cull a few blossoms from Henry's greenhouse and set them in among the blooms delivered by the flower shop without need-ing to roll them up.

By the time they'd finished the arrangements it was time to dress, and Dorina was excited to do so. She would be wearing a delight-ful scarlet and jade caftan that Henry had lent her, after Jonas had declared her wardrobe charming, but not nearly comfortable enough for the sort of intimate evening they had planned. Dorina had had her doubts ... but when she saw what Jonas had picked out she was ever so glad to don it. It was so comfortable it seemed almost sinful—the yukata had been too much like a robe for Do-rina to feel as though she could meet strangers in it, but the caf-tan was structured and modest while feeling like she was wearing nothing at all. Beth pinned her hair minimally, just enough to keep it out of her face, and set a little matching hat on her head that completed the ensemble beautifully.

"It looks well on you, miss," said Beth.

"It does, doesn't it?" Dorina smiled at herself in the mirror. "I suppose I can see what my sister sees in those awful bloomers she loves ... I feel delightfully free in these trousers." She spun round, keeping an eye on herself, pleased.

"When you've finished, Lady Henry said to meet her by the door."

"By the door!"

Henry insisted on receiving her guests that way when her society met—"We are all of us equals, and I am perfectly equal to opening a door a few times" was her explanation.

"You look well," said Dorina, though to be honest, Henry looked decidedly odd in her swanky London foyer; she had donned a tweed country suit. But they were all to be comfortable that night, she reminded herself. "Do you like the caftan?"

"Charming," Henry replied. The way she said it reminded Dorina of a cat's purr. Oh, how she longed to hear Henry say her name in that tone!

The doorbell rang. Feeling suddenly nervous, Dorina felt herself begin to perspire. She dearly hoped to impress Henry and her friends by being witty and interesting and possessed of intriguing opinions on subjects people cared about ... The problem was, she still had no idea what this little gathering was all about, save that it was an *appreciation society*. Henry had avoided her questions all day when she'd tried to ask anything about it, even who would be attending. She'd decided, therefore, that it must be a group of the most famous artists and musicians and actors and bons vivants of the age, and Henry wanted to surprise her.

"Ah, Mrs. Dhareshwar!" cried Henry as she opened the door to reveal a stout, handsome Indian woman in an electric-pink sari trimmed with intricate loops of gold braid. Her umbrella, too, was colorful—a bright blue with floral pattern in silver. "Welcome, welcome!"

"Harry," she said, kissing her hostess on the cheek. "How are you this evening? You look absolutely ravishing, as always." She turned to Dorina after shaking out her umbrella and placing it in the stand. "And who is this? A new protégé?"

"May I present Miss Dorina Gray. Miss Gray, Mrs. Kamaladevi Dhareshwar," said Henry. "Miss Gray is to be our guest this evening, Kamaladevi. She's Basil's niece."

"Fantastic!" Mrs. Dhareshwar embraced Dorina. "You'll have *such* a good time, my dear; Henry always puts on absolutely delightful programs. Never the same thing twice."

"I've been looking forward to it since the moment she mentioned she curated an appreciation society," said Dorina.

"An *appreciation society!* Well, that's as appropriate a description as anything, isn't it?" Mrs. Dhareshwar winked at Henry.

"If you'd like to go in, Jonas is pouring champagne," said Henry, studiously avoiding Dorina's curious gaze.

Mrs. Dhareshwar laughed a light, tinkling laugh. "I wonder which of those two things you think will tempt me more. Jonas is—" A knock at the door cut her off, and Henry opened it to reveal a tall, thin man with thick brown muttonchops and a stoop. Except for his height he was unexceptional in every way; Dorina thought he would not look out of place in a shop or bank. He boasted no colorful umbrella, just plain black.

"Mr. Seward!" Henry greeted him with a handshake. "So glad you could make it; I know your back has been troubling you."

"Wouldn't miss it," he said in a nasal drone. Dorina couldn't imagine this man appreciating anything beyond a Sunday roast and the evening papers. But, remembering how she'd told her sister not to be a snob, she pushed the thought aside.

"Mrs. Dhareshwar!" he said, embracing her. "And a new member!"

he said, turning to Dorina. "Enchanted, my dear." He shook her hand in a gentle, avuncular manner.

"She's not a member yet," said Henry. "She is my guest. Basil's niece."

"Oh, is Basil here?" asked Mr. Seward.

"I'm afraid not," said Henry.

Dorina wasn't the only one to notice the shift in Henry's mood. "Mr. Seward, will you escort me into the parlor? I hear there is champagne," said Mrs. Dhareshwar diplomatically. With a nod, Mr. Seward took her arm and led her through.

"Mrs. Dhareshwar runs a successful textile-importing business. She took it over after her husband passed away and has done fantastic things with it," said Henry before Dorina could ask. "The coverlet on my bed—if you noticed it—that's one of hers . . . Oh, and that robe you had on, the golden one, I had that made up out of something special she brought back for me the last time she was abroad."

Dorina was surprised to find that Mrs. Dhareshwar was a businesswoman; she didn't seem the type at all. Then again, Dorina didn't know so very much about merchants. Maybe they were all bright and bubbly and elegant and interested in . . . *appreciation*, whatever that might mean.

"As for Mr. Seward, he's my banker," said Henry, her good mood apparently restored by Dorina's surprised expression.

"A banker!" she cried.

"Yes, he's fantastic at it. At least, I think he is . . . I always have enough money to do what I like, so that seems a good indication of his prowess. He's also such *fun* to go to the opera with. Tremendous ear. In fact, if you have a good time tonight, one of our meetings later this summer is to be musical in nature. We always have a theme, you see . . . and tonight is to be the first in a series called 'The Five Senses.' The theme is scent, and I've arranged a program around that, with Mrs. Hill's help—the florist we met, earlier. Mr. Seward is arranging everything for sound in a month or so. It should be fantastic. I'm *so* looking forward to it."

"I see," said Dorina. She was now acutely aware of her own snobbery, as well as how mistaken she had been about the nature of this gathering. It made her uncomfortable, realizing both things at once.

But she was simultaneously thrilled to hear that Henry was already amenable to her attending a second time . . .

Mrs. Hill soon arrived, with another large bouquet under her arm, which Henry gratefully received. As they took them into the back together, Dorina was left alone to greet a German gentleman by the name of Dr. Sauber, who made Dorina giggle when he announced that he studied "the female orgasm."

"My dear girl," he explained to her as she covered her mouth with her hand, "you may think that in the modern world we need not concern ourselves with such matters, but I assure you, female sexual pleasure is still tragically disregarded in most marriages. In fact, I would assert that sexual enjoyment in women is less valued today than it was one hundred years ago, which is a terrible step backwards for society. In the eighteenth century, it was believed that women needed to orgasm to conceive. Sadly, as our understanding of biology advanced, we gave up the idea of orgasm being necessary, and now consider it a happy accident—if we consider it at all!"

"That *is* a tragedy," said Dorina, with as straight a face as she could manage. She'd never heard anyone speak so openly of such things in her life.

"Thus, I have made it my life's work, researching and publishing on this very topic—and tangentially, discrediting the notions of hysteria and frigidity—in order to help women assert themselves in and outside of wedlock, rather than accepting a life of sexual deprivation and—"

"Doctor! Miss Gray is seventeen years old," said Henry, looking rather miffed as she rejoined them.

"Good! Good!" he cried. "I have observed that a sexually satisfied young person is more likely to become a sexually satisfied older person. She cannot begin at a better age!"

"Begin?" Dorina arched a single eyebrow. "Who said anything about *beginning*?"

"Ah!" Dr. Sauber took off his spectacles and polished them with his handkerchief, peering at her intently. "Do I take this to mean you are already familiar with how to induce an orgasm in yourself?"

"And in other women, whom I believe would all consider themselves quite satisfied." Dorina was enjoying herself, and Henry's reaction. She'd never seen her friend look so uncomfortable!

"Fascinating! A sapphic seducer! Miss Gray, I would love to interview you. Would you consent to talk to a researcher about your experiences?" He leaned in. "I come up with pseudonyms and identities for all my subjects, so if you are worried about your parents or friends, I assure you, no one will know it is you. You could be anyone you like!"

"But I'm already exactly who I wish to be," replied Dorina, shooting a sidelong glance at Henry.

"Charming!" cried Dr. Sauber. "Henry, your friend is delightful."

"Thank you, Doctor," replied Dorina. "And I would love to help you in your very important researches . . . but I must confess some trepidation. I would need a chaperone, I think, especially if I will be talking about *intimate* matters."

"Ah, perhaps Lady Henry will consent?" cried Dr. Sauber.

"We'll discuss it later," said Henry. "Won't you go in, Doctor?"

"I will," he said, winking at Dorina as he bowed.

Henry had a rather prim look on her face after the doctor left them. "Don't," she said when Dorina opened her mouth.

"How many more?" she asked, all innocence.

"Three."

Momentarily, Dorina was introduced to a Miss Hyacinth Travers, a columnist for a women's magazine who published helpful household hints and tips for homemakers. She was wearing bloomers and a large, shapeless shirtwaist Evadne would have found no fault with, and was taller and rather more masculine than her companion Mr. Robert Blake, a graying man of about Dorina's height who illustrated children's books. Dorina immediately got a strange feeling about them, as if they were in some sort of relationship, and wanted to know more, though of course she didn't ask.

More importantly, the presence of a writer and a visual artist reassured Dorina that she hadn't been totally mistaken with her assumptions about the party, even if they weren't quite the sort of writer and artist she'd thought to meet. Before she could remark upon this, the final guest arrived.

"Mr. Walmsley," said Lady Henry. "Good of you to come."

"Wouldn't miss it," he said, and refusing her aid, used his cane and the doorjamb to step up into the entryway.

Dorina was startled by his appearance. Not because of his cane — her uncle had come back from the Sudan with a wooden leg — but because this fellow looked as if he suffered from some sort of wasting disease. Unlike the rest of the guests, who had, like Henry, been attractive and healthy-looking, Mr. Walmsley's sandy hair was without vibrancy, hanging limply over his forehead; he had flesh, but it looked unwholesome, bloated even. His color was bad and his face careworn, lined — no, *creased,* like a dog-eared page in a book. And he walked as if he felt pain with every step, and from every part of him.

"Let me introduce Miss Dorina Gray, who is my guest for the evening," said Henry, shutting the door behind the final arrival. "Dorina, this is Bertram Walmsley."

"A pleasure," he said, but did not extend his hand. Dorina didn't find this surprising; it seemed to take all his effort to remain upright.

"The pleasure is mine," she said.

"Go on in, Bertram; we'll join you in a moment." The man nodded, and disappeared after a brief and awkward fumbling with the parlor door.

"What is he, a greengrocer? A poet? Both?"

Henry took Dorina's arm. "Neither. He's a gentleman—another client of Mr. Seward's. Now, Dorina, before we go in . . ."

She sighed. Another lecture!

"There is only one thing I insist upon: be satisfied with what you receive."

"I beg your pardon?"

"You are my guest, yes, but you must not request anything other than what you will be given. And I must insist you not take anything you are not personally served, or ask to see anything more than you are allowed to see. And I ask that you apply this behavior to everything, including leaving if you are asked to."

Dorina was actually surprised by this. "All right," she said. "I promise."

"Good girl. And you're not alone—so don't feel like this is because of your age, or your sex. Mr. Walmsley is also a junior member, and must follow the same rules. All right?"

Dorina was too excited to argue. "All right," she chirped.

"Then let us go in," said Henry.

And they did.

HENRY'S CHINOISERIE PARLOR WAS ALWAYS impressive, with its black lacquered wooden furniture and golden wallpaper adorned with scenes of fecund fruit trees and bright-plumed exotic birds, but in the candlelight it really came to life. Modern electric bulbs illuminated the space efficiently from the corners, but the long tapers still cast their warm, flickering light over everything from the deep-upholstered chairs and sofas to Jonas pouring drinks for Miss Travers and Mr. Blake. He was doing something with sugar cubes, a clear glass bottle with a dropper, and champagne. Everyone had a glass of the stuff, which fizzed delightfully and produced the most intoxicating aroma of spice and sweetness as they talked to one another. Save for Mr. Walmsley, everyone was already deep in conversation; he sat alone on a settee, observing, not only without a companion, but also without a beverage. Thus, when Henry went to talk with Dr. Sauber, Dorina decided instead to be a good hostess, and gently sat down beside the wracked-looking man.

"Would you like a drink?" she asked. "I'd be happy to fetch you something."

"I don't need you to *fetch* anything for me," he snapped. Dorina must have looked as taken aback as she felt, for he sighed, and added, "I simply mean that I am able to get what I want, for myself, when I want it."

"I never doubted it," she replied. "But, as I'm parched, please excuse me."

"Wait," he said, putting his hand on hers as she began to rise. "Please—Miss Gray, was it?" He smiled, but it looked more like a grimace. "I apologize. I am so accustomed to people taking pity on me that my first impulse is always to refuse them the opportunity to do so."

"I see," said Dorina. "Well . . . I confess I thought to be helpful, but not out of pity."

"Oh? What then?"

"Experience. I was once corseted so tightly for a party, I sat by myself the whole night because I feared I would faint if I stood. I was so thirsty, and eventually I became terribly cold, and I just wished someone would . . ." She trailed off, for Mr. Walmsley did not seem particularly enthralled by her tale. "Well, I know they're not the same thing, but it impressed upon me the importance of making sure people are having a good time when they're sitting alone. Forgive me if I was in error."

His hard expression softened. "Thank you for explaining yourself," he said, "and in spite of my ungratefulness, I do appreciate your concern."

"Does that mean you would like a drink?"

He hesitated, then nodded. "Yes, thank you."

Dorina approached Jonas, who was sipping on his own cocktail, lounging against the bar. "Might I trouble you for two of those delightful-smelling concoctions — for myself, and for Mr. Walmsley."

"Of course; I've another bottle of champagne chilling," said Jonas, and after uncorking it, poured two. He did not do the thing with the sugar cube and the substance, but remembering Henry's admonition, she did not press him, merely thanked him and returned with the two glasses.

Mr. Walmsley had obviously been watching her, but when he accepted his drink, he sipped and said only, "Good champagne."

"Of course," she replied.

"And yet . . . on its own, it does not seem to satisfy our hostess." His eyes flickered to Lady Henry. She was currently deep in some sort of intense conversation with Dr. Sauber, who was gesturing wildly whenever she gave him the opportunity to reply. Dorina longed to go over and listen in, but she realized by talking to Mr. Walmsley she had the opportunity to learn about this little gathering — the truth about it, not just what the full members would reveal.

"I . . ." She coughed into her hand, realizing she didn't quite know what to say. "I'm just happy to be here."

"Of course." He toasted her with his glass. "To good things," he said, and drank.

"I beg your pardon?"

"Good things. The ones that come to those who wait."

"Oh, I see." Dorina wasn't sure she liked Mr. Walmsley. "Have you been waiting long?"

"I suppose not, in the grand scheme of things. But it does make one curious, doesn't it? To be invited to a gathering like this, and not be allowed to participate in what makes it truly exceptional?"

"What do you . . ."

"I believe we ought to go in, don't you?" said Mr. Walmsley, nodding to Henry. Dorina looked up and saw Henry, gesturing at the door. She kept her sigh to herself—was anyone here anything less than completely cryptic?

Dinner was delicious, but Dorina scarcely tasted the artfully prepared dishes; she was too occupied listening to the conversation of the other members. Though their professions and appearances had surprised her, their banter was of the sort she had always wanted to engage in. They were all of them witty, thoughtful, arch, and intelligent . . . and yet, now that she had found herself in the center of exactly what she'd dreamed of, Dorina found she had nothing to say. She ate and drank more than she was accustomed, just to have something to do with her mouth other than speak— it was terribly intimidating, being in the midst of such a cultured group. They did their best to draw her in to every topic of conversation, but her voice seemed to be frozen in her throat.

When the sweets were served, Dorina couldn't help but notice hers and Mr. Walmsley's looked a bit different. Their tarts were the ones she and Henry had bought earlier at the Borough Market, whereas the others, while similar, were just a touch browner on the sides. Curious. She caught Mr. Walmsley's eye, and he nodded ever so slightly to her before digging in.

The tart was delicious, regardless. As Dorina was deciding whether or not she would disgrace herself if she picked up the last of the crumbs with her finger, Henry, who had been seated at the head of the table, stood and called for everyone's attention.

"Welcome, all," she said. "I am so very glad you were all able to make it tonight, for we shall begin our series on the five senses, isolating them, one by one, in order to fully explore and appreciate them. I think I can safely say, being among like-minded individuals"—this drew a chuckle from the group—"that life itself is the first and most delightful of arts. To live—to live *well*, I should say—is to create art with one's body ... with one's soul.

"As we have Miss Gray with us tonight, joining us for the first time, I would like to say a few words on the mission of tonight's program, and the mission of our group in general, if everyone is amenable." Nods, smiles all around. "Well then: let me begin with the senses. The senses are how we appreciate life. In spite of this, the senses are often maligned, misunderstood. The worship of the senses is considered to be frivolous at best, and immoral at worst. The art that tantalizes our eyes, the music that delights our ears, the scents that ensorcel our noses, they are celebrated only when they are under the control of some sort of governing body, whether it is the Royal Academy ... or the church. To *that* I say—no. As I am in polite company, at least reasonably so, I shall restrain myself.

"Instead, let me say that I propose that we, as aesthetic adventurers, indulge our senses unrepentantly. Outsiders would decry this as sinful, for people these days are afraid of their senses—their sensations—their *passions*. Fear keeps them from truly understanding themselves. I reject this. I say, we must not starve our senses, we must not suppress them, we must make them ... well, I do not like to say *spiritual*, but we must make them an object of worship. We must give in to beauty, surrender ourselves to pleasure and enjoyment. We must return to hedonism, but we must also make it our own—for we are not sentimentalists, seeking to recreate an emotion time and again. It is our holy duty to create a new hedonism, a philosophy of passionate experience."

"Hear, hear!" cried Mr. Blake, the children's book illustrator. He pounded his hand on the table, surprising Dorina—the rather goat-faced man was perhaps the last of the assembled she would expect to interrupt their hostess so enthusiastically, save perhaps for Mr. Walmsley.

"Puritanism is uncomely, and until I see evidence of an afterlife, and the God who requires abstinence to experience it, I reject it," continued Henry, after nodding her thanks to Mr. Blake. "But, while a solitary rejection can be ever so satisfying ... I am very glad indeed that I have found you all to help me reject it." There was applause from everyone at this. "Most of the assembled have chosen to devote ourselves to *experience,* and that is beautiful— more noble to my mind than rejecting what this life has to offer. Sweet or bitter, vulgar or refined, the mission of this group is to reject personal asceticism, which produces nothing but unhappiness, and instead concentrate our attentions on *life,* every aspect of it. We have devoted ourselves to lifting veil after veil of the dusky gauze that others would use to swaddle the world. We embrace the fantastic. We call forth the gods of the old world and the new, the gods of dark and light, of pain and pleasure, of love and hate. This is the only way to quiet the restless mind, to light the flameless tapers of modern propriety, to see fresh colors and new shapes, to embrace the strangeness that is fundamental to any romance."

Was it Dorina's imagination, or did Henry's eyes flicker toward her as she finished?

During the pause, Dorina looked around the room, watching through the haze of spicy smoke from cigars and cigarettes, to see the effect this queer speech had on the assembled. They were all of them enthralled—even poor Mr. Walmsley looked as rapt as anyone else.

"I have spoken long enough, and I'm preaching to the converted," said Henry, "so let us adjourn, and begin the program. Ah—but while we ready ourselves, I wonder if our newest likeminded friends, Miss Gray and Mr. Walmsley, would mind doing me a favor?"

"Of course," said Mr. Walmsley, as if used to such requests.

"Jonas mentioned that he left the bouquet of flowers Mrs. Hill brought for us in the foyer, after putting them in water. Would the two of you be so kind as to retrieve them for me, and bring them into the parlor? We're focusing on scents this evening, and I'm sure they smell delightful."

"With pleasure," said Mr. Walmsley, immediately if unsteadily lurching to his feet. Dorina also got up, confused, but she followed him happily enough.

"Thank you, my dears," said Henry, and shut the door firmly behind them.

"I felt just as dazed, the first time they politely suggested I might go elsewhere for a bit," remarked Mr. Walmsley as Dorina blinked, not actually sure how she had been ushered out of the dining room so quickly. "Console yourself knowing that one day, if you are judged worthy, you shall be allowed to remain."

"How will they judge us?"

He shrugged. "I've been coming for months and have no insight."

Months! Dorina cringed inwardly. She would be leaving London in a month and a half, meaning she might never know. And it wasn't as if Henry had been enthusiastic about her attending in the first place . . . likely she'd put her off indefinitely.

"Don't worry," said Mr. Walmsley. "It's not *you*—it's not your youth, it's not your innocence, your lack of cultural knowledge—"

"What do you know about my cultural knowledge—or my innocence for that matter, I wonder?"

He held up his free hand. "Nothing. The remark was an impertinence; I apologize."

They walked slowly to the foyer. Mr. Walmsley said nothing further. Eventually, his studious silence made Dorina repent.

"It's my turn to apologize," she said as she collected the flower arrangement.

"It's all right," said Mr. Walmsley. "We both have chips on our shoulders, for we both feel as if we have something to prove."

Dorina opened her mouth, but then closed it. She'd never thought about it like that, but he was right.

They continued down the hall together, toward the parlor. Neither spoke, until Mr. Walmsley cleared his throat.

"I think it's nice," he said.

"Pardon?"

"That we have something in common."

"Oh." She glanced over at him. He was smiling, and she saw that he was handsome—or at least, he had been, at one time. There was a softness to him, an openness, behind the wooden wall he'd put up. "Yes . . . it is, isn't it? Both being in the same situation, and all . . ."

"Not quite." A little of his stiffness came back. "I was vetted by Mr. Seward, who is my banker; you were brought by Lady Henry, who is your friend."

"Friend . . ." Was that true?

"You think it is the perception of your youth that is causing Lady Henry to push you out the door; truly, it is her taking her time deciding whether you can be trusted."

"Trusted for *what*, though?"

They had reached the door. With his free hand, Mr. Walmsley knocked twice.

"That's the question, isn't it?" he asked as the door opened.

THE PROGRAM WAS OVER TWO hours in length. Thinking back on it, Dorina couldn't quite recall what they had done to fill the time. Not that she had been bored; rather, her memories were hazy, confused. They bled together like the colors of a kaleidoscope. All she could distinctly recall was that sometimes they inhaled vapors of various colors or perfumes of varying vintages, odors bitter, sweet, and sour. Sometimes there was silence, enhanced by ear-muffs—to allow them to isolate their olfactory senses—and at other times, there were chimes or pieces of music to listen to, or things to touch while they were blindfolded, all efforts to enhance their experience of the scents.

She did note—and remember—that she had detected no difference in the other members of the society after she and Mr. Walmsley joined them again. They did not seem to be drunk or otherwise intoxicated; they did not look flushed of face or breathless, or queer in any other way. Well, queer*er,* as they were a curious group to begin with.

No, they all seemed exactly the same as they had at dinner—an affable, intimate company, like some Dutch oil painting, but rather more attractive. What they might have done while isolating themselves from Mr. Walmsley and herself, she couldn't imagine.

"Did you have a good time?" asked Dr. Sauber after the festivities had concluded and Dorina was reviving herself with a glass of very cold, very sweet white wine.

"Yes," she said. "It was wonderful. But confusing, too . . ."

"Confusing how?"

"Well . . . I hope to become an art critic," said Dorina, with a flash of guilt—she had recalled that she was here, at a fancy party, rather than interviewing her uncle, or taking notes on his works.

"Really?" said Mr. Blake, who had meandered over, a small stemmed glass of some brightly colored Italian digestif pinched between his fingers.

"Yes . . . I mean, I think so . . ."

It occurred to Dorina in that moment that these people had talked to her all night, been interested in her and her opinions and her conversation, without her having announced this loudly and first thing. They had cared about what she thought without her framing it as being about her goals in life. Something to think on, later, when she had a moment.

"You *think* so?" asked Miss Travers.

"I thought so, I should say . . ." said Dorina, a bit overwhelmed now that they were all crowding around her. "Now, I am not so sure."

"You mean in the wake of tonight's entertainment?" Dr. Sauber leaned in closer, but not in a way that made Dorina feel as though he was being inappropriate toward her, unlike what she had perceived in so many of her friends' uncles and brothers and cousins.

She shook her head. "What I mean is that I have spent so long learning to see the beauty in everything. But the more I read, the more I learn. And the more I learn, the more I realize I am required to dismiss and discard, as well as embrace, if I am to be taken seriously."

"Surely you preferred some of the night's experiences to others?" asked Mr. Blake.

"Yes, but the pungent aromas made the sweet ones sweeter, and the sweet ones made the savory ones richer! Even the unpleasant scents worked with the nice ones, like they were all notes in some divine chord . . ."

A swift look passed between Dr. Sauber and Mr. Blake, but just as soon their attention was on her again.

"You have deduced one of our purposes," said Dr. Sauber as Dorina looked back and forth between them, eyebrow arched.

"Lady Henry was speaking of something similar, earlier, but this idea of the aesthetic whole, it is crucial," said Mr. Blake, jutting out his chin just like the goat he so resembled. "What is beauty without ugliness? What is kindness to someone who has never experienced cruelty? Only light can produce a shadow."

As she nodded her agreement, she noticed Mr. Walmsley watching her; he drained his glass, and turned away. From his gestures, Dorina guessed he was saying his goodnights.

"Would you please excuse me for a moment?" Dorina rose, and

before they could reply, she walked over to where he was limping to the door.

"Departing already? And without saying goodbye?"

"I'm afraid I'm not much of a conversationalist," he replied. "While I find myself in sympathy with the philosophy and goals of this organization, I do not much like talking over my experiences. I'm sorry."

"Don't apologize," said Dorina.

"I must seem so insensible to you, but I can only be who I am."

"You mistake me. Some people do not like talking about their sensations, their emotions. It does not mean they are any less potent." For some reason, Evadne came into her mind, but Dorina pushed away the thought for the present.

"You are generous, my lady." He bowed to her awkwardly, steadying himself on his cane. "It was a pleasure meeting you—I mean it. I hope to see you next time."

And with that, he left her. Dorina stood alone, flummoxed, and then turned around, almost bumping into her hostess.

"Mr. Walmsley is an unusual fellow," she remarked to Henry. "But, as we managed to each offend the other, and accepted the given apologies, perhaps we shall be friends."

"I hope so. And what of the rest?"

"They are . . ." Dorina looked around at the little groups. Mr. Blake and Dr. Sauber were still deep in conversation; Miss Travers was laughing at something Mrs. Hill had said, as Mr. Seward freshened their drinks at the bar, and if Dorina wasn't completely mistaken, Mrs. Dhareshwar was just shy of drooling over dear Jonas.

"She looks ready to pounce," remarked Dorina.

"Oh, that's Kamaladevi," said Henry. "Apparently, for her at least, Jonas evokes certain . . . sensations."

"I wonder what his are?" He was smiling and seemed to be

responding to her overtures with politeness and humor, but she could sense no reciprocation of her obvious desire.

"Jonas has very particular taste."

"Oh?" Dorina gave Henry a saucy look. "I wonder what the particulars are?"

"Are you interested?"

"I'm afraid I too must scarper," said Mr. Seward, interrupting them before Dorina could protest. "Early day tomorrow . . . but really, Harry, you outdid yourself tonight. Really looking forward to next time."

"And when is the next meeting?" asked Dorina.

"Usually every two weeks, but of course, things will interfere," said Mr. Seward. "I hope you'll be in attendance, Miss Gray?"

"I'll speak to her guardian about it," said Henry.

"Who, Basil? Well, get him back, too. He's missed. Good night!"

"Good night," said Henry.

"Why *did* Uncle Basil leave your group?" asked Dorina, knowing Henry could not escape with a parlor full of guests.

"Personal reasons," she said smoothly. "Ah, Mrs. Hill looks to be leaving. Shall we?"

An hour later, they had at last got rid of Dr. Sauber; he had remained behind, after everyone else had gone, declaring he would remain until Henry had "absolutely, unequivocally" promised him that she would indeed oversee an interview with Dorina. Jonas thought this was absolutely hilarious; Henry, less so.

"His discretion really is absolute," said Jonas after Henry finally pushed the doctor into his coach.

"I'm not the one who's worried," said Dorina.

"At last," groaned Henry, darting back inside. She shook the rain from her shoulders with a swift, almost feline gesture, and glanced up at the clock on a pedestal table. "I thought he'd never go. Well, well . . . did you have a good time, Dorina?"

"Fantastic." Dorina had been waiting for this moment all night. "But . . . it's ever so late," she said, affecting a yawn. "I wonder if it would be easier if I just stayed the night . . ."

"Not at all. James will be happy to take you home."

"But the rain . . ."

"Has turned into a pleasant steady drizzle. James is well prepared, I assure you, and it is not far to go. Jonas, won't you be a dear and tell him to bring the coach around?"

"At once," said Jonas. He cast a sympathetic look Dorina's way once he was out of Henry's sight and disappeared into the interior of the house.

Dorina wasn't finished trying yet. "Are you certain? It'll be less trouble for everyone if—"

"I'd have to send a servant round to Baz's to tell him where you were anyway," said Henry, "which would be just as much trouble."

She spoke crisply, almost dismissively. It was the first time she'd been so brusque with Dorina, and it brought a blush to the younger woman's cheeks.

"Of course," she said. "I'm sorry."

Henry glanced at her, and cracking open her cigarette case, withdrew one. She lit it off the big cut-glass lighter that squatted on a pedestal table. "Never apologize for wanting what you want, or for going after it."

Dorina had really no idea what to say to that!

"I'm glad you had a good time," said Henry. "You did very well —everyone remarked that you'll be a delightful addition to our group."

Dorina almost asked if she meant a full member, but decided against it; Henry was so mercurial. "I'm glad," she said demurely. "It was . . . a wonderfully unique experience."

Henry took a step toward her, closing the gap between them, and raising her hand, brushed a strand of hair out of Dorina's eyes.

"Good," she said as Dorina inhaled her smell, smoke and spice and some subtler scent that made her think of both perfume and something good to eat. "I like providing those. Ah, I think I hear the coach—good night, Dorina."

And she went straight up the stairs, taking two at a time, not even looking back. Dorina watched her go, and stood shocked for fully a minute before realizing no coach was anywhere near the door.

She had gone from astonishment to fury by the time James came around. She spent the entire drive home fuming, let herself in noisily just to be obnoxious, and stomped upstairs.

It wasn't until after she'd undressed and thrown herself into bed that she realized how stupid she was being. She'd played this game with other girls! The ones who needed a bit of urging she was kind to; the eager ones, she tormented until she was assured of her position.

Henry was playing games with her! The ruddy nerve!

But to what purpose? Dorina drifted off while considering the possibilities, but knowing one thing was certain:

One can only win the games one plays.

5

As a child, did you have feelings that you could
not understand? Questions no one could answer?
Demons will certainly provide answers. As to
whether they are correct, that is something one
must decide on one's own.

— *On the Summoning of Demons*

H ER FIRST FEW DAYS in London had been some of
the longest of Evadne's life. With nothing to do that
pleased her, and no one nearby whose company she enjoyed, the minutes had dragged and the hours had seemed inter-
minable. She'd had nothing to look forward to but time away from
Lady Henry, and the prospect of that being her entire summer had
made nothing so attractive as going to bed to seek what oblivion
she could in sleep.

Once she began fencing at the academy, Evadne's days took on
new meaning. She rose earlier than Dorina so she would have time
to do the exercises Mr. Cantrell had recommended in order to
strengthen the muscles associated with fencing. And for the first
time in her life she went to bed later than her sister so she could
get in some extra practice—going over what she had learned in
clinics, practicing techniques she strove to perfect in her lessons.

Also on Mr. Cantrell's advice, she had caved and was now using
Lord Oliver's rapier for home practice. The heavier weight of the
blade had so quickly built up her strength that she ardently wished
she'd thought to try with a real sword years ago.

Before heading back to Swadlincote she would buy her own, returning Lord Oliver's to Lady Henry, apparently unopened. That hadn't been her intention when she began using them, but when Evadne had opened the box, she had found Lord Oliver's fancy Chinese sword packed alongside the rest. She had been mortified to see it nestled in among the less valuable swords, for of course its inclusion had been a mistake. *Yes,* she had thrown it on the bed with the rest, but it was because Jonas had distracted her, and she had forgotten to put it back on the wall where it belonged. She didn't even want it—as good as she'd felt while holding it, she'd felt revolted by it once she'd put it down. In fact, she had not touched it again since that first time.

But she could not quite bring herself to return it. It was simply too embarrassing to admit the mistake. Henry and Jonas likely thought her a scoundrel—she had been given the pick of Oliver's practice swords, not display pieces off his wall. So, for this reason, she planned to return the unopened box at the end of the summer. That way, they need not discuss the matter at all.

In the meantime, she used the rapiers daily and in secret, lunging, performing little accuracy drills, sometimes just standing and holding the sword for various lengths of time. She could already tell she was in better shape than she had ever been before; her dresses were looser in the waist and tighter across the shoulders. To her surprise and pleasure, Mr. Cantrell had noticed, too. He had remarked—politely—on her fitness level, at which point she had confessed how much she had been practicing. He had congratulated her, given her a few more pointers, and begun driving her even harder.

She was glad to have Mr. Cantrell's advice and instructions to think about, as meals at Basil's house had become painfully quiet affairs, with only the most basic of pleasantries being exchanged among the three of them as they ate. It struck Evadne as somewhat odd, the quietude. The coolness between herself and her sister was natural, given that they were not on particularly good terms with one another, but when days of silence at the table became a week, and then a second, Evadne could not help but be curious about the strange silence between Dorina and their uncle. The two of them were barely speaking, and when they did, it was terribly polite and stiff. It made Evadne wonder if they, too, had had some sort of falling out — and the longer it went on, the more obvious it became that this must have been the case. They saw nothing of one another; Dorina never went into his studio, nor did she seem to be researching or writing much for her monograph.

Evadne chose to ignore the situation. She was good at that — never being interested in the sorts of things she was expected to care deeply about had accustomed her to disregarding just about everything.

But no longer. The more Evadne fenced at the Westminster Academy, the more she realized how disconnected she had felt from her life — and how frustrating that had been. It was so pleasurable, being a part of a community, knowing there was a place she could go, every day if she chose, where she could be herself, and where people were happy to see her. It gave her a sense of purpose, a sense of belonging. She felt as though at long last she had woken up from a dream where she'd had no power to direct the action, no ability to control what happened to her.

She realized, too, that she had felt that way for a very long time. It had begun before their mother had announced that Evadne should be her sister's chaperone in London — before Freddie had told her of his engagement. In fact, the more she thought on it, the more Evadne began to wonder just what she had been doing for so long, why she had let so many days pass her by. It seemed incredible she could have ever wished there were fewer hours in a day, rather than more.

"That was sloppy, Gray!" snapped Cantrell after disarming her so violently her epee went spiraling across the floor, landing several feet away. "I've told you before that your defense was weak, and here you are, dropping your arm at a crucial moment!"

Evadne massaged her shoulder; there was a bud of pain where he had tagged her that she knew would blossom into a spectacular bruise. *Saint George* his friends might call him, but Mr. Cantrell was exceptionally hard on her, uncompromising and ferocious. He was a little terrifying, actually—just as she imagined a real saint would be, if he taught fencing.

She liked it. Liked it a lot, actually. Probably more than she should. As it turned out, all her life she'd been looking for someone who cared about her enough, found her worthy enough, took her seriously enough to be really honest with her. She just hadn't realized it until Mr. Cantrell showed her how she'd longed for it —*needed* it, in order to bring out her best.

"It *was* sloppy," she agreed, moving to take off her mask.

"Did I say we were finished?" He raised his sword, saluted her, then used the tip to point at her cast-off weapon. "Pick that up! You're not leaving before you get this not just *right*, but *perfect*, five times in a row. We will reset back to one even if it's the last go-through. Do you understand me?"

Evadne gladly picked up her sword to try again, eager to show him that his faith in her was justified. She burned with the desire to impress him, longed to earn his approval—or at least some acknowledgment that she'd done a bit better.

Her focus was so complete she did not realize that once again the entire school had paused to watch them fence, including Mr. Perkins. Only when she removed her mask did she see them, standing against the wall or draped over chairs or standing with their epees bending into the floor, smiling, frowning, brows raised or furrowed.

"That was five," said Cantrell unnecessarily. "The last was not as good as the rest, but I'll count it. You seem tired."

"I'm not tired," she said, drawing deep from some well of ferociousness inside her. Truthfully, she *was* exhausted; her arms felt like jelly and her legs, something even more jiggly—blancmange perhaps. She was sweating buckets, but it made her furious he'd found fault with her *again*, after his lecture, when she was trying so hard.

He really was an astonishing teacher. His approval made her feel worthwhile; his discontent with her made her fierce. Both were highly motivating.

"You *are* tired," he said, finally smiling. "And that's all right."

"Let's do it again! From one, if you think it's necessary."

"You need a cool drink, and to sit down for a moment." That was Mr. Perkins, now beside her, his callused hand on her shoulder. "It is possible to work too hard, Miss Gray . . . and the improvement in your fencing I've seen in such a short time makes me think you are working very hard indeed."

"Not *too* hard," she insisted.

"Gray knows her limits," said Cantrell, thrilling her by calling her by her surname, without title—just as he did the rest of his students. He flipped his sweaty hair off his forehead, and flashed her a look sharper than any blade. "If she says she's all right, I trust her."

"Over the years, I have seen quite a few students burn themselves out," said Perkins, "and I would hate to see such a promising young lady—no, a promising *student*—do so."

"But she is not *your* student," said Cantrell quietly.

"*Everyone* is my student at this school, because it is *my* school," replied Mr. Perkins, quieter still. "I would prefer if you chose to remember this, George . . . It would make everyone's life so much easier."

Evadne didn't know what to do. She liked Mr. Perkins, and her feelings for Mr. Cantrell were stronger still . . . but no one who spent any time at all at the Westminster Fencing Academy could possibly make them both happy, that was clear enough. Their methods of instruction were similar, but just different enough to cause strife, and both were possessive about to whom the best students "belonged." Evadne was an unusually a clear-cut case—she had come for Mr. Cantrell, and while she had taken a few lessons with Mr. Perkins, it had been a frustrating experience for them both. She was "George's Girl," as Mr. Perkins had once put it rather pithily.

Evadne had tried to ignore the inappropriate thrill that phrase had given her, pushed away the joy she had felt when Mr. Cantrell did not deny it, but had instead looked pleased. *Very* pleased.

Of course, since that moment she had thought about being "George's Girl" every day, several times a day, alone and in company, when she was practicing, or just having a cup of tea. *George's Girl.* She'd never been *anyone's* girl before, and while of course she was George's Girl in a platonic, student-teacher way, it felt good. More than good. It felt wonderful, like she was wanted. Like she was valued. *Desired,* even.

She also felt important watching Mr. Perkins and Mr. Cantrell face off over her. The two of them cared what she did, and how she did it.

George's Girl or no, it was Mr. Cantrell who cracked. Looking exhausted, he nodded his assent with a wince; reaching into his jacket, he withdrew his pouch and took one of his pastilles without a glass of water. Her heart went out to him. Her teacher's digestion was always plaguing him.

"You're right," he conceded after swallowing. "Perhaps my enthusiasm for Gray's potential is clouding my judgment."

A flash of annoyance passed over Mr. Perkins's face, but just as quickly it was gone. He glanced at the clock. "It's late," he observed tactfully. "I wonder . . . Miss Gray, would you like to get a bite to eat with us? Before you go home? Strange hour, more of a meat tea than a supper, but I daresay you must be hungry after such a spectacular display."

Evadne looked to Mr. Cantrell. He nodded ever so slightly. The secret permission gave her another thrill . . . which was odd, as she very rarely enjoyed being told what to do.

"I'd be delighted," she said, her former compunctions about dining in public forgotten in her eagerness to spend more time—casual time—with Mr. Cantrell. Anyway, Basil had mentioned at breakfast that he intended to go out to his club that night. As for Dorina, likely she had her own plans—and, even if she didn't, she wouldn't want Evadne hanging around anyway. "I'm not needed or wanted anywhere."

"Of course you are," said Cantrell. "*We* want you."

"The only thing is, I'm afraid I must go home and change. I came in my practice clothes," said Evadne, turning toward the changing room to hide her blush at his words.

"Oh, *pfft*, we're just going down to the pub. They know us there, and don't mind at all if we come in after practice," said Mr. Perkins. "They're used to it."

"Well . . . all right," she agreed. "I'll just put away my things, and—"

"Tootles, come take Gray's things and put them up for her," shouted Cantrell, and Frank Tunesbury, one of the school's less talented students, came to take her epee, mask, and gear.

"I'll go on ahead," said Mr. Perkins as the rest of the school took this as a cue that they should begin to clean up for the evening. "See that everything's settled, and join me when you're ready."

Mr. Cantrell called a few people to him—Trawless the secretary, and three of the most senior students, Phillip Bourne, Ger Stockton, and Adam Reid. Evadne had crossed swords with all four of them over the previous weeks. At first, she had lost more matches than she'd won against them, though the balance was about even now. All were very good, though Evadne came to understand that they, too, had their faults, which was reassuring. Reid was a gorilla of a man; he went for brute force when finesse would be better. Bourne tended to drop his sword hand when flustered, and Stockton's footwork frankly needed to be rebuilt from the ground up.

Trawless was perhaps the best, though the least aggressive of the gang; he was graceful, and had a keen interest in the nuances of fencing, rather than merely executing the sorts of brutal attacks and wicked parries that ended matches more quickly but less beautifully. But irrespective of any of their strengths or weaknesses, she had come to enjoy their company; they were friendly young men who had learned quickly that if they laughed at her or treated her "like a girl" she was likelier to beat them during a match. They had come to respect her for this, and now she was more or less one of them—in that when they took tea breaks, they invited her to join them, and tapped her more to practice with them than many of the students who had been there longer.

"Where are we eating?" asked Evadne. Mr. Perkins hadn't mentioned a location.

"The Red Lion," said Cantrell. "It's not far."

"And after?" grunted Reid.

Was it Evadne's imagination, or did Mr. Cantrell glare at Reid? She couldn't be sure; his annoyance passed quickly, if it had even existed.

"We'll see," he said simply. "For now, get yourselves together. We don't want to keep him waiting long. Well, Gray," he said as they went off on their various errands, "invited to your first dinner at the Lion . . . quite an honor, given you haven't been with us a month."

Evadne didn't know what to say. She was glad she hadn't realized how significant an invitation it had been at the time, or surely she would have been too embarrassed to accept.

"Perkins likes the shepherd's pie there, and the beer," said Cantrell carelessly, not noticing her confusion, or choosing to ignore it. "Usually he goes home before us . . ."

The way he trailed off made her suspect he was trying to tell her something indirectly. "Do you do something afterward?" she asked. "I'm happy to take a cab home, if it's all right to leave my things at the school overnight. I can get them—"

"Gray," he said, and again that shiver went down her spine at the way he said her name in that clipped manner. She looked into his blue eyes, the whites of which were almost blinding in their purity. Oh, but she liked to look at him! The curve of his lips, the way his eyebrows tapered to sharp points, the shadow of golden stubble along his jawline. "I am not telling you because I want you to leave us—I am telling you because I hope you will wish to join us."

"Oh," she said softly.

She saw his hand move, and almost flinched when she felt his fingers on her chin, but then he tipped her face upward . . . He was taller than her, and his grip was strong; she couldn't turn her head to look away, so she turned her eyes to the wall to avoid meeting his.

"Will you come?"

"Yes," she whispered. It was perhaps the first time in her life she'd agreed to something without knowing what she was getting herself into. It was thrilling.

"Excellent," he said, releasing her and stepping away just as the other chaps came back. Evadne wasn't offended; she might not be as wise in the ways of the world as these Londoners, but she knew very well that if any of her new friends suspected she and her tutor might have some sort of interest in one another beyond fencing they would immediately return to treating her as the girl of the group. "Well, are we ready?" he said to them. "Shall we go?"

The night was warm; the walk, pleasant. She felt no fear of strolling through Westminster after dark, not with these companions. The pub was respectably situated at the corner of Parliament

Street and Derby Gate, just across from the Foreign Office, practically in the shadow of Big Ben. It felt younger than the pub back in Swadlincote, but still had the smoky, slick, almost oily feel to the tables that Evadne liked. She ordered a glass of claret, rather than accepting a mug from the pitcher of bitter Mr. Perkins had ordered for the table, but she helped herself to everything they'd ordered—shepherd's pie, as Mr. Cantrell had predicted, plus a roast chicken, some cold ham, and a salad of summer vegetables.

Her eyes were bigger than her stomach; she ate lightly, though the food was good. Her thoughts were not on her meal, but rather on what she might be doing after.

After . . . with Mr. Cantrell.

Cantrell clearly did not share her concern; he kept the conversation lively all the night long. Evadne could scarcely listen, however—she saw mainly their mouths moving, their teeth when they smiled, their eyes as they glinted over the edge of their mugs. Only when Mr. Perkins called her name did she realize how far away her mind had been, and she turned to him, apologizing for her inattention.

"No, no," he said softly, so that she had to lean in to hear him. "I know how you feel. I'm not much of a conversationalist myself." Evadne didn't quite know how to take this—it was a confidence, but not a compliment. "But, I wanted to say . . . I'm sorry to have gotten into that scrap in front of you, with George . . . He's a fine teacher, and you've done well under him. But I confess I'm a bit envious he's the one who snapped you up . . . It has been a long time since I've seen anyone improve as rapidly as you have."

"Thank you," she said, and as if seeking to excuse her own ability added, "it's been a long time coming. All those years of practice . . ."

"Ah, but I've always said that practice makes *permanent*—not perfect," said Mr. Perkins, shaking his head. He paused to drink deeply from his mug of bitter; Evadne had noticed Mr. Cantrell refilling it all night, and more often than he did for his fellows.

"You arrived on my doorstep with mistakes in your form that were not your fault — they were simply the result of your lack of instruction. But you have quickly overcome any bad habits, and worked hard to obey the instructions George's been giving you. There's no reason a woman can't fence, and well, I just . . . well . . ." He took another long pull of beer; Evadne caught Mr. Cantrell's eye, and he winked at her. Blushing, she turned back to Mr. Perkins.

"Can I get you anything, Mr. Perkins?"

"What? No." He was tipsy. "You're a good girl, Evadne — I beg your pardon, I mean, Miss Gray. Sensible. But you have to be careful . . . burn out . . ."

"What do you mean?"

"Eh? Nothing, nothing . . . just an old man's worried rambling. But, really, you know, you *can* practice too hard. The body is like a fire, you have to feed it slowly, steadily, or it burns too hot and fast . . . and then all you have left is ashes."

Evadne again looked over at Mr. Cantrell, who rolled his eyes and shook his head slightly. Evadne tried not to smile.

"I know you think I'm an old man," he muttered.

"Not at all," she assured him.

"Eh?" He looked up at her, eyes focusing. "What have I been saying, I wonder? Drank a bit too much . . . should get home. Do you trust these young rascals to see you safely to your uncle's? You could come with me . . ."

"I haven't quite finished my meal," said Evadne, gesturing to the cooling potatoes on her plate. "I'm sure I'll be all right."

"Of course. You can defend yourself, after all." He patted her hand as he lurched to his feet. "Well, my boys, I'm off. Take care of her, will you?"

"Of course, Mr. Perkins," said Trawless.

"She's in good hands," said Cantrell, looking Evadne in the eye until she turned away.

"Tomorrow, then . . ."

And he was gone. He'd left money on the table, a generous amount to pay for what they'd eaten, but they left it all—which likely accounted for the quality of service they'd received from the Lion's staff, and their willingness to tolerate a rowdy bunch of sweaty athletes when most of their clientele were decently dressed professional men eating a quiet meal.

"Shall we?" Cantrell stood, and the rest of the group followed. Evadne got to her feet as well, feeling tingly from head to toe.

"Where are we going?" she asked as they walked toward the door. She hung back slightly; the rest were in front of her and Mr. Cantrell, which is likely why he felt at liberty to put a hand on the small of her back.

His touch sent a shock through her body, a tiny spark, like a candle's flame when it hits an uneven part of the wick. Her body was suddenly alive with sensation, and all the hairs on the back of her neck and along her arms pricked up as he leaned in to whisper, "Why, back to the school, of course."

THE ACADEMY WAS DARK WHEN they entered; the only light was what came in through the slits in the drawn curtains, long blades of brightness that cut at weird jagged angles over the desk in the foyer, the potted plant, and up against the door that led into the studio. All six of them waited in the warm darkness while Trawless fumbled with the key.

Finally he got the door open and they shuffled inside, stepping carefully up onto the practice floor. No one spoke, nor did they move to find a light, save for Mr. Cantrell, who darted into the kitchen to grab a gas lantern. The flame made Evadne's eyes water until he pulled the hood, at which point he silently led them down a creaking set of stairs into the basement of the studio. She knew no one else was inside, but the sounds all made her worry they would be overheard. They were clearly up to something secret.

Once they were all assembled, Mr. Cantrell lit several candles.

As the room gradually brightened, Evadne saw the cellar was cluttered with the sort of detritus one might expect: fencing equipment that needed repair, an old lamp, a box that looked to be some sort of lost and found, and a low table that listed to one side on an uneven leg. There were a few chairs, too, but they looked newer, or at least less dusty than the rest. The men jockeyed to offer her one before they would take a seat themselves.

"Perkins's knees give him trouble; he hasn't been down here in a year," said Cantrell as he settled in. Evadne looked questioningly at him, and he explained further, "It wouldn't do for him to know what we were doing."

This made her uncomfortable. It *was* Mr. Perkins's school, as he'd said earlier . . .

"But," she began.

"You know how he feels about dueling," said Trawless.

Dueling! Was this a dueling club? She wasn't quite ready for such a thing, and turned to her tutor. "Perhaps I've made a mistake, Mr. Cantrell, I—"

"Gray, I would not ask you to allow *me* such a familiarity, but if you would consent to call me George—or at least drop my honorific, it might be easier . . . at least under these very particular circumstances," he said over her objections.

This intimacy shocked her. *George's girl*—and now she would call him George. At least in private. Among less intimate acquaintances, she'd stick to his last name.

Needless to say, all thoughts of departing left her mind entirely.

"Well!" he said, after she nodded, "welcome everyone. I've called you here tonight for two reasons. One, because I have a new lead. Two, because I feel, due to the strength of our adversary, we could use some more power . . . which is why I've invited Gray to join us."

"Very jolly!" declared Reid.

"The more the merrier," said Bourne.

"Adversary?" said Evadne, blushing, hoping to redirect their attention.

"Yes, adversary. This is not a dueling club, Gray, dedicated to the winning of petty victories over one another. This is an organization of like-minded individuals who have decided to hone their fencing for a very specific purpose. This is a rare thing . . . We do not often invite new members into our, ah, *inner circle*. The reason is"—he hesitated; she smiled at him, nodding, to encourage him —"what we are doing is illegal."

Evadne's heart began to beat a bit harder. Saint George, asking her to do something that was against the law?

"What do you mean?" she asked, voice trembling.

"Sometimes, when there is a real and terrible danger lurking at the edges of society, but the police will do nothing about it, it falls to spirited and . . . *morally flexible* individuals to help," said George. "We here in this basement are true patriots, Gray—brave citizens of England willing to risk our bodies, and even our lives, to keep crown and country safe."

The little hairs were pricking up on the back of Evadne's neck again. She rather wished George had told her *why* he might risk his body and life before telling her that he did—and expected her to, as well . . .

"What we do—myself, and my companions—may be vigilantism, but I assure you, it is crucial. My work began in my days in divinity school. I had a teacher who . . . well, he introduced me to certain fascinating truths about the world. *Secret* truths. Did Freddie ever mention anything about . . ."

All Freddie had ever mentioned of George was that he was a scholarship student, an excellent fencer, and a "queer duck." She shook her head.

"Well, he was never a good enough fencer to be invited to our society," said George carelessly. Evadne smiled in spite of herself at this dig at her former crush. "Well then, I imagine what I tell you next will come as something of a shock. Gray, the threat I spoke of—the canker that gnaws at the heartwood of our nation . . . it is . . . how shall I put this? It comes from the evil in men's hearts, but also from another source. A source beyond our understanding. Beyond our world, actually." It was the first time Evadne had seen George nervous, and it astonished her. Then again, what he was saying was astonishing. *Beyond their world?* What could he mean? "I am perfectly serious when I tell you that we here, in this room . . . we are committing to stamping out fell beings who influence this nation's citizens, who turn them from God and from country, who infiltrate and insinuate themselves into our hearts and minds. I'm speaking of . . . *demons*."

Evadne's mouth hung open, but she had no words.

"Yes—demons," he said, anticipating her question. "I am being entirely serious, Gray, I assure you."

"He is," said Trawless. "We've all seen the evidence."

The rest of them were nodding. Evadne didn't know quite what to think, but in the darkness, with these intense people and George's face lit from below with candle and lantern light, it seemed entirely possible that there were demons out there, *real* demons. Not just metaphors for human wickedness, as Dorina would say, but beings who fought for souls and power, as she herself had suggested in the National Gallery what felt like ages ago now.

"Evidence," said Evadne, knowing she must say *something*. "Evidence that they exist, or evidence that they interfere with . . . ah . . ." She couldn't quite bring herself to speculate on how or when or why beings might do such a thing.

"Why wouldn't they?" was George's answer. "They are obscene. Their wants are what men call sin, and they will be satisfied only when we are all in their thrall. They wage their own wars among themselves on their own plane, but they also do battle in our world by gaining power over men and turning our will to theirs. I have seen what they can do, and I will *never* be satisfied until I know England is cleansed of their influence!"

Evadne glanced around, and saw the upturned faces of Bourne, Stockton, Reid, and Trawless—their attention was unwavering; their devotion, unquestionable. There was no doubt they believed.

Whether or not *she* did . . . that was another matter.

On one hand, she had heard the village vicar lecture about resisting temptations and the burden of all men to eschew demons and their tricks, to guard her soul against wickedness and influence. On the other, well, she had never seen any evidence of actual demonic beings. Just human weakness.

"You doubt me," said George shrewdly, looking right at her. She opened her mouth, then shut it, and shrugged.

"I have never seen a demon," she said carefully. "But . . ."

"But?" George's eyes met hers, and he stared at her with such intensity that she felt her pulse quicken as when he had caressed her chin.

"I suppose if you could show me . . ."

"Oh, I will," he said. Evadne found his intensity mesmerizing. "I have never gone after a diabolist without evidence."

"Our Saint George only hunts real dragons," said Trawless, winking at her, though his expression was serious. "He's not fooled by lizards with costume wings."

"What's our latest target?" asked Stockton.

"In good time," said George. "First, Gray, if we are going to discuss this further in front of you . . . do you agree to complete secrecy about this matter?"

"Of course," she said. "I wouldn't betray your confidence. And anyway, I have no one to tell."

A sad smile twisted George's perfect lips. "Yes, so many of us come to this school, and yet more specifically, this sort of calling, from a place of loneliness. The truth is, Gray, some men and women serve the greater good by living traditional lives. They go to church, learn their lessons, become husbands and wives ... mothers and fathers. Others—those of us who are less suited to *conventional* lives—are forced by our difference, and often by our *excellence,* to serve the world in an unconventional way. For those of us with our sort of talent, we must become rather like knights-errant. But there is no less honor in walking the warrior's path—in fact, I believe there is a great deal more, for it takes bravery and generosity to give up what we are told we ought most to want."

Evadne listened, enthralled. The speech was exactly what she wanted to hear; it was a gift given to her, put directly into her hands, by someone who understood her better than anyone else—even those who had known her all her life.

"All right," she said, nodding slowly. Honestly, she would have agreed to anything at that moment—she could judge for herself, once she saw this "evidence." "What must I do?"

He was pleased, she could tell, and that in turn pleased her. Folding his hands behind his back, George began to pace.

"As I have said, I have located our next target. The trail I followed began with the disappearance of three children, all of a similar age. You may have seen it in the papers—we check the broadsheets for such crimes. Of course, some sensational or confusing acts of violence are the work of men—the Whitechapel murders, for instance—and on the other hand, common-seeming tragedies have demonic origins. So we have to be careful." He rummaged about in the lost-and-found box and produced a few old newspapers. Spreading them across the table, he beckoned his followers to come and see. Pencil circles surrounded three similar headlines. "All of these children are young, between six and eight, and all disappeared during the new moon. The body of the first was found a month later, significantly decomposed. The second was found no less than two weeks after the disappearance, and it—forgive me

—*the body* of the child was relatively fresh. Pristine, almost. I believe this indicates our diabolist kills them during the full moon.

"Now a third has gone missing, also during the new moon . . . and tomorrow it is full again."

"Tomorrow!" said Evadne.

"You wanted evidence? I will provide it within twenty-four hours. We must move quickly—it is during a ritual that a diabolist is the most vulnerable. They are also at their most powerful, but the power makes them less in touch with their humanity. They take greater risks, they forget their limits. That is why we must strike when the time is exactly right. He will not begin before the moon is up, and if we infiltrate his stronghold when he is already giving himself over to his master, but has yet to harm his victim, we will be victorious.

"But," he added, glancing at Evadne, "we may not save either—man or child. The stakes are high, which means the consequences of failure are dire."

"Where is he operating out of?" asked Stockton.

"An old house close to Seven Dials. We shall convene here but depart in separate cabs—it won't be noticed, because of the frequent comings and goings of those who live there."

"It is a notorious area," said Evadne.

"Yes, and I believe he has been using this anonymity to his advantage—but it will prove to be his downfall," said George.

"How on earth did you find him?" asked Evadne.

The rest of her companions chuckled.

"George has a bloodhound's nose for this sort of thing," said Trawless, smiling at Evadne.

"It's all just logic and research," said George crisply as he produced a map of London from the same box of odds and ends. After unfolding it over the newspapers, he pointed to an incomplete hieroglyph he had drawn in red ink. "The first child was found here," he said, pointing at a dot, "and taken from here." His finger moved to another, at an acute angle to the first. "The second was taken here." He pointed to another dot, and then to a fourth. "And reappeared here." His finger moved yet again. "As for the third child, she was taken from here, but has obviously yet to reappear. But, if we connect these dots"—he drew with his finger something that Evadne knew was part of a symbol, even if it was difficult to visualize exactly—"we can see the center of it . . . and when it began to take shape, I began to hang around the area, see if anything hinted at where he might be lurking. It was easy enough to see, once I was there."

The feeling of respect was palpable from his fellows. Evadne, too, admired his pluck and his reasoning. It was obvious George knew what he was about. The thought sent a chill down her spine as much as it thawed some of her reluctance to believe something so incredible as a demonologist lurking in a London garret, taking children for some diabolic purpose.

"So . . . what exactly are we going to do tomorrow night?"

She was surprised by the steadiness of her voice as she spoke. Perhaps she really had been born to walk this path.

6

A demon's whims are laws to everyone except themselves.

— On the Summoning of Demons

ALL EVADNE HAD TO DO to prepare herself for a night of demon hunting was get dressed and arrive at the school on time.

Getting to the academy was easy enough. As to what she would wear . . . that had presented a bit of a problem. The men were perfectly comfortable fencing in evening dress — if the knees of their trousers and the elbows of their jackets were a bit worn, they'd only look more natural where they were going. As for her, it would be difficult, if not impossible, to fence in a full skirt, not to mention dangerous, given that she'd never practiced anything like that. Her bloomers and petticoat — the typical ensemble she wore to practice — would stick out terribly in a seedy neighborhood like that, and her plastron would not fit under her shirtwaists, leaving her open to injury.

In the end, they decided Evadne would simply cover up with a cloak. George volunteered an old one of his that they could easily abandon if necessary. If she kept it buttoned, it would also hide her weapon. The men all had sword canes, impressive pieces whose shafts had been specially constructed of a resin that made them a defensive tool in combat. But even if she could have carried a cane and not looked queer doing so, Evadne had not been trained in such a way — George confessed he had meant to do so, only this had come up so soon after he realized her potential. She would just have to make do with her own weapon, and rely on her nimbleness to keep her out of harm's way.

Out of harm's way. While George seemed confident they would have the advantage, for there were six of them and their target appeared to operate in isolation, there was a chance any of them might be hurt—even killed. As this was Evadne's first time, they would of course be looking out for her, but just the same, there was undeniable risk involved.

The previous night, upon returning to Uncle Basil's house after her most extraordinary conversation with George, Evadne had marveled at both her choice to help him and her ease at making it. She had never done anything risky like this, not really—unless she were to count the time she had swum into the sea on that mistaken errand to save Dorina. The idea of it had made her feel excited in the same way fencing did. She'd felt *alive*. She'd decided to trust herself.

And of course, to trust George . . .

As she didn't have to leave until half eight, the following night she ate with her uncle and sister. The meal was tense. She wasn't able to get much down, being so anxious. And yet, her secret anxiety wasn't so wholly occupying that she failed to realize she wasn't the only distracted one.

Uncle Basil seemed even less present than usual. He kept sighing, eyes flickering toward his studio, not paying attention to either girl. Dorina, too, was quiet, browsing a copy of some book of poetry called *Les Fleurs du Mal* as she picked at her food. For some reason—perhaps it was the gilt cover, the elaborate binding—Evadne assumed it was some trash given to her by Lady Henry.

When the clock struck eight, Evadne excused herself. Only then did Dorina look up.

"Off to bed?" she asked, surprised.

"No." Evadne had already decided on her lie. "A fencing instructor from Italy is visiting—he's friends with Mr. Perkins. There's a lecture tonight."

"Oh." Dorina nodded. "All right. Well . . ."

"Hmm?"

Her sister hesitated, and Evadne, impatient to be gone, glanced at the clock.

"Have a good time," said Dorina, and returned to her book. She sounded sad, or at least disappointed.

"Are you doing anything tonight?" Evadne asked her sister, more for politeness' sake than any real interest.

"No," she said. "Just reading."

Evadne almost asked if Lady Henry was busy, but then she realized she didn't really have to ask. Of course that must be what was happening—if she were free, Dorina would have been by her side.

"Enjoy your book," she said, feeling guilty for some reason she couldn't quite explain.

"Enjoy your lecture," said Dorina.

Evadne was of two minds as she went to change. Dorina had been reaching out to her, for the first time since their dreadful fight. If it had been any other night, she would have reached back. She missed her sister—even missed squabbling with her. The silence between them had grown heavy, freighted.

Then anger flared. Why should she always have to work around Dorina's schedule? What of *her* interests, *her* priorities? This was something important, something significant, something meaningful she was doing with her friends—*of course* Dorina would choose that night to pretend like she actually wanted to behave like sisters.

Evadne undressed quickly and savagely while thinking these thoughts, but after stripping down to her pantalets and chemise, she sat on the edge of the bed. Part of her wanted to cancel on George—to stay, to see what Dorina might like to do. Sadly, that was impossible—and anyway, if she stayed home, she and Dorina were unlikely to end up reconnecting on some beautiful sisterly level, as if they were characters in one of Dorina's sentimental three-volume novels. Likely they would just fight.

If Evadne was going to fight that night, she would fight demons.

Well, maybe. Evadne was still going back and forth on that, actually. She both wanted and did not want to believe that she might see something . . . *unusual.*

Another chime from the clock reminded her of the crucial timing of her adventure, and she pulled on her clothes and then hurried to replace the practice epees in her bag with the real rapier of Lord Oliver's that she'd been practicing with. Slinging it over her shoulder, she ran downstairs—and nearly crashed into Jonas Fuller, who was standing awkwardly in Basil's foyer.

"Miss Gray!" he exclaimed as she skidded to a halt.

"What are you doing here?" she snapped. He winced; true, it wasn't the most polite greeting she could have offered him.

"I was, ah, in the area," he said, blushing red as a beetroot. "I thought I'd stop by and say hello . . ."

"It's nearly half eight," said Evadne, desperate to be gone. Why was Jonas here, right when she needed to be on her way to see George?

And, of course, to do good in the world by saving children, and so on and so forth . . .

"I'm sorry, of course; I'm aware it's late," he apologized, clasping his hands in front of his belly, then over his plump behind, then back again, "but I wanted . . ." He stopped.

Evadne made a little impatient sound in the back of her throat. "Wanted what?"

"To see you," he said, all in a rush.

Evadne blushed now, remembering Dorina's ridiculous allegation that Jonas *liked* her. Could it be there was some merit in what she'd said? Only then did she notice that for the first time since she'd met him, Jonas didn't look completely perfect. His dark hair was a bit mussed, and his suit didn't look as if he'd just pressed it five minutes before arriving. Sweat beaded his forehead though the night was cool.

"Are you quite all right?" she asked, actually concerned by these small but significant lapses.

"Yes, of course," he said, proper again, then shook his head. "No," he confessed. "Miss Gray, I—I *had* to see you."

"Why?"

"I've . . . you've . . . you haven't been by," he said. "With Dor—Miss Dorina, I mean."

"I've been busy," she said.

"I know you do not care for Lady Henry's company," said Jonas, and Evadne went pink again. "I just," he said over a protest that sounded insincere even to her own ears, "had rather hoped you might . . . well . . . come along anyway . . ."

"For what purpose?" The chime of half past the hour was maddening—she needed to be gone, and he was still hesitating. "Jonas, I'm very sorry, but I'm headed out and I really must . . ."

"Oh!" He seemed to notice her bag and cloak for the first time—also most unlike him. "Where are you going? Might I escort you? The hour is late, and . . ."

"Oh, I'm only going to the academy. There's an event tonight."

"Why take a cab when I could take you there in Henry's carriage? I must head back that way anyhow."

Evadne did not care to accept the favor, but looking at the clock, she knew she was now compelled to. "Thank you," she said. "That's very kind."

Jonas grabbed her bag before she could protest and slung it into the carriage with surprising ease; he was stronger than he looked. Also before she could protest, he took her by the hand to help her up.

The pressure of his fingers on her palm was pleasant and firm, but once he released her Evadne pulled away. She found she liked him less, rather than more, after this uninvited intimacy—the feeling of his skin on hers lingered, leaving her feeling unsettled, even a bit unclean. She very much did not enjoy having liberties taken with her person—at least, not by Jonas, who apparently believed her physically incapable of getting into a carriage without assistance.

George would never assume she was so weak.

Evadne fumed as Jonas told the address to the driver. They sat in silence for a time as they rattled along. Evadne knew it would be polite to find something to talk of, given his kindness to her, but she could not think of anything to say. He kept stealing glances at her, and it made things awkward. She willed the horses to trot faster.

"I'd like to apologize to you," he said at last, startling her.

"What? I mean, I beg your pardon?"

"I must apologize for offending you."

"It *is* polite to ask a lady if she likes to be touched before doing so," she said primly, looking out the window of the carriage to the dark city beyond. She hoped this would put him off, but no such luck.

"Oh, I beg your pardon," said Jonas. Evadne realized he had meant something else, and turned to meet his eye. "You are correct, of course. But I was speaking of our time at the museum, Miss Gray."

Evadne cringed inwardly. She did not wish to go over the incident another time, not at all, and certainly not while she needed to be collecting her thoughts in anticipation of her potentially dangerous evening.

"Oh," she said, gaze falling to the toes of her indiarubber-soled shoes. "Well, thank you . . . but I had already forgotten it."

"Have you?" She glanced at him; he was smiling ruefully. "I do not mean to question your truthfulness, but before I said what I said . . . forgive me, but I admired you so much, when I saw you fencing. The precision of your footwork . . . the movements of your wrist . . . I found it—*you*—so intriguing. I experienced a keen desire to get to know you better. And if I may be so bold, you did not seem displeased by the idea . . . until I went and ruined things like a silly ass." She chuckled at that until he said, "I still wish to know you better, Miss Gray; every time your sister has come to call, I have harbored a hope that you might come along with her . . . Every time we have visited your uncle, I have wished to see *you*. Terribly selfish, I know, but there it is."

Evadne had never felt so confused in her life. It wasn't that she actively *disliked* Jonas. She had resented him for his remark, true, and unfairly—she acknowledged that, to herself at least. And his pleasant openness during this conversation reminded her of why she'd been so at ease with him, all those weeks ago.

And yet, he was a valet, a vassal of the aggravating Lady Henry. They were much like one another—in their manners, and also in the way they made her *feel*. Greasy, unclean . . . To see more of him would mean seeing more of the lady, and that she could not brook. She decided to let him down. Gently.

"I have no objections to getting to know you," she said, "but our schedules are such, it might be—"

"We can make time," he said eagerly, leaning forward. Even as she once again saw how his smile made his plain face something close to handsome, Evadne realized, horrified, that she had given him the wrong impression. What could she possibly say now to dissuade him?

"Ah," she said, but the carriage saved her, slowing and then stopping outside the academy. "I'm sorry, I must be off, I'm already late. Forgive me."

"Another time, then, Miss Gray." His delight was painful for her to behold. "I say," he said as she grabbed her bag, and he looked to the dark front window of the academy, "are you certain the event is tonight? It looks closed up!"

"I'm sure they're in there. Thank you for escorting me," she said brightly, and leaping out before the footman could help her, she hurried inside.

Everyone else was clustered in the dark foyer, anxious like hounds before a hunt. George canted his head at her after she closed the door, smiling faintly.

"Who was that who brought you here?" he asked, jutting his chin at where the carriage was pulling away.

"A family friend," she said, hoping the darkness concealed her blush. She didn't want him getting the wrong idea about Jonas. "I told him there was a conference here tonight."

"I suppose we should have had a light burning, then," mused George. He shrugged. "Ah well, no matter. Let us be gone. But first . . ."

He produced a large cloak and threw it over her shoulders with a flourish. As he fastened it under her chin, Evadne couldn't help but notice it smelled pleasant, like him—a manly smell, with a faint hint of some spicy cologne. It made her feel quite funny, to be surrounded by something of his.

Actually, it felt wonderful.

She was thankful for the pleasantly cool night air that kissed her face as they walked deeper into Westminster to catch cabs. Trawless and Reid hopped in the first that appeared, after George handed them each something along with offering a murmured admonition. Bourne and Stockton took another, after the same strange exchange, which left Evadne with George.

"I'm proud of you, Gray," said George. She fought the urge to say *call me Evadne* as they climbed inside a summoned hackney. "Impressed, I mean. Few people would be brave enough to agree to do something like this."

"Perhaps it's not bravery; I'm still not entirely certain what I've agreed to." All she knew was that they weren't going to *kill* the man. George had been very specific—they were to interrupt whatever unholy ritual he was attempting to conduct that night, and capture him. A dead man couldn't answer questions.

"Questions about what?" she'd asked.

"About his patron demon. About his plans. Whether he has any associates." George had sighed. "No one believes in demons anymore. That's not going to change anytime soon. I have tried and *tried* to come up with some way—*any* way—to get the state involved, or the clergy, but there's no way that doesn't result in me being hanged . . . or locked up in Bedlam. The fact of the matter is, the world has moved on. We are so certain we live in an age of reason, but that simply isn't the case. If men were truly *reasonable*, I could show them evidence of what I know and not be accused of being a diabolist myself, or a madman. It's a shame. I am all too aware that we are vigilantes. If we're caught doing this, *we'll* be the ones to go up before a judge."

That hadn't occurred to Evadne, but at her worried frown he'd patted the back of her hand.

"It's a risk, but it's an important one that good men—good *people*—must take. While what I've done—what we're doing—is illegal, technically, I'm certain I have done good in the world. We have, my group and I. We are an invisible knife that cuts away at an unknown cancer. We will not be thanked, we will not be congratulated. Our only reward will be knowing the nation is healthier for our actions."

They rattled past the heart of Seven Dials, where the shabby buildings converged in a seedy, dark starburst. As they turned down a yet more wretched street, Evadne spied women without escorts, and shiftless people squatting on doorsteps, even a man urinating against a building.

"We're getting close," said George.

"Yes, I see." Evadne's heart fluttered.

"Nervous? Take this, it'll help." He offered her what appeared to be a Communion wafer, save that it did not have a cross stamped on it.

"What is it?"

"Protection."

She stared at him, still not reaching for it. "Protection of what sort?"

George looked amused. "Demons give their followers . . . *gifts*. Rewards for their service. Every demon's is different . . . Sometimes it is unnatural beauty; sometimes it is something more advantageous in a fight, like the ability to mesmerize people, or become invisible. I like to be cautious. After all, we know this man is sacrificing children, but we don't know which demonic entity he's working for."

"How many demons are there?"

"How many people are there?" He shook his head. "They— demons—cannot live in our world without help, without something to host them. Their bodies cannot survive here, but their will, their thoughts . . . *those* can cross the boundaries of our separate realities. That is what a diabolist summons: a demon's intelligence—its will."

"I see," said Evadne, even though she didn't, not really.

"It is a tricky thing to negotiate. No human can communicate directly with a demon; that would kill someone if they tried. We mere mortals can only experience their thoughts, their feelings. The awareness of their desire. That's why it's so easy to be tricked or betrayed by their race. Think of it this way: if it's difficult for one person to tell if another is lying, even when they're speaking face to face, then you can see the impossibility of understanding diabolic deals that are communicated largely by emotion or sensation."

Evadne took the wafer and contemplated it. "I still don't understand why someone would do this," she said.

"Communicate with a demon? Of course you don't. You're like a hothouse flower." Evadne didn't appreciate this compliment; it reminded her of Lady Henry, and therefore, her sister. George must have noticed, as he amended himself. "What I mean is that you are an innocent — a ferocious innocent, though, like" — *Please don't say Athena,* thought Evadne — "Jeanne d'Arc. Pure, martial, full of ideals, but unable to comprehend the true villainy of the world."

"That's possibly overstatement."

"Is it? What care you for what a demon might offer? You do not wear cosmetics, so you must not yearn for eternal youth. You will step out in clothes other than the latest trends, or what is fashionable within some social circle, so you're obviously unconcerned with fame or beauty. You are devoted to hard work and earning what you want, so pleasure or wealth or whatever else, obtained by mesmerism or some other means, would not tempt you." He shrugged. "Demons prey on our lower natures, and you don't seem to have one."

Evadne thought of words she'd said to her sister in anger; her resentment of Freddie; her neglect of her mother, who had so desired a letter; her treatment of Jonas. But the compliment George had paid her was too delicious to deny, so she did not.

"I'd advise eating that now, so you have a bit of time to digest it. That's the building there." He pointed past her ear, out the cab window. She didn't turn; she'd see it soon enough.

"What will happen to me if I . . ."

His smile was playful. "Has everything I've shown you, or done, served to make you healthier, stronger, and better?"

"Yes . . ."

"Well?"

Evadne's eyes tracked back to what she held in her hands.

"It's a holy wafer. If you don't trust me to protect you, do you trust . . ." His gaze flicked heavenward.

She made her choice, put it on her tongue. It was vaguely sweet, and melted away quickly into a paste.

The coach rolled to a stop. George hopped out, paid the cab-driver, and then turned to offer Evadne a hand. She frowned, re-membering her earlier thought that George, unlike Jonas, would not offend her independence, and elected to alight upon the street without aid.

"Old habits die hard," said George. "You're right, Gray, I wouldn't offer assistance to any of the others; it was an unworthy impulse. But let me say, in my own defense, that I did not offer you my aid because I think you weak . . . rather, well . . ."

He trailed off, leaving Evadne breathlessly curious. She tried to get herself under control; the others were leaning up against an ad-jacent boarding house. Though ordinarily her comrades appeared quite gentlemanlike, tonight they did not look like men she would approach, even if she were in desperate need. They looked seedy and threatening as they waved without much interest at George, who ambled over. Evadne tried to imitate his casual gait, but she was too nervous.

"It's that one," said George softly, nodding at the tallest of the buildings in the row.

"Do you know which floor?" asked Reid, his thick brow furrowed.

George shook his head. "I suspect the roof," he said. "If it is to be done *on* the full moon, why not *under* it?"

"See?" said Trawless to Evadne. "He understands the way they think."

Evadne nodded, though that still really remained to be seen. Their talk in the cab had convinced her that George knew quite a lot about the subject. Whether it was a subject worth knowing anything about, that was another matter. Surely alchemists believed their own claims.

She was ready to find out for certain. Energy filled her; she felt strong and powerful, ready to do . . . *something*. Everyone else was in the same place, stomping and champing like standing horses. George popped one of his pastilles, winced, and then after massaging his throat, went up and tried the doorknob.

It was open. He raised a finger to his lips, and clutching his sword cane at the ready, eased it open.

The house was dark; the hall, empty. They made for the stairs off to the left, but then a woman—older, hard-faced—came out of one of the shut doors, and looked understandably surprised to see them. When her eyes found Evadne's face in the crowd, she smiled cruelly.

George broke off from the group and went over to her. "Dear lady," he said, extracting a wallet from inside his jacket, "forgive our intrusion, but we mean you and your house no harm. We merely wish to gain access to the roof." He produced a ten-pound note; this liberal sum, more than his reassuring tone, seemed to assure the landlady of George's sincerity. She reached for it, but he held it back.

"What do you want with the roof?" she asked, her accent coarse and thick, eyes on the money.

"To look at it," said George, carefully keeping impatience from his voice.

She peered at him, mouth twisted with suspicion.

"Surely you have been paid less to accommodate far more unusual requests," said George.

Her laugh was somewhere between a donkey's bray and a fairytale witch's cackle.

"Right," she said. "I'll take you to the attic. There's a window that leads onto a ledge; from there you can get yourself onto the roof to do whatever you want with that one." She nodded in Evadne's direction; Evadne almost flew at the horrible old woman. She was full of hot, angry energy, could barely keep still, and the idea of attacking this wretched crone who had implied—she didn't want to *think* about what the woman had implied—would make her feel much, *much* better. But Trawless put his hand on her shoulder, and shook his head slightly.

"Do you have a ladder that might enable us to scramble onto the roof a bit more easily?" said George, ignoring the woman's vileness.

"No," she said, to Evadne's surprise. "Someone took it, a few days ago, and hasn't given it back."

"Who is this someone?"

"New tenant," said the woman. "He's only been here a few months, keeps mostly to himself. Borrows the ladder occasionally. As he pays for the privilege, I don't ask what he does with it —something you gents can likely understand."

"Indeed," said George as Evadne bristled. "Well, shall we repair to the attic?"

Her eyes dropped to the note. He gestured up the stairs with it, and she nodded.

Evadne was on the tip of her toes as she followed the woman upstairs; she had to fight with herself to not take them two at a time, to jump up and down, bounce, or otherwise tire herself out. The others, save George, seemed in much the same state. Her nervousness had evaporated. She was now ready for whatever might occur. When she saw that the window was already open, the cool summer wind blowing the sheer curtains like ghostly arms, she felt no apprehension whatsoever; all she wanted was to get up to the roof and see what was there.

"Thank you, good lady," said George. "But I'm afraid we must part ways here."

"Never happier," she said, and left them, the note clutched in her dirty fingers.

Evadne had never climbed out of a window before, much less onto a narrow cornice, but she did so without fear. George had gone first, and when she emerged to see him urging the rest of them up the very ladder they had requested, he had a look of savage triumph on his face.

"Just as I suspected," he whispered. "Stay out of sight. I'll go up first, you follow then fan out behind me. Weapons in hand. Evadne . . . get your cloak off but keep it close; you can throw it if need be."

A scream cut the air—a child's cry, and George turned pale.

"Now!" he said, and scrambled up the ladder.

They all followed without hesitation; Evadne pulled off the cloak when she reached the top, winding it around her fist, and kept close to Trawless, who was just in front of her.

There were chimneys and other structures that threw weird shadows across the roof; they darted from one to the next until Evadne saw a brief flare of light. Getting closer to the center of the roof, she saw more clearly that they were candles, arranged in a pattern—the pattern George had divined on his map. An odor reached her nose. *Flowers.* It was not a smell she associated with this part of London, or its rooftops; her shoes were already black with soot, and everything she touched soiled her fencing gloves.

The flowers were piled in sad, wilted heaps between the flames, and in the center of it all was a child—a girl, naked and obscene. Her body was on display in the most profane way Evadne could imagine: on her back, arms and legs spread, her pale hair like a halo on the dirty ground.

To think, she had doubted George could produce evidence of people consorting with demons!

To Evadne's astonishment, the girl did not look terrified. Her eyes were blank as she stared up at the night sky without seeing it. Her jaw was moving, but she was not speaking—she was *chewing*, slowly, like a cow with its cud.

"I know you're here!" called a voice from the darkness—a voice with an animal quality to it, rather like a bark. Evadne couldn't locate its source until the speaker moved, rising up from the ground like some terrible ghost. Cloaked, on his knees, he looked malformed; his long fingers, thin and bony like a skeleton's, held a flower of the same sort that lay heaped on the ground. He fed it to the child, and she ate it mindlessly.

"You are accused of consorting with demons," said George, his sword in one hand, cane sheath in the other.

"Accused by whom?"

Strangely, Evadne felt no fear of this man, but she was appalled to see he was naked under the robe. In spite of this, she forced herself to keep her eyes on him.

He threw back the hood, revealing a gaunt and terrible face. His hair was close-cropped and patchy, as if with mange.

"By we six," declared George. "You have kidnapped and killed several children already—we will not allow you to complete whatever you are attempting here. Do you surrender? If you come quietly, no harm will come to you."

"I do not surrender." His voice really did sound odd—uncanny. The hairs prickled on the back of Evadne's neck, and she shifted from foot to foot to keep warm.

"You are outnumbered, sir!"

"Ah, but it is *you* who are at a disadvantage!"

From nowhere, he produced a knife, an ugly-looking blade that had the horrible appearance of bone. As he held it aloft it gleamed in the moonlight, and then it flashed again—down, into the girl's stomach. A hot putrid stench obscured the sickly aroma of wilting flowers as her insides spilled out.

"No!" George bounded forward, they all did, but it was too late. The man was upon her, and he was *eating* what he had torn out of her, slurping it up with as much gusto as a hungry mutt at a bowl of offal. It got all over him, down his front, even his man's parts, but especially his face and neck, before George got close enough to kick him off the girl. Rolling him over with his foot and pinning him, George held him at sword point.

"Do you yield, sir!" he cried, blade at the man's throat.

The man laughed, and then something happened Evadne would never have believed if she hadn't seen it with her own eyes.

At first she thought it was just the steam rising from the girl's sliced-open body, which, being warmer than the night, was releasing little tendrils of hot smoke. But no—the man's body shivered and split apart like a melon falling off the back of a cart. George cursed and stepped away as each of the chunks writhed and re-formed into ... Dorina would call them *homunculi*. Evadne had no idea why her mind went to that place at that moment, but she had spent many hours of her life looking at Dorina's books of Renaissance triptychs full of little children with the faces of old men. But these weren't old men ... No, each wore the face of the man who had killed the girl who now lay still, dead, eyes open, mouth gaping, on the roof of the boarding house. They were naked, and their hands were too big, and their feet were too big. Everything about them was wrong, the way they writhed about before getting up, the way they shook themselves like wet dogs, the way they started jabbering with their too-familiar mouths that were full of unfamiliar pointed teeth as well as multiple tongues. Their language actually physically hurt Evadne's ears, and her eyes and nose, as well.

Evadne thought about George's earlier promise that they would not kill the man, just bring him in to present him to the police, but things had gone wrong—wrong enough that he ran one of the horrors through with his sword and yanked it back, his rapier blade covered with steaming purple blood. The homunculus squawked as the blade pierced its chest; after he withdrew it, it writhed horribly, and then it went still.

"Get them!"

George's command ought to have been unnecessary, but it woke Evadne from her stupor. She had been frozen, numbly staring. It was time to act.

Seeing the destruction of their fellow, the homunculi went berserk, running all over the place, scattering like frightened children on their short, fat little legs away from those who hunted them. Evadne set her sights on one of the scuttling horrors and chased it down. She had never been so swift in her life, or so strong, or nimble. Yes, she slipped in soot as the thing started to scale one of the chimneys to get away from her, but she caught her balance and threw her cloak at it, covering it. It scrabbled at the cloth with its huge fingers as Evadne yanked on it, reveling in the sheer might of her arm, pulling it down to her level with one tug.

It fell with a thump far too heavy for something so small. Writhing under the cloak, it uttered a little mewling cry, wordless but full of significance. She commenced stabbing it, over and over again—her arm felt as if it would never grow tired. She only stopped when the thing's purple blood was seeping through the rips in George's cloak, pooling underneath it. It did not shine, like oil; rather, it seemed to suck in light.

She turned, sickened. A quick look over her shoulder showed Stockton was in a bad way. One of the creatures was worrying his calf with its teeth. He couldn't quite get his sword around to stab it, and it was ignoring the strikes of his cane sheath. The rest of her friends were occupied with homunculi of their own, so she took a step to aid her friend until she heard George call, "Gray!"

Another of them went scurrying past her, and without hesitation she ran after it. Unlike the first, when it heard her footfalls, this one turned and began to speak to her, its tongues slithering and slipping over one another. She saw the motion with her eyes, but she also felt it inside her mind. It reached its hands out to her, hands that were the size of an adult human man's. Evadne saw it coming for her as she felt wetness on her face, under her eyes, beneath her ears and nose. She reacted out of instinct, getting her arm up before lunging at it with all her might.

It was the most basic of fencing attacks—get your arm up, then step and thrust—but long, ago, Freddie had taught her well when he said it would save her more often than any fancy attack or parry. Endlessly, she had practiced *arm up, step, thrust* until it became pure instinct, and she was grateful, for it saved her then. She was strong, she was fast, and her blade pierced the creature's left eye with such force that it broke through the other side of its skull, where it fountained gore from both ends, spraying her and the ground behind it. The enraged thing kept speaking, kept struggling on her blade until it died.

She stared at the sight, completely horrified.

Then George was by her side, his hand on her shoulder. She startled away from him, dropping the blade, nearly casting it away from her. He raised his hands in a gesture of peace.

"Sorry!" She shook her head. "It . . ."

"That did not go well," he admitted. "We were too late. Or rather, I did not anticipate what would happen if he began the ritual too early."

"Too . . ."

"Early." George picked up her rapier, and with his foot, slid the carcass off the blade. Wiping it on the creature's skin, he handed it back to her. "I very much doubt he intended to destabilize like that . . . I don't know to whom he was praying, so I can't say what his goal was, but I'm guessing it wasn't"—he gestured to the massacre—"*this.*"

"Destabilize." She sounded stupid even to her own ears.

"They come from another plane," he said, "something parallel to ours, but that can only intersect in certain, strange ways. As I said, they cannot live here. When they do come over, it's . . . toxic to us —and to them. Those *things*, they would have died soon enough, but possibly not before making mischief. They would have been slowly poisoned by our air, our voices even—they cannot hear us without pain, nor we them. That's why when it spoke . . ." He wiped under her eye with a callused thumb and showed her.

It was blood.

Evadne touched her ear, and her fingertips glistened when she pulled them away. That was when she began to shake, to quiver like the last leaf of autumn clinging to a beech-tree's branch.

"Steady!" He took her hand in his, and squeezed it. "We are not yet done!"

Then he pressed something into her palm—a bottle—and bid her sprinkle it all over the roof. "Holy oil," he said when she looked at him uncomprehendingly, but after that, it made enough sense for her to follow his orders.

She felt herself drawn to the worst of the carnage—meaning, the child. She went over, drawn to the awful tableau as equally as she was repelled by it, and looked upon the ruin.

The presence of the flowers made the disemboweled girl appear yet more horrifying, surrounded by their beauty, loathsome in her nakedness. Evadne sprinkled some of her holy oil on her broken body, fresh tears mingling with the drying blood caking her face.

Beside the broken thing that had been a child was the knife. Disgusting as it was, it was also strangely compelling. It whispered at Evadne, practically begged her to pick it up and hold it.

Evadne stripped off her glove to grasp it.

As soon as her fingers touched it, a vision came to her of what ought to be done with the knife. She saw all the children of London at once, her mind's eye tracking from one to another to another in impossible succession. There they were, in their beds, in their rooms, in factories and on the streets, in loving homes and wretched ones. So many children! Surely, *some* could be sacrificed . . .

"They shall come to me," she intoned. "Their power shall be mine, their youth, their innocence, and from that I shall shape a—"

A stinging slap across her cheek startled her, and the blade went clattering to the roof, skittering away from her.

"Evadne!"

George was looming over her, his hands on her shoulders. Her cheek ached, but the sound of her name in his mouth alarmed her more.

"What?"

"You picked it up, you silly girl! Why would you do that?"

"It . . . I don't . . ." She gasped. "I'm sorry!"

"It's my fault. I should have wrapped it up first thing. Demonically tainted objects can seduce the unwary, and they suggest their purpose to those who touch them." He looked at her keenly. "But only certain people see clearly the visions such items would impart; others just feel a sense of purpose, unconsciously, that motivates them. You must be particularly sensitive, Gray . . . You were speaking the demon's will aloud."

Evadne sank to her knees. Being attuned to demonic influence was not a talent she desired. Her hand felt greasy; she felt unclean, knowing that she was somehow *particularly sensitive* to commune with beings like she had just seen.

He knelt beside her. "Gray. It doesn't mean anything about you, your future choices, your fate. It is a great asset, actually, to those who follow our path. What did you see? You said their innocence would . . ."

"I don't know . . ."

"Perhaps it's better that way." The set of his mouth was grim as he stood, but it quirked into a smile as he offered her a hand up, then withdrew it before she could move. Evadne cursed her earlier reaction to his aid—the touch of human skin might have felt good after her otherworldly experience.

"Well," he said as the others came to them, empty bottles of holy oil in their hands, "is everyone all right?"

"One *bit* me," said Stockton, whose pale face glowed like the full moon now hanging above them.

"Did it break the skin?"

"Not sure."

"We'll check it out back at the school. Anyone else hurt? No? Did any of them get away?"

They all agreed none had. Evadne hoped they were right. One of those things, loose in London! Even for a short time! Though, on the other hand, it might show all the unbelievers what was really lurking out there, for George had been right.

Demons did exist.

"Gray?"

"Hmm?" She realized she hadn't been listening.

"Ready to go?"

"Go?" She looked to the body of the girl. "But what will we do with ..."

"Burn her."

"Surely—"

"Even if we could find her parents, if she were yours, would *you* want to know? If you were the police, would you believe us—believe our explanations as to how this happened?"

She saw the wisdom of this, but not the burning. "But the building ..."

"The oil will only burn that which is already corrupted," he said. "We'll find his room, too, and burn that. There will be ashes, but it won't take the house."

It was a sign of the shocks she'd suffered that Evadne did not protest more as they descended the ladder. She went last, and looked up before descending; George was standing over the body. He made a strange motion with his hand, at which point brilliant green flames erupted and spread over the rooftop. She shook her head—he must have struck a match, she reasoned, and slipped down the ladder and through the window.

George stayed behind to inspect the man's room, but told everyone else they ought to disband quickly. Evadne did not make a fuss; as exhilarated as she had felt, she was now heartsick. Images of what she had beheld kept flashing behind her eyes. Trawless got her into a cab, and rode with her back home.

"Are you sure you wouldn't rather go to the school?" he asked. "We could clean you up there . . ."

"No one will be awake," she said. It was too late, and even if Dorina was up, she wouldn't come out to greet her sister. Evadne could slip easily into the bathroom and wash herself and get the worst of what was on her clothes out with no one the wiser.

"If you're sure . . ."

She was—and she was proven right. Trawless said something as she disembarked from the cab, but she scarcely heard it. It was like being asleep, then awake, then asleep again—like those dreams she had occasionally where she couldn't open her eyes to see what was happening. It wasn't until she was soaking in the tub that the enormity of what she had seen hit her, and then she wept, silently, scrubbing at herself until the water was cold, her skin was raw, and she was weak and shivering.

She wrung out her gear in the disgusting water, not wanting any questions asked of her tomorrow by the maids. Then, somehow she got herself into her nightclothes, once the evidence of where she had been and what she had been doing had been largely disposed of. The bed looked so welcoming, and she longed to collapse into it . . . but her eyes tracked over the box on the floor where the unusual hilt of Lord Oliver's Chinese sword could just be seen, and her fractured mind suddenly remembered what George had said:

Demonically tainted objects can seduce the unwary, and they suggest their purpose to those who touch them.

The memory of the only time she'd held the sword came back to her potently—she had known just what to do with the blade, how to hold it in her hand, how to wield it. The similarity of the experience to picking up the dagger on the rooftop startled her the more she thought about it. Lord Oliver's sword hadn't suggested she use it to murder anyone, or do anything other than celebrate the beauty of graceful motion, and yet the sensation of being *informed* had been so similar . . .

Was the sword tainted with demonic essences? Could Lord Oliver have trafficked with demons?

What of his sister?

A cold chill crept over Evadne that had nothing to do with lingering too long in the bath. She struggled to recall what Lady Henry had said that day they were at the National Gallery . . . They'd had a conversation about demons, the three of them, and Lady Henry had been rather flip about the subject. At the time, Evadne had chalked it up to her loucheness paired with a city-dweller's amusement over provincial beliefs, but now . . . now that she thought about what they'd said, compared to what George had said . . .

Dorina had explained that Bacchus's followers were given powers, *gifts* . . . exactly what George mentioned with regards to diabolists. While the god of wine was on the surface one of the friendlier-seeming in the Greek pantheon, he gave his acolytes the ability to rend, destroy, tear—to throw off the fragile mask of humanity and eat the flesh of men. And rather than finding this ghastly, Lady Henry had suggested that it must be a pleasurable experience, for "why else" would anyone agree to do it . . .

Her eyes tracked back to where the Chinese sword lurked. It had made her feel so *queer*, but she had been distracted from really thinking about the sensation by Jonas's interruption. Holding the object had not been unpleasant . . . but after, the sensation of having been affected—*contaminated*—was palpable.

Just like with the dagger.

And it might be only her imagination, but had she felt something similar the few times Lady Henry had touched her? And Jonas? Surely not . . . it had likely just been the imposition of his touch that had disgusted her earlier that night, the lingering sense of him on her skin. Then again, while she had thought nothing of it at the time, beyond being annoyed by it, now . . .

George hadn't said demonically tainted *people* were divinable by those like her—those who were particularly sensitive—but it made a certain kind of terrible sense.

What of her sister? Dorina was so under the influence of that woman already . . . Evadne shivered again, colder still as she tasted salt water; the memory of trying to save her sister when she wasn't in any danger came back to her in that moment. Was she making the same mistake? Seeing danger where it wasn't?

Would she again end up a laughingstock for her concerns?

It was worth the risk, she decided, remembering the sight of that poor child's broken, torn body, the scurrying things that had fought and bitten, the dagger that had called her to do evil. First thing tomorrow, she would speak to Dorina, warn her. Dorina would surely scoff at her, would laugh and tease, but what was that to Evadne?

She had killed demons. She could brave a talk with her sister.

Evadne got into bed, sore and trembling and so very tired, resolving to get up early and make her sister understand the danger she might very well be in. Unfortunately, she slept until noon the following day, and by the time she woke, weak-limbed and plagued by headache, Dorina was already gone.

7

Reader, be not afraid of this book. All your life, you have likely cultivated a passionless interest in trivial things. That is what man does, for matters of high import terrify us. All that will change, and quickly, as you read on. But, reader, beware: this book will not give you answers. It will merely tell you what questions you ought to ask.

— *On the Summoning of Demons*

HENRY HAD INVITED DORINA to a second meeting of her appreciation society. The theme was *sight,* which excited Dorina's sensibilities more than scent — though of course she had had a lovely time during the previous meeting. Still, expanding her appreciation of the visual could not but help her in her professional aspirations.

Not that she had necessarily been paying much attention to said professional aspirations. She had simply been too busy — preoccupied, really — with Henry.

They had seen one other nearly every day of late, but ever since realizing Henry was toying with her, Dorina had been letting Henry make the arrangements. The older woman had determined the days, the times, and, mostly, what they would do. This was by design, of course; Dorina had made sure to seem more distant on purpose, though she remained enthusiastic and excited about all the sights Henry showed her, and was active and engaged during their conversations. And she made sure to turn Henry down every once in a while. Take last night — Henry had been going out to dine with Mr. Blake, to talk over a bit of this evening's program, since he was in charge of it. In truth, Dorina had longed to go, but as it would be nicer to experience the program without foreknowledge, she had declined, to Henry's genuine surprise . . . and disappointment, if Dorina were any judge of such things.

And, really, she was a *very* good judge of such things.

The day of the meeting Henry was expecting several deliveries, and would be at home because of it; Dorina had agreed to keep her company. Henry's coach was to fetch her around noon, to retrieve her and bring her to Curzon Street, so that morning Dorina had gotten herself together with all haste, including packing her ensemble for the night.

She was very excited about what she would wear. Henry had escorted her to one of Mrs. Dhareshwar's fabric showrooms the previous week, and Dorina had despaired of ever being able to choose among the silks and cottons and brocades for a caftan of her own. In the end, she had decided to splurge and have two made up— one a bluish-green brocade with a gold interior, and another, a little more exotic in style, in a parrot-green silk with a pattern of yellow and white ginger blossoms and a coral-pink interior. Lady Henry had seemed surprised at Dorina's choice, but Dorina had pretended not to notice, and simply quipped that she'd fit right in at Henry's home in such a garment.

She had selected the ginger caftan for that evening. She folded it carefully in a little bag, and on top of it put some older clothes in case Henry was of a mood to do some gardening. Nestled alongside her garment lay a few other items, including some elaborate Chinese hairpins Henry had bought her and the copy of *Les Fleurs du Mal* which she was still reading.

Evadne hadn't come down to breakfast, which surprised Dorina. But when she had remarked on it, Basil mumbled that he had been just going to bed when he heard Evadne return. The lecture at the academy must have run late. Still, it seemed odd to Dorina that even now, close to midday, her sister yet slumbered. Before

descending, Dorina raised her hand to knock and say goodbye—
she would be the one out late tonight—but thought better of it.
Likely Evadne needed her rest.

It was too bad, really . . . She had hoped to spend some time
with her sister the previous night. It seemed amazing that they
had exchanged little more than cold pleasantries for so long, but
Evadne had been gone so much of late, and distant when she was
home. *Tired,* she said. Sweaty, too, though she did not articulate
that. Anyway, Dorina missed her.

Henry was indeed digging in her greenhouse when Dorina arrived, but as she was just finishing up, Dorina did not join her
hands with Henry's in the dirt. Instead, she read more of the astonishing book of poetry Henry had given her, reveling in its
beauty and decadence. Thankfully, Henry's copy had the French
and English side by side, so Dorina could check her imperfect
knowledge as she went along—she had never been much interested in languages until she resolved to be a critic, and though she
had revisited her old schoolroom French book, it had been too late
for her ever to become truly fluent.

"You're enjoying it?" asked Henry, coming to squat by where
Dorina lounged on an iron bench wrought in the shape of ginger
blooms and roots.

"Of course," said Dorina. "Though I must say, his idea of our
sort is a little . . . far-fetched."

"Our sort?"

"I've been with quite a lot of girls, but I've never kissed—or
been kissed—like a waterfall, whatever that means, nor have I
spent a hot night with a friend before a mirror, caressing the ripe
fruits of my womanhood." Henry was looking at her, clearly torn
between amusement and something else, Dorina couldn't quite
say. "I suppose perhaps I'm just too English for such a thing. It
seems very French, for all it's supposed to be about Greeks."

Henry laughed, and lit a cigarette. "It's a shame your tastes run to art. You'd make a spectacular literary critic."

"No better than an art critic, I'm afraid."

"You haven't given up your ambition?" asked Henry.

Dorina shrugged. "A critic should know something before she opens her mouth, and the more I learn, the less I'm sure I know anything at all."

Henry took a long drag without saying anything. Dorina wondered what she might be thinking, but a ringing at the front door distracted them both.

"The first of Robert's deliveries," said Henry, dusting off her hands on the wide canvas trousers she liked to wear when gardening. "I'll just go and see what it is. Would you like to come?"

"Oh no. I like a surprise," said Dorina, deliberately keeping her eyes on her book. "You have a good time . . . I'll be here when you're finished."

Henry hesitated, but she did not argue—just nodded and promised a speedy return. Dorina smiled as the older woman turned away, and watched Henry's narrow backside as she strode out of the greenhouse.

Henry might be the more experienced of the two of them—possibly, Dorina didn't know, for Henry had never discussed affairs of that sort with her—but Dorina was certain she was gaining ground, step by step. This was a good thing. Dorina might be able to act cool and collected around Henry, but inside, she was a furnace. She wanted Henry so badly that she had to stop herself from inhaling her scent too deeply, wanted her so badly that she thought she might go mad from desire if Henry didn't crack soon. Henry's hands, with their perpetually grubby, short-clipped nails, inspired daydreams as hot as any night of Baudelaire's imagining; the sight of her clavicle when she pulled off her cravat produced a reaction indescribable in polite company, but certainly noticeable to Basil's laundress if Dorina hadn't taken the time to rinse out her pantalets.

She dreamed of Henry at night, likely due to certain personal attentions Dorina often paid herself before bed, only to awake desperate, unsatisfied, her head aching, and often with a soreness in other, more private places. She had never in her life desired anyone so intensely. Girls, to Dorina, were fundamentally fungible — or at least, her interest in exploring the variety nature had generously produced had kept her from falling head over heels for any individual specimen. Thus she was totally unequipped to deal with her infatuation; only her experience in tempting the untemptable guided her in how to keep herself apparently cool and calm around the object of her affection.

This was why of late she had been warmest toward Henry in a crowd, or when there were things to distract her from her desire to do things like lick Henry's earlobes or nibble on her prominent wrist bones. It was simply too difficult to be friendly and intimate when they were alone without betraying herself. In a crowd, however, she could lose herself.

Henry was busy with deliveries the rest of the afternoon. Just as Dorina was regretting her decision to be standoffish, Jonas returned with a few items for the party, and then Mr. Blake arrived early to see to the preparations.

The gathering went spectacularly well. The members were again all in attendance that evening, and the dinner, if possible, was more delicious. Once again, Dorina and Mr. Walmsley were exiled for a brief time before the entertainment began, but they were not sent on some errand; rather, they were sent ahead to the gallery where Mr. Blake had set everything up.

"I've never seen an ice sculpture before," said Dorina, standing before the magnificent Chimera that had been wheeled in just before the guests began to arrive. The cold it radiated was intense.

"No?"

"We had some elaborate parties back in Swadlincote, but being rather provincial, we made do with more easily managed adornments." Dorina smiled at her companion, who stood defiantly before the piece, leaning on his walking stick. Tonight, he looked exhausted as well as in pain, but had been putting on a brave face all evening. Poor fellow . . . she wondered if there was some way she could get him to sit down without insulting him. Hopefully, Mr. Blake had been considerate of everyone's needs and planned for a seated affair. But for now . . .

"Ugh, I ate so much at supper. Thank goodness I've something loose to wear!" Dorina sighed. Normally she was not one to discuss her digestion with near-strangers, but it was as good an excuse as any to take a seat. "I simply must get off my feet . . ."

"Shall we take a seat?" A smile hovered at the corners of Mr. Walmsley's lips. He knew she was trying to accommodate him, but apparently she'd made less of a hash of it than last time.

"Please," she said, with overexaggerated relief.

"I'm pleased to see you again," he said, after settling himself as comfortably as he could. "Not everyone is invited back a second time, you know."

"No, I didn't."

"Oh yes. It's what you say, what you do . . . here, but also afterward. Some people are just unsuitable."

"I wonder why?"

Mr. Walmsley shrugged, winced. "Some people are hedonists in their fantasies, but haven't the stomach for the lifestyle."

Dorina had no idea whether she was truly up to snuff. She certainly liked to think so, but she would ponder that later. For now, she was deeply curious what Mr. Walmsley had done to prove himself worthy, for he seemed as receptive to pleasure as a pair of old boots.

"Perhaps that is also how they determine who gets to stay when they close the doors," mused Dorina.

"You still don't know?"

Dorina glanced at him. "No, why should I?"

"Given your friendship with the lady, I just assumed . . ."

"Oh, she tells me nothing," said Dorina as lightly as she could, to bury her disappointment. "She scarcely believes I'm old enough to attend these meetings, much less understand anything deeper about their purpose."

"So you do think there's something more? Something . . . else?"

"I really couldn't say." Dorina felt like he was pushing her, but to what end, she couldn't guess. She decided to turn it back onto him. "What do you suspect?"

"It could be anything. Drugs . . ."

"They don't seem drugged."

"No." He chuckled. "Perhaps I'm wrong, and they're just a dues-paying club. The most expensive ingredients or what have you go into their special drinks, so they're all in there squabbling over whether or not to hike up the rates because of the price of saffron or pearl dust." He leaned in close to her. "But I don't think so," he stage-whispered.

They didn't have time to discuss the matter further, for the rest of the party joined them then, and the program commenced. It was exhilarating, even more delightful than their exploration of scent, and by the end of it Dorina felt intoxicated, even though she had barely sipped her wine at dinner.

After it ended, Dorina wished she'd drunk more, rather than less. Her stomach turned to a fluttery, flimsy thing when the guests began to depart. It was now or . . . not *never*, but definitely *later*, and she didn't know how much longer she could go on without satisfying her lust for the divine creature who was just closing the door behind Dr. Sauber.

"I think we ought to do it soon," said Henry.

"What?" said Dorina. She was hanging back by the foot of the stairs, steadying herself on the balustrade.

"The interview," said Henry. "Dr. Sauber seems most eager to talk to you, and I can't have him staying so late every time we meet. I need my rest."

"Oh, of course . . . any time, really."

Henry cocked her head at Dorina. "Are you quite all right?"

She was showing her hand too soon. "Only a little . . . over-come." She didn't want to say anything about drink; it was an easy way for Henry to dodge her impending pass. Tired was also bad; it suggested bed, but not in the way she had in mind. "You of course are an old hand at such remarkable displays and delights, but I am still quite the novice."

"A natural reaction," said Henry. "Well, perhaps you ought to scurry home."

"Don't send me home," said Dorina, stepping forward, away from the safety of the railing. "Please. At least, not yet."

Her tone must have conveyed *something*, for Lady Henry paused before nodding. "Let's have a drink," she proposed. "I'm sure there's a half-bot of champagne left around somewhere."

"I don't want any more to drink," said Dorina, taking another step forward. Her hands were shaking; she was tingling all over. "I want . . ."

"Shall I call for the carriage?" Jonas poked his head in. Dorina could have killed him in that moment, remorselessly and quickly, if she'd had a pistol or some other dangerous implement at hand.

"Not yet," said Henry quickly, barely looking over her shoulder at her valet and friend.

"I beg your pardon," he said, and withdrew.

It had broken the tension, but it had also broken Dorina's hold over Henry's attention.

"Dorina," she said firmly, "I think you and I ought to have a talk."

"A talk?"

"Yes." Henry had gone so white that she looked almost ill, with her too-fair hair and her refusal to wear any rouge. Her blue eyes, normally so bright, looked paler, like the sky on a very hot day in the country. "Dorina . . . dear heart . . ."

"Call me that again," moaned Dorina, closing the gap between them. Grabbing Henry's hands, she raised one to her lips and kissed the back of it. "Oh, Harry, let me hear it from your lips once more."

"Dorina," she said firmly, extracting herself from Dorina's grasp. "You must stop this."

That was not at all the reaction Dorina had expected. "Stop what?"

"This madness. We cannot . . ." She shook her head. "I don't think you understand how bad an idea it would be for us to . . ."

"To what?" asked Dorina, trying to sound playful, but her mouth was so very dry all of a sudden. "I just want you to call me *dear heart* again."

"Dorina—please."

It hit Dorina then. She was being rejected.

She had never been rejected—*really* rejected—in her life! It was outrageous, incomprehensible. All she'd ever had to do before was butter up a girl, and from there everything had been easy enough. Just nature taking its course.

This wasn't how she'd expected her night to end. Henry had been so increasingly awkward, anxious to get her attention. Dorina had sensed she was ripe for the picking, but she must have been deluding herself. And rather than Henry's denial putting her off, Dorina felt more desperate than ever, perhaps because she couldn't anticipate any relief from her passion, only more long days wanting, waiting . . .

"No?" Her voice sounded small, especially in Henry's big, high-ceilinged foyer.

"I'm far too old for you, for one," said Henry gently.

"I don't care about that," said Dorina, more fiercely now. "Who cares about that? Not I!"

"And there are other things . . ."

"Tell me!"

"I can't." Henry seemed regretful for some reason. Dorina wanted so badly to kiss her, to make her smile.

"Do you like me? That way?" she demanded.

"That's not the point."

"Of course it's the point!"

"Dorina . . ."

Dorina felt a surge of hope. Henry *couldn't* say she didn't like her!

Dorina reached out, placing a trembling palm on either side of Henry's narrow face, and drew it slowly, so slowly, toward her own. Kissing the older woman, she drank in the taste of her, vaguely gingery—no surprise there. As she lapped at Henry's mouth, Henry groaned, her lips parting; Dorina took the opportunity to plunge her tongue into the dark cavity, exploring. Finally, Henry yielded, and wrapping her arms around Dorina, she drew her closer, embracing her, all bones and tweed against Dorina's flesh and silk.

"This is wrong," she murmured into Dorina's mouth. "I shouldn't be doing this."

"I really couldn't disagree more," answered Dorina, and pulling away from their first wonderful embrace, she led the older woman by the hand to her own bedroom.

EVER SINCE HER FIRST ORGASM, Dorina had chased the next one, and the next, and the next. No encounter had ever sated her, not really, not wholly. Simply put, a tumble with another girl was one of her favorite things in the world, only a hair below discovering a new artist, and well above almond-paste croissants —meaning, among the ranks of things she could never get enough of. But that night, when at last they fell apart, Dorina felt as if she might understand what satisfaction meant, and she fell deeply, happily asleep, her limbs tangled with Henry's.

She had odd dreams. Lost in a maze, she wandered, thirsty and alone. Someone was calling to her, but in a language she could not understand. Maddeningly, she sensed if she could only comprehend the words they would tell her how to escape, but as hard as she listened, the language was beyond her. At some point she cried out, half-waking in frustration, but Henry's arms found her, and her warm body pressed close lulled Dorina into a deeper, dreamless slumber.

The next morning she awoke in an empty bed. The covers had been thrown aside, and there was still an indentation where Henry had slept. Dorina stretched luxuriously, like a cat in the sun, and after rolling around a few times to make sure she wouldn't fall back asleep, she got up.

There was a note on the dresser:

I've gone out with Jonas. Beth knows you'll want breakfast. Make yourself at home. I've sent word to your uncle you've stayed the night, so don't feel like you must hurry back.

—Harry

Dorina tried not to feel hurt that the missive was so brief, and didn't mention anything about . . . well, *anything*. Then again, what would her lover have written, really?

Someone had left a dressing gown for her, and Dorina belted it around herself before ringing the bell for Beth. Then she lounged about, picking up Lady Henry's belongings, smelling her perfumes, poking around her fantastic bathroom while she waited. It wasn't long before Beth brought up a tray with tea, toast, and a nicely done egg.

"Lady Henry said to tell you she won't be long," said Beth, her face betraying no surprise at Dorina's having stayed the night, and in her mistress's bed.

"Thank you, Beth," said Dorina. "When did she go out?"

"Oh, not an hour ago."

After breakfast, Dorina put on the skirt and shirtwaist she'd worn yesterday, which had been neatly pressed for her, and wandered downstairs. She was starting to become impatient for Henry's return—felt a bit injured, truth be told, that Henry hadn't woken her before going out.

Dorina smiled to herself. Usually *she* was the one who disappeared conveniently after a rendezvous.

The remains of the party had been cleared away from the salon, and the dining room was neat and tidy. Truly bored, Dorina was just crossing the foyer into the library when there was a knock at the door.

She opened it and to her surprise, it was Hyacinth Travers. She was dressed in a fashionable walking suit in the most delicious charcoal gray, with blue silk accents and agate buttons; Dorina instantly coveted it. She had a brown paper parcel under her arm, and was in the process of shifting it into her hand when she noticed Dorina.

"Dorina!" she exclaimed. She seemed alarmed, not just surprised . . . but then her eyes narrowed, and she laughed a little laugh. "I wasn't expecting you . . . but why I wasn't, I don't know."

"Ma'am?" said Beth, from behind her.

"It's Miss Travers," called Dorina over her shoulder, then turning back, said, "Will you come in? Henry isn't here right now."

"I'm afraid I can't, I'm on my way in to the office . . . just passing by. I had something of Henry's I was returning." For some reason, Miss Travers seemed rather reluctant to give it over.

"I'll take it up to her study," offered Dorina. "She should be home any minute."

After a moment's hesitation, Miss Travers relinquished the parcel. "Thank you, Dorina. I'm sorry I can't stay . . . next time?"

"Next time," Dorina agreed.

Though she was curious why Miss Travers had seemed so awkward, the package quickly claimed her attention. It was a book, that was obvious—a slender hardback volume. The paper had slipped a bit, for Miss Travers hadn't tied it up with string, and as Dorina walked it upstairs to Henry's study, she saw the corner of the cover. Bound in gilded leather, illustrated with winding vines and flowers, and printed with black ink so bright it looked almost wet, it was astonishingly beautiful. Dorina found she couldn't resist peeking at the title.

"*On the Summoning of Demons,*" she read aloud as she traced her fingers over the embossed letters.

No wonder it had been wrapped in brown paper! Surely this book was not meant to be seen by just anyone's eyes. If it was a joke, many wouldn't think it a funny one—why, how Evadne had reacted to the conversation topic in the National Gallery!

While Dorina felt a sense of guilt over opening the package, she was unable to resist her curiosity. Henry had never mentioned demons again, never ever, not after their conversation that day at Kew. Could she have been putting her off? Did Henry really believe in magical beings?

She opened the book. The first few pages were blank. There was neither dedication nor epigraph, neither author nor title page. When it began, it began as such:

Pity the disciple who doubts, the skeptic who would believe, the convict of life embarking alone in the night, under a sky no longer illuminated by the consoling beacons of ancient faith. Such is the natural state of man when it first becomes known to him that demons exist. They are neither metaphors, nor evil agents of the Devil, nor good angels sent by God to guide man, as some have

imagined. They are both more and less than any of that—they are
creatures of will and temper, of want and ruin, of charm and hun-
ger, of pique and cunning as we mere mortals are, and yet funda-
mentally different.

*   For those men who would know more of their race, for his own*
purpose, I have written this book . . .

Dorina settled into Henry's chair behind her desk, entranced.
The style settled down after a bit, she was pleased to note, and it
became even more engaging.

According to the golden book, demons inhabited another
world, one separate from that of men. Like humans, they possessed their own inner lives, their own politics, their own laws and
desires and needs and hopes and rages. But unlike humans, they
were able—with help—to pass between the worlds, at least in
part. Only their minds, or at least fragments of them, were able to
endure the strain of crossing over.

They were similar to us, declared the book, yet fundamentally
different. Demons were possessed of reason, and had moral and
ethical concerns. But, cautioned the unknown author, these concerns were not as men's; their ideas of morality were not necessarily congruent with men's, nor was their conception of evil, or
justice. Like humans, demons were neither wicked nor good; each
of them was unique and made independent decisions about how to
live its life. Some had no interest in humanity and our world; others were *obsessed* with us, fascinated by our art, our culture, our politics, our desires. Still others took that obsession further, attempting to meddle in our world to please themselves—or as a means
to meddle in their own.

A demon that resided partially in the world of men was weakened in its own, more vulnerable to the sorts of rare but serious
diseases that affect their race . . . or more commonly, to attack by
one of its fellows. These attacks could be carried out either in their

world or in ours, and were often deadly, for demons could be griev-
ously wounded, even killed. While it was more difficult to snuff
out their light, it could be done, and such attempts were usually
made when a demon was reeling from the trauma of being severed
from a human with whom it had struck a bargain. And yet, for
some of their race, the ones fascinated by men, the risk was worth
it to touch our minds and live with us—just as the risk of persecu-
tion, discovery, and even death was worth it for some men.

Dorina turned page after page, intrigued by this information,
though she was not entirely convinced of the truth of it. The author admitted that his or her own knowledge of the subject was
necessarily limited, which made her suspect much of the information was really just guesswork. Then again, the author did al-
lege that contact with demons was inherently and absolutely dangerous—to speak directly with a demon would essentially cook
the human brain, destroy the body. That *would* account for many
gaps in men's knowledge . . . a natural, or rather supernatural, de-
terrent. Apparently, when a human communicated through a medium, which was the only way humans could speak with their race,
he or she ran the risk of shattering the self completely. Few over
the centuries had tried; fewer had succeeded. Fewer still succeeded
in the long term; the temptation to go further, to learn more, was
always present, and if it was not resisted, self-destruction was the
inevitable result.

The prose was not exactly transparent. Dorina was about to set
the book aside when at last she reached just how a human might
contact a demon. Then, she could not but read more:

*If one wishes to speak with a demon, the body must be tempered
like a cook tempers an egg for custard. The flesh, the bone, the mind
must all be inoculated with a small bit of demonic essence, or the
mind will curdle, so to speak. The easiest way, honored by time, is*

to commune with one of their race via the consumption of a sacrament contaminated with their unique essence.

Plant matter is the safest and easiest method by which to achieve this, for animals of all sorts are far more likely than plants to be destroyed by demonic contact. A would-be diabolist therefore conducts a ritual to lure the demon into some sort of plant, and if the demon is interested, and successfully summoned, the plant may either be consumed in the moment, or planted for the purposes of propagation. Even someone with only a window box may — if they are clever, and have a green enough thumb — cultivate an endless supply of demonically infused plant matter.

By consuming a small amount of said plant, over time the human body becomes sensitized to the toxic presence of the demon. Not all survive this diabolic grand feu — but if one does, one becomes a remarkable vessel fired for a remarkable purpose. And like clay, one takes on new, often useful, properties.

Now I must say beware to those who would seek such a result. While one receives gifts from demons, such as beauty, strength, or insight, there is always a cost. The cost can be physical, or mental; regardless, it will *be paid — and in full.*

It is also good to understand that demonic essence possesses an addictive property. While a tiny amount of demonic essence may suffice at first, the human body is supremely adaptable. It craves what pleases it; it will need more over time. But increasing the dose risks the body's integrity, and one must be very careful never to go too far . . .

"Too far," murmured Dorina, but then a noise startled her, and she looked up to see Henry in the doorway. She was holding a box of pastries from Dorina's favorite bakery.

"What are you doing?" she asked calmly. *Too* calmly. There was steel behind her words, not mere conversational interest.

Dorina swallowed. She'd been caught. She should have heeded that nagging sense of guilt, that sensation of *maybe I shouldn't be doing this.* But she hadn't. What good would lying do now?

"Is it real?" she asked boldly. "Is this what you all do? Your appreciation society, I mean. Do you traffic with demons?"

8

With demons, as with men, real communication begins where intellectual expression ends.

— On the Summoning of Demons

H ENRY HAD AWOKEN EARLY to find Dorina curled into her, the girl's soft body a warm, substantial weight in her armpit. Awake, Dorina was always a simmering pot on the edge of boiling, but asleep, she looked at peace. A slight smile gently turned up the corners of her mouth, and when Henry moved, hoping to free herself—her arm was numb, under Dorina's head—the girl snuggled in yet closer.

Henry, however, was not at peace. She ought to be. What they'd shared last night had been one of the most astonishing experiences of her life. She was used to taking the lead, or at least being equally active during her affairs. Dorina, however, had practically devoured her, barely letting her do a thing. No one had ever been so free with her, or so *rough*. It made her wonder if her previous lovers had been intimidated by her status, her title. Not Dorina. The girl had bitten at her lips—jammed her fingers inside her as though she were desperately attempting to catch some precious object that had fallen down a drain before it slipped away forever. Henry had been shocked at first, to be treated so outrageously by this naïve country strumpet, but she had never come so hard, writhing as Dorina stared at her, watching her reactions with eager concentration. Her body had been a violin, and Dorina's touch, a bow . . . but that implied too much separateness. They had been one flesh, just like they were taught in Sunday school.

Well, maybe not *quite* like in Sunday school.

Even so, she knew she'd made a grave error, giving in, giving over. Her demon companion contradicted her, which it very rarely did; it thought she'd finally made the right decision. But where Dorina was concerned she could not trust it, could not ask its advice. It liked the girl—as much as it could "like" anything. Perhaps it would be better to say it approved of her.

It *wanted* her.

Henry had hosted her demon for years now, close to a decade, and she had always been able to keep its will separate from hers. It was important to her to be able to identify the ways in which they were distinct, even if she welcomed its intrusion into her thoughts and feelings.

It wasn't the demon that made her anxious about Dorina. She hadn't lived as a monk since her decision to let it into her mind; she had had several affairs of varying lengths. The most successful had been with Hyacinth Travers, but when they had mutually decided they were better as "just friends," Henry had not felt too many regrets. She was past the time in her life when she always needed someone in her bed when she woke up. While it was pleasant, especially in the winter, she liked her mornings to herself, so much so that she had considered whether or not she ever wanted another romantic relationship. They only led to hurt feelings.

How could her affairs not? Hyacinth had been the only woman who had known—had *understood*. The others were just acquaintances, lovely and pleasant ones, to be sure, but none of them had had the temperament or the sort of spirit Henry liked to see in potential members of her society. How could an affair last with someone who was not a part of it? So, in the end, she'd let them all go, for their sake as well as hers. They were hurt by her attention to other people, other matters. And she knew that they would never understand how not only her mind but her physical body was different than other women's.

She wasn't old; she neither looked nor felt like she was past her prime, but her life would be shorter than most. That had been part of the bargain she'd struck. The demon would preserve her. She would never grow sick or elderly, or become enfeebled, but she would live for fewer years because of it. They all would, every one of her friends . . . which was why they were, admittedly, a fairly close group. The shared presence in their minds was a kind of companionship, but the body as well as the soul has its needs. Even so, all of them, over the years, had come to the conclusion that it simply wasn't possible to carry on with anyone who wasn't a part of their enhanced existence . . . even Dr. Sauber, bless his soul. Then again, the man had been voluntarily celibate before he even joined them. He claimed retaining his "vital essences" kept his mind clear.

As Henry looked at Dorina, and began the process of extracting herself without waking the girl, she felt nothing but regret for what she would have to do. Dorina was so young, so innocent. She thought she was such a worldly creature, with her love of art, and her unapologetic attraction to and experience with women . . . How little she really knew!

How little Henry wanted her to know.

She had to end it. She would do it gently—of course she would —but this had to be their last meeting. She would send Dorina back to her uncle, and never see her again. Dorina would protest Henry's decision, second-guess her, but this was how it had to be. Henry knew her own heart too well—she would not be able to resist a second, and then a third night, and so on and so forth, and given how much everyone liked Dorina, how much the *demon* liked Dorina, eventually she would insinuate herself into the group . . . and then there would be no turning back.

Yes, she had to end it, and she had to do it *now*, before either of them became too attached.

Henry grabbed clothes and dressed in another room, then wrote a note in her study so the scratching would not disturb Dorina. That's when she got Jonas up and shooed him out of the house, even though the other part of her urged her to give up this madness—to take off her clothes, get back into bed . . .

"I'd assumed you'd sleep late today," he said, yawning, as they trotted down Curzon Street toward the Shepherd Market. There was a bakery there whose almond-paste croissants Dorina craved constantly, and Henry thought to pick up a box to share before they said goodbye.

"You thought wrong," she said waspishly.

"You're not going to deny something happened, are you?"

Henry shot him a look.

"Then what's wrong?"

Henry stopped in the middle of the busy lane. "Are you so thick?" Her voice did not sound like her own, was not her own. She did not quarrel with Jonas. They never had, not even after Oliver's death, when they'd neither of them been themselves for many months.

"Let's assume for the moment that I am," said Jonas evenly. "Explain to me what you're feeling."

Henry shook her head. "Not here," she said. "Let's . . . let's get a coffee at the bakery, and we can talk there."

But it wasn't any easier to talk about once they were settled in the cozy little shop, with its red and gold wallpaper and ornate stained glass windows. Jonas claimed a table in the corner; she returned with two coffees, her hands shaking a little. A pinch of ginger snuff helped her feel a bit better, but also depressed her. She stared at the delicate white china, and the deep blackness it contained so easily, brooding over it until Jonas interrupted her thoughts.

"Is she awful in bed?"

The demon was more amused by the question than Henry.

"It happens. Even the ones who seem like they'd be fantastic, they're just—"

"Don't be . . ." She stopped herself from snapping at him again. "No," she said primly. "That is not the issue."

"So she's good, then?"

"Jonas!"

He smiled at her. She realized what he was doing, and smiled back sheepishly.

"Let's just say she didn't make it easy for me to end this."

"What? Why? Why are you ending it, I mean?"

"You can't be serious," she said. "You know I can't—" The presence in her mind disagreed vehemently. "Or rather, I *mustn't*," she amended. It had nothing to say to that. "How could I? How could I do that to her?"

Jonas cocked his head. "I'm not sure I follow you."

"What are my options? Hide myself while continuing on with her, as if I wasn't what I was? She deserves better than that." Henry's hands tightened on her cup of coffee; mechanically, she brought it to her lips and sipped. It tasted of ashes. "And as for the other . . . it is impossible."

"It doesn't have to be."

"I'm a gardener. No matter how beautiful a bloom is, when you snip it free and put it in a vase it withers and dies."

"But if you leave it, that same blossom will just rot on the stem."

"It takes longer."

"Ah," said Jonas. He understood now; she saw it in his eyes. He looked sad. "And you don't want to give your bloom the choice?"

"I know what she'd choose!" exclaimed Henry. Then lowering her voice, she said, "It is obvious to you, me, and all of us that Dorina is . . . she's not a blossom. She's a damned *tuning fork,* and our meetings have struck her like a mallet." The demon agreed wholeheartedly with this sentiment, to her dismay rather than her pleasure. "There is nothing in the world that would suit her more than . . ." Henry shrugged. "But how can I do that to her? How can she know what she really wants at such a young age? How can she know what she *will* want, a year from now, ten years from now?"

"How can *you?* Happily married women in their middle years have affairs; men late in life go back and pick up the instrument they hated practicing in their youth. Perhaps Dorina knows what she wants now, even as young as she is. Stranger things and all that."

"Oh, I know that. But you know what it would mean for her."

"I also know that she's a very intelligent young woman — precocious, even. So few people trust young women. Are you one of their number?"

"Don't you *dare* appeal to that part of me."

"What, your better nature?"

Henry sighed. "I take your point, but . . ."

"Do you love her?"

The question shocked Henry, even as it delighted the presence in her mind. *It* knew the answer.

"Do you? If you don't, then . . ."

"I think I do," she said, hating herself for dissembling even that much.

Jonas knew what she meant. His amused smile spoke volumes.

"Then there doesn't seem to me to be a problem. Take it from one who has fallen very hard for one whom he senses will never return his affections." He held up his hand as Henry opened her mouth. Poor Jonas; she could absolutely see what he saw in Evadne, but she could never abide that sort of rejection and coldness. She would have given up the chase a long time ago. "Things are good, Henry. Your path is clear. You know what you feel about her, and you know what she will say if you offer her what you can offer her."

"It's not as easy as that!"

"It could be."

"If I love her," said Henry, "then what I ought to do is send her away, and you know *exactly* why."

Jonas reached across the table and took Henry's hand in his. "You can't blame yourself forever. Oliver—"

"Let's get those pastries and head back," said Henry suddenly. She didn't want to have this conversation, not now, not ever. She didn't blame herself for what had happened. Why couldn't Jonas—why couldn't Basil, or Hyacinth, or anyone else—understand that she didn't blame herself! It was just that she had suffered the consequences of her choices in ways none of them had, and it had changed her, just as the demon's presence in their lives had changed them.

"All right, Henry," said Jonas sadly. "I just hate to think you'll go your whole life alone."

"I haven't!"

"You cut Hyacinth off and she would have stayed with you forever."

"We mutually decided—"

"Tommyrot." Jonas's bluntness shocked her. "She let you think that because you were grieving, but you hurt her badly. She's over you now; she and Robert have taken up together in some strange way—I don't know the details and I don't wish to—but I do know that she was devoted to you, worshiped you, and you fed me the same line when you booted her into the street."

"I don't have to take this," said Henry. She was actually annoyed now. "I don't have to listen to you going on about my faults."

"I'm not, you silly ass," he said, gentler now. "I'm trying to say that I love you and I want you to be happy. You've cocooned yourself in isolation because you're frightened, and I understand why . . . but you once told me that Oliver knew what he was doing, and that you let him do it because he went into it with his eyes open."

Henry kept her eyes on her coffee. She missed her brother more than she could ever say, so she had never tried. Perhaps she should have told him that, before he . . . She closed her eyes momentarily, and let go the thought, for she knew in her heart that there was nothing she could have said, could have done, to change Oliver's mind.

The demon agreed with her.

"Henry." Jonas brought her attention back to himself. "Maybe you doubt Oliver now; maybe you don't. Maybe you doubt yourself . . . I can't say. What I do know is that you have a chance for something *good* with this girl. I know she loves you; anyone who's around the two of you for five minutes can see it. And it's not some young person's obsession—she hasn't taken to borrowing your clothes, or affecting your style or mannerisms. She just likes to look at you; she hangs on your every word, respects you even when she disagrees with you. And you love her, too. You're making this difficult for yourself, for the two of you, and you don't have to."

"You can't make an impossible thing more difficult," said Henry. He sighed. "As you say."

Jonas didn't have to understand. She knew she was doing the right thing.

She had kept her mouth shut during their walk home, thinking about what she had to do, and why she had to do it. Jonas had a gift for conversation, and perhaps for philosophy, too . . . but neither conversation nor philosophy was what was needed now. Only strength of will and self-knowledge.

But then she had come home to find Dorina with the one book she had vowed the girl would never read. And what did she say, but:

"Is it real? Is this what you all do?"

Who had given it to her? Hyacinth had had it last . . . Anger flared in Henry's breast, but she saw the brown paper on her desk, and she knew then Dorina had unwrapped it, never knowing she was reading the most deadly book in the world—the only book in Henry's library she would have denied her.

"Can . . . I do it too?"

Henry walked to her desk, and setting down the pastries, took the book out of Dorina's hands, shut it, and set it down.

"Are you angry with me?" Dorina was obviously quite anxious for her to say something, but Henry didn't know what to say. She'd come here to end this, to keep Dorina safe, knowing it had been her own fault that she was at risk in the first place—and the silly girl had gone and taken the first step into death and peril on her own. "If you're angry with me, it means it must be real. But how can that be?"

Henry sat on the edge of her desk, steadying herself with her hand. Dorina sat back in the desk chair so that Henry wasn't looming over her.

"It is real," said Henry.

She couldn't lie to the girl. She'd know. She was very perceptive.

"Is it ginger? Have you . . ." Dorina's eyes flickered to the closed book. "Did you conjure demonic essence into ginger?"

Henry nodded.

"Your candies . . . your snuff, your cigarettes . . . when you close the door on Mr. Walmsley and me, you were eating this special ginger?"

Henry nodded again. "You have the measure of it."

"Well . . . can I have a cigarette?"

"Good God, Dorina! No!" Henry sprang off the desk and began to pace, rubbing her hands together. "Of course not! You read the book—at least some of it. Don't you know what you're suggesting?"

"You're right, you're right," said Dorina. Leaning forward, she opened the book and pointed at a page. "I ought to ask, what was the . . . bargain? What did you get, and what did you give?"

"That's not how it . . ."

"It's not?"

Henry ran her hand through her short hair. The girl was impossible—and even worse, the demon was laughing at her, at them both.

"So what does it give you?"

Henry looked at Dorina. The girl wasn't smiling, she was deadly serious. This was the worst possible moment, the worst possible conversation. Once Dorina knew, there was no going back.

Tell her. Let her choose for herself.

Henry walked over to the armchair where she liked to read and almost collapsed into it. "Dorina . . ." She sighed. Against two such strong and willful characters, she could not prevail. "All right."

"All right what?"

Henry shot her a look, and the girl quieted down. "Demons are defined, in ways that we as humans are not, by their obsessions. In their own realm . . . Well, I don't actually know all that much about it, so let's confine our conversation to what I do know."

Dorina nodded.

Henry's head suddenly felt heavy. She rested it in the palm of her hand. "Some demons crave power. Some crave worship. Some crave . . . *experiences.*" She looked up, cocking an eyebrow at Dorina. "The demon . . . the one I . . . the one that is part of me, it . . . it is concerned with experiences. An *aesthetic adventurer,* I suppose you could call it. It cares nothing for pride, power, adulation; it is at war with no others of its kind, and craves nothing more than the friendship—after a fashion—of those humans who would cohabit with it, and it enhances our appreciation of the world. It expands the senses, gives us a deeper understanding of art, culture . . . everything we touch, or see, or smell . . . taste . . ." She saw Dorina's eyes shining like stars, and Henry hated herself then, hated her weakness. Of course once Dorina knew this, she would be satisfied by nothing but initiation. It was awful; part of Henry at last admitted she had known this would happen eventually, even though she'd denied it to herself while they had gotten to know one another better, even as she'd let Dorina kiss her, and lead her to bed.

"I want to do it," said Dorina. "It's *always* been my dream . . ."

"You didn't even believe in demons a month ago." Henry had to smile, remembering their brief conversation in the National Gallery. Had that been Henry—or her companion? Which of them had been baiting the hook?

Dorina rose, slippers *shoofing* across the Oriental carpet, and came to rest on the arm of Henry's chair. She put her tender hand on Henry's tweed-encased shoulder, slid down onto the seat beside her and nuzzled her neck before Henry pushed her away.

"Stop!" she said, almost leaping from the chair. "You don't understand, Dorina—it's not so simple!"

"Is there a ritual or something?"

"That's not what I mean!" Henry felt faint, like her head was a buzzing hive of bees. "Dorina, please . . ."

"What is wrong?" she asked gently, and Henry, for the first time in she couldn't remember how long, began to weep.

"Henry!" cried Dorina. "My goodness! I never expected . . . What have I done?"

"Nothing," she sobbed, leaning into the girl. Her body felt so good, damnably so—and being held while she wept felt even better.

"Tell me," said Dorina. "When you can—take your time."

"It shortens your life," explained Henry once she could, after dabbing at her eyes. "You remain young, and beautiful, but you die early. How can I let you *die*, Dorina? You are so young . . . You have your whole life . . ."

"How much does it shorten your life?"

"It's difficult to say. It might only be a few years . . . or . . ." Henry sniffled, and blew her nose on her pocket handkerchief.

"Dorina, here is what I have been trying to say: I have lived with this demon for almost ten years. I was the one who summoned it; I founded my group; I introduced them all. And by and large, I think it has made their lives better."

"Yes, and they all seem so happy!"

"But Oliver . . ."

Dorina's hand found hers, and squeezed. "What happened?"

Henry took a deep breath. "He wanted to know the demon better, more completely. He did not feel as if he could truly appreciate all that it gave us." Henry swallowed; it seemed incredible that not an hour ago she'd been buying almond croissants, thinking to break things off with this girl, and now she was telling her everything. "He began taking bigger and bigger doses. He claimed it expanded his mind, gave him new senses beyond those that ordinary men possessed. It made him . . . I can't explain it to you. And eventually, he took so much, such a large dose, that he . . ." She tore her hand away from Dorina and buried her face in the silk of her handkerchief. "When I found him, his eyes . . . he was bleeding out his ears, his nose . . . everywhere. But he was smiling."

The demon responded to her distress, tried to comfort her, but she pushed it away. Its infinite patience and understanding irked her—but it understood that, too. Infuriating creature.

"Oh, Harry," said Dorina. "I . . . I'm so sorry."

"I showed him, Dorina. Oliver, I mean. I showed him what it was; I gave him his first dose. It will be on my conscience forever. You see now why I can't . . . if you were to . . . if I lost you, the way I lost him . . . if I had another death on my hands . . ."

"I would never do anything like what he did," said Dorina.

"You can't know that!"

"I can't know if I shall be murdered on my way home. Henry, I want to do this. I want to know."

"If you don't like it, if you want to stop . . . Basil, he was a part of our group. But after Oliver . . . he couldn't stomach it anymore. He went through a withdrawal. I helped him, but it was horrible."

"Is that why he's so frail?"

Henry nodded. "Exactly."

Dorina squared her shoulders. "I still want to," she declared. "It's my choice to make, and . . . and if you don't help me, I'll find a way to do it myself!" She eyed Henry, seeing the effect her words produced. "Who knows which one I'll find, or what it will do to me . . . I'd rather meet yours—"

"It's not mine! If anything, *I* belong to *it.*"

The demon agreed.

"It seems lovely. I mean, I'd rather meet the one you know personally," she said. "Who knows, maybe I'll meet one of the horrible ones you mentioned. *Or* . . ." She smiled deviously. "You could introduce me, introduce us, and we could have a lovely time. Why, we could go back to the National Gallery . . . see what is to be seen . . . but through enhanced eyes . . ."

Henry shrugged helplessly. "I came back and I was going to send you away, never see you again . . . and now I find I am bound to you more tightly than ever."

"You were going to what?" Dorina sank to her knees at Henry's feet. "Last night was the most wonderful of my life," she said softly. "Please don't send me away. Henry . . . I love you."

"And I you," said Henry, raising her up. "Dorina . . ."

"Let me choose for myself. I choose you . . . and it," she whispered. *"Please?"*

The demon in Henry's mind stirred, urging her to give in.

"I am outvoted, it seems, for it wishes to meet you too," she said helplessly. "All right, Dorina. May I be forgiven, but all right."

"Do I get a cigarette?"

"No," said Henry firmly. "You may try a candy, and then we'll go to the National Gallery."

Dorina kissed her. "Henry," she whispered, "you won't regret this."

I already do, she thought, but she knew this was a lie, as her intention to keep Dorina away from her life and her ways always had been.

The demon . . . it just laughed, and urged her to hurry. To its mind, she had already waited far too long.

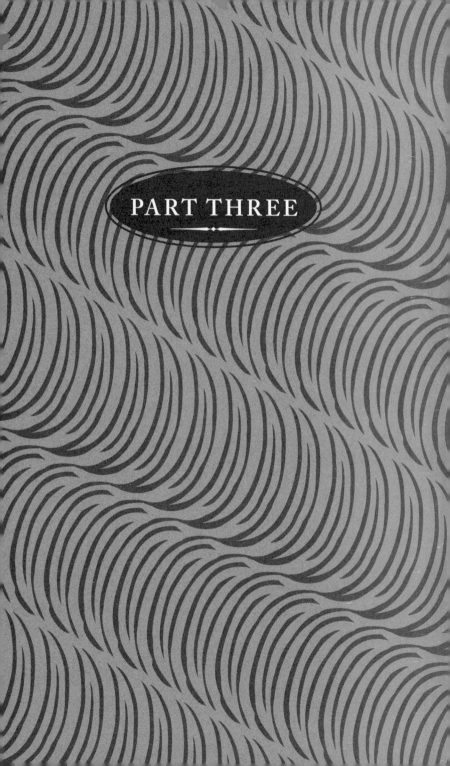

PART THREE

1

What is this morning—or yesterday afternoon—or last
week? We have lived since then.

— On the Summoning of Demons

W HEN EVADNE WOKE TO FIND her sister gone, she
immediately resolved to go and fetch her back again.
It was of the utmost importance that they talk. But
every time Evadne tried to stand for more than a moment, much
less dress or walk, she felt too sick to manage it, as if she suffered
from flu or some other sort of fever. Her bones ached inside of
aching muscles; her neck felt like a vise pinched it right below
her head. There was another clamp around her temples, one that
opened and closed at odd intervals. She did not want to eat, even
though she was hungry; didn't want to drink, even though her
throat was parched. Everything she lifted to her lips tasted wrong,
but by midafternoon she felt so listless she knew she had to take
something.

A little beef tea seemed like a good thing, unseasonable as it
might be; she took it down to her uncle's studio with her, where
he was painting. She hoped conversation would distract her. It was
difficult to swallow when all she had to think about was her sister,
and all she had to look at was Lord Oliver's sword.

Basil did not seem well, either. When she finally made her way
downstairs, wrapped in a warm robe though the day was hot, mug
in hand, she found him sitting before his picture of Oliver Wotton. Even Evadne, who cared little for art—or the Wottons—was

taken aback by its beauty every time she saw it. Today, it seemed lit from within; it shimmered with its own luminescence.

Her uncle held uncannily still, holding a brush in his hand, its bristles caked with drying paint the exact hue of the peacock feathers featured on the painting sitting on his easel. He had an untouched cup of tea balanced on his thigh, a film drifting like clouds across its surface.

"May I join you?" asked Evadne.

He nodded, but said nothing and did not look at her. That was not so very unusual; he was a quiet man. At least, he was these days. Once, he had been outgoing and gregarious, but whatever illness had touched him had left him introspective, with tongue leaden and slow. And he did not seem to be recovering; if anything, he looked worse than when they'd first arrived.

She had intended to ask if he would dispatch a servant to try to bring her sister home, but the soporific quietude of the studio and the warmth of her drink proved overpowering, and Evadne fell asleep on the couch. When she awoke, it was dark again, and cooler. She felt confused, and a little annoyed that he had left her — left her and gone out to his club!

Evadne did not know what to do with herself, so she went to the kitchen and asked for a little more broth. It helped, but as the minutes turned into hours, and the hours became long stretches where the only noise was the ticking of the clock, and still no Dorina, even the light soup became as the richest supper, churning and swirling inside her unpleasantly. She waited, worrying, until it was too late to send someone, for the servants had all gone to bed.

She listened to the slow chiming of the quarter-hours in Basil's sitting room, bundled, feeling as wretched as she'd ever felt in her life. She thought only of Dorina — fearing for her, rather than wondering why she did not return, worrying about what might happen to her sister in the house of someone whose brother trafficked with demons, someone who seemed likely to do so herself.

Would Dorina come home? Or would she go missing, just like the girl whom Evadne and her companions had failed to rescue? Would she find her sister on a similar rooftop, body on display and guts spilled free as forces beyond the understanding of men worked their will through her flesh?

Sleep did not come. At least, it did not come until it did, catching Evadne by surprise, and leaving her with a crick in her neck when she finally woke up in the wee hours, as the windows were just beginning to brighten.

Evadne felt a bit better, even after sleeping on a sofa in a dressing gown. She had an appetite, and made her way to the kitchen, where she procured tea and toast. Solid food helped even more, and her aches finally began to melt away as she stood, stretched, and decided she would take a bath.

It was the sight of the tub that did it—all the memories of her awful night on the rooftop came back to her. She'd been so focused on needing to tell Dorina of her suspicions and make sure her sister understood the danger she was in that she'd scarcely thought about what had granted her this burdensome knowledge. The image of that homunculus, its teeth bared, its eye pierced by her sword's blade . . . She fell back against the wall of the bathroom, reeling. The smell of that unnamed girl's entrails, the perfume of the blossoms, the viridescent color of George's fire that had burned it all to ash. What had once been that girl, had been those *things* . . . it was all just particulate matter now. It had changed into something wholly different, as she had, and over the course of just a few hours.

Sometime later she sat on her bed, hair piled on top of her head, body clean, if damp, with very little memory of how that had happened. Then, just as strangely, she was dressed and downstairs, waiting for her sister with *The School of Fencing* open on her lap. She tried to read it, but even the familiar words would not make sense.

The bell rang, and Evadne was on her feet and running for the door before she realized Dorina would not ring the bell. Indeed, instead, she found George there. He looked about as she felt—exhausted.

"Gray," he said.

She stepped out to meet him, rather than inviting him inside; she felt awkward having a man over without asking her uncle's permission. In fact, it was odd he'd come to find her at all—it was terribly improper. How had he known where she was staying?

Of course—he must have looked at the paperwork she'd filled out. And anyway, why was she worrying about this when they'd slain actual demons together?

"Mr. Cantrell," she said. "How are you?"

"It's Mr. Cantrell, is it?" He seemed amused, and a little sad.

"George," she said softly. "I'm sorry. I've had a difficult . . ."

"I can imagine. I came by to apologize. Had I known, I never would have . . ."

"How is Mr. Stockton?"

"He's fine, just fine."

"And you?"

George smiled at her. "You're worried about me? Gray, you're too good. I came here enquiring after *your* health."

"I have been very tired and sore, but I believe I've weathered the worst of it." Evadne did not meet his eyes. His presence pleased her, but it also alarmed her.

"Forgive me." His tone brought her attention to the present. "You do not seem yourself. Is it just exhaustion, or is something bothering you?"

How could she open her mouth? If she did, she had no idea what might come tumbling out. It wouldn't be pearls and flowers —more like toads and snakes. If they had been sisters in a fairy tale, Dorina would be the one rewarded with extra graces for her winning personality; Evadne, the one condemned to being yet more loathsome for failing to appreciate the import of some crucial interaction.

"No," she managed at last, with a shake of her head. "Just a bit tired."

"I can imagine. That was quite a first adventure," he said, a little more warmth in his voice. "Thank goodness we were successful!"

"You would call that a success?"

"Yes," he said gravely. "Though only a partial one, naturally. I had hoped to take him alive, as you know. But the most important thing is those creatures were destroyed, and their contagion cannot spread. After you left I burned everything on the roof and in his room that might be used for fell purposes." He sighed, but to Evadne's relief he did not try to touch her to comfort her—it would be an embarrassment, to be touched by a man in the street, and she felt grateful to him for understanding. "Sometimes, that is what we who are called by duty to defend the world of men call a success."

She had nothing to say, given that she was not as convinced on this side of her adventure that this was indeed the path she was born to walk.

"It's not strange, you know, to have second thoughts after . . ."

She glanced up, as George had somehow divined her thoughts. He smiled at her gently, his handsome, craggy face softening.

"There are many who never go on another mission after seeing something like that. Most are lucky enough that their first few experiences aren't so hideous, which is why I wanted to say if you did not wish to—"

"Hello, Evadne!" cried Dorina. Startled, Evadne looked wildly at the street, and saw Lady Henry's carriage rattling away. She hadn't noticed it pulling up. "How are you! What are you doing outside? And . . ." Dorina stared at George for a moment, and he back at her.

"Dorina! Ah, this is my . . . friend, Mr. Cantrell," she said awkwardly. "Mr. Cantrell, this is my sister, Miss Dorina Gray."

"Charmed," said Dorina, offering her hand promptly, like a man would. George took it, shaking it firmly to Dorina's obvious approval.

"Have we met, Mr. Cantrell?" she asked. "You seem familiar . . ."

"I fear I've never had the pleasure."

"Do you have a brother?"

George shook his head. "An only child, to my parents' dismay."

"Well, you must just have one of those faces," she said, shrugging. "Shall we go in, then?"

Evadne's face went red. Dorina—inviting a stranger into her uncle's house! Thankfully, George must have noticed the awkwardness.

"I'm afraid I was just going," he said. "I hope to see you back at the academy, Gray, when you're feeling better."

"Oh, you're Evadne's fencing teacher! *That's* why I knew your name," said Dorina, mortifying Evadne—how dare her sister say she'd spoken of this man at home . . . even if she had. "Lovely to meet you. Evadne, you're not well?" Dorina, of course, looked the very picture of health. Beside her, Evadne knew she must look even worse than usual.

"We'll discuss it later," Evadne said through her teeth. "Good day, Mr. Cantrell. I will return when I am able."

"Good day, ladies," he said, tipping his hat specifically at Evadne, and then at the two of them.

"You must really be feeling badly if you didn't invite him in," opined Dorina as she bustled inside. "I can't see why—he was clearly *dying* to speak to you more, only you were so cold! Are you not yet over Freddie? You ought to try. He seems awfully nice, and if you won't be kind to Jonas you might as well—"

"Dorina, you didn't come home last night."

"Yes, but Henry said she'd sent word."

It must have been delivered straight to Basil, and she had not heard anything about it. Infuriating man! But really, it wasn't Dorina's whereabouts that Evadne cared about so much. The real issue was . . .

"Dorina, we need to talk."

"Oh?" Dorina seemed distracted, happy and thoughtless as usual. "About what?"

"About . . ." The words wouldn't come to her mouth. "About the company you keep," she managed. "Shall we repair to somewhere not the foyer and . . ."

"The company I keep?" Dorina eyed her. "Oh dear, are you cross I stayed over with Henry? It was only that it became so late, and—"

"Dorina, be serious! I am being serious," snapped Evadne. "I'm not talking about anything so frivolous as one of your affairs—"

"Affairs!"

Evadne took a deep breath. "Please, will you come upstairs? Can we talk? In one of our rooms?"

Dorina already looked rebellious. This was not going to be easy.

"If we must," she said, icy where she had lately been so warm.

Evadne trailed behind her sister up the stairs, as if she were the one in trouble and Dorina about to deliver some necessary lecture. It was infuriating, but then again, she was dealing with Dorina.

"Would you like me sitting in a chair, or on a bed? Would you prefer to be in your room, or mine?"

"Dorina . . ."

"What?" Dorina just looked at her. It occurred to Evadne that her sister was carrying a bag. "Your room," said Evadne. "You can unpack while we talk."

"How kind of you."

Evadne almost gave up right then and there. Dorina was being impossible, and didn't seem especially receptive to any advice or confidence. Perhaps she should try again later, see where Dorina was that evening, or tomorrow.

No. She had to do this. She had to tell Dorina her suspicions. A vision of the dead girl again welled up in Evadne's mind, like tears, like blood in a wound. She could not put this off. Who knew what might happen if she bided her time, waiting for the perfect moment?

Evadne hadn't been inside Dorina's room for some time. Their estrangement had been sudden and mutual. Not that they had ever spent much time running in and out of one another's rooms, like sisters they knew socially tended to do.

"Well?" said Dorina, throwing her bag on the bed. "What do you have to say about the company I keep?"

As much time as Evadne had spent thinking about informing Dorina of her suspicions, she'd actually not quite gotten around to *how* to begin the conversation, where to go with it, where to end. She stared at Dorina, standing stupidly in the middle of the floor.

"Are you going to actually say anything, or did you just need me to know you don't approve of Henry? Or my, as you call them, *affairs*? I already knew that."

"Dorina, this is very serious." Evadne paused. "So, the two of you . . . you're . . ."

Dorina whirled, a little paper bag of candy in her hand. She opened it and the strong smell of ginger filled the room; she popped one in her mouth, but put the rest in a drawer in her desk without offering Evadne one.

"So what if we are?" she asked after swallowing.

"I'm not angry," said Evadne, even if in all honesty the idea of such a thing made her heart beat a bit faster. She was supposed to be standing guard over Dorina here in London, not sitting idly by while her sister got into complicated and confusing situations just like this one. If only she'd written her mother for advice!

"Thank goodness," said Dorina loftily.

Evadne took a deep breath. "I'm not angry, I'm just . . ." And then she stopped.

It occurred to her that it might actually be a terrible idea to talk to Dorina about all of this. Her sister would inevitably re-

peat whatever Evadne said to her friend—her *lover*—and if Lady
Henry had known about her brother's diabolical experiments, or
even participated in them . . . that might put both sisters in danger. If, God forbid, Lady Henry was planning to do something to
Dorina as disgusting and dangerous as that nameless demon-wor-
shiper had done to that poor girl on the rooftop, Evadne's warnings might force her hand, make her act all the sooner.

Evadne made her decision in that moment—she would pretend to be upset about Dorina's relationship, and instead she'd
tell George of her concerns. Talking to Dorina would necessitate
Evadne confessing her involvement with an organization that by
its very nature must be kept secret. Why, after all, would she know
so much about the matter? What could she point to but a sword
she should never have had in her possession in the first place,
much less touched? She ought not to call attention to it at all, for
as neither Lady Henry nor Jonas had requested its return, it would
be better to keep it secreted away until she could tell George about
it and get him involved. His expertise would be invaluable when it
came to handling such a delicate situation.

"Just *what*," said Dorina, as Evadne hesitated.

"Just . . . our mother . . . she sent me here, you know, to look after you . . . and I feel like I've failed. I've let you run wild, and—"

"Run wild! To museums?" Dorina's hand flew to her throat in
mock alarm. "The scandal!"

"It's not just to museums, you know. You've been spending a lot
of time with Lady Henry, and now you seem to have grown closer.
I doubt Mother would—"

"Are you threatening to tell Mother about all this?"

"I feel as if I should."

"Evadne!"

"What? It's not as if being called home would impact your career—you haven't even been working on your article."

Dorina, flushed of face, slammed some sort of hair ornament

into her jewel box. "You're so . . . spiteful! I can't believe you hate Harry so much that you'd try to separate us. But you do love to tattle."

"I don't hate her," said Evadne, surprised. "And I don't love to tattle!"

"Oh, well, I can't imagine why I'd come to such conclusions!" Dorina sneered at her.

"Just because I don't want to see Lady Henry every day . . ." Evadne sank onto Dorina's bed, the closest available surface. "I didn't mean to give the impression I *hated* anyone." Though of course, she knew she had—even the polite Jonas had remarked on it.

"No?" Dorina was actually angry—her fists were balled, she was standing ramrod straight, eyes blazing. "Maybe you just don't realize you hate *everyone,* me included!"

"Dorina! I love you . . ." As she said it, she realized it, *really* realized it. She had always loved her sister, even if things were difficult between them. The thought that she might be involved with something that could get her killed—to see her sister lamented, and then forgotten—it was unbearable. "No matter what, I love you."

This softened Dorina's hardness a little, but not much. "So, you *love* me so much that you're going to try to separate me from someone with whom I've really connected?"

Evadne had so much she wanted to say, but she'd done what she needed to do. She'd antagonized Dorina to avoid bringing up her suspicion that Lady Henry was potentially involved in, for lack of a better way to put it, *occult matters.*

"I just don't know if you really understand what you're getting yourself into," said Evadne, being completely honest. "She may not be the person you think she is. There may be things you don't know about her . . . things you never suspected. She's already scandalously exposed you in several public places, before you are even officially out . . . She has no respect for society, and therefore no respect for your future. She's also far older than you, Dorina. Even if you don't care about that now, you may one day." Dorina looked mutinous. "You haven't known her for long, that's all, and I'd hate to see you risk your entire future for someone you barely know, and who doesn't seem to care about you. At least not in respectable ways."

"I may not have known her long, but I know her perfectly," said Dorina coldly. "She is open and honest with me. She understands me better than anyone ever has. And the society *she* keeps would never judge me for going into public places or whatever you're fretting over. They're above such things."

"The society she keeps? You mean that group you go to?" Evadne realized she'd never once asked what they got up to. "What sort of group is it?"

"Oh, it's terribly immoral," said Dorina. "We have a nice meal together, and then we do something scandalous, like discuss aesthetics, or the nature of beauty, or the way we interpret the world through art. So risqué!"

"It doesn't sound so risqué . . ."

"Oh, but it *is*," said Dorina. "Everyone's terribly louche. Why, one of the members is a children's book illustrator. With that sort of company, I'd be surprised if it wasn't secretly a cabal of demon-worshipers!"

Evadne froze. "What on earth do you mean by that?" she said, deadly serious.

Dorina looked alarmed. "Nothing," she said, but so quickly Evadne couldn't help but wonder. Her sister's face was a mask, composed, calculated to deceive—not at all her usual open, vivacious self.

The memory of a scent sickened her—the flowers the diabolist had heaped around the girl before he did what he had done . . .

Could Dorina already be corrupted? Was Evadne too late? Or

was she still shaken by her adventure and seeing demons everywhere? They'd never needed to worry about such things back in Swadlincote—hadn't ever suspected there really were such things—but here in London, corruption and evil seemed to lurk everywhere . . .

It was too big a tangle for her to unravel on her own; she was new at this, and she needed help. Thankfully, she knew someone she could turn to, and there was no time like the present to ask about it. She would not sit idly by and wait for Dorina to be hurt. Her resolution to let her sister swim out into the middle of the ocean, come what may, was swept away like a wave erasing writing in the sand. She would do what she had to do.

Evadne stood and shook out her skirts. "I'm sorry I said anything," she said. "I was just concerned."

"Well, don't be."

Evadne nodded, and took her leave of her sister—but she did not go to her room for more time than it took to collect cab fare and her shawl. Tired as she was, she was determined to make her way to George as soon as she could.

GEORGE WAS FINISHING UP HIS last lesson of the day when Evadne arrived at the school. She elected to wait, but not to practice while she did. Mr. Perkins seemed surprised when she turned him down for an impromptu match, but she begged off, explaining she was without her gear. He didn't seem to believe her excuses, however, so she escaped into the kitchen just to get away from his worried frowns and sidelong glances.

She was just sipping a cup of tea when George came in, sweaty and still looking rather tired. She poured him a cup, too, and he seemed to revive over it, after dropping in one of his pastilles.

"You said you wanted to speak to me?" he said.

Evadne nodded. "About something that happened the other night."

He looked angry, to her surprise—a wrathful saint, instead of the gentler version to which she had become accustomed. "We can't talk about that now, Gray," he snapped. "Perkins might—"

"It has to do with my sister, George," she said, desperate. "I don't know where else to go, who else to talk to." Surely he would not put her off. She could not bear this alone, not any longer. She had to speak of it or she would burst.

"Your sister?" He was all attention now. "She seemed like a lovely girl, from the brief moments we spoke. What could she possibly have to do with—"

"Dorina has become close with Lady Henrietta Wotton. The lady is an unusual person, to begin with . . ."

"Oh yes," said George knowingly.

"She knows I fence," said Evadne, feeling more enthusiastic now that she'd found a toehold. "And when she found out, she offered me Lord Oliver's swords."

"Is that where you obtained that rapier?"

"Yes. And also another sword . . ." She took a sip of tea, as her throat felt dry. "A Chinese sword."

"Saber or double-edged?"

"Double-edged, straight. It was so beautiful. And when I took it down off the wall, it felt so *good* in my hand. It felt *right,* and I knew just what to do with it. But afterward, I felt . . . unclean. Greasy and odd. I never wanted to pick it up again. I thought little of it at the time, and while the experience was quite unusual I had no way of explaining what I had felt. I brushed it off as nothing. But now, after what you said about that dagger, the one I . . ."

George leaned closer. "What do you mean?"

"The sword didn't give me visions of anything terrible," she said carefully, trying not to think of what she'd seen on that rooftop. "But when you said what you did about diabolical objects *suggesting a use* . . . well, it just reminded me, and I began to fear that my sister . . ."

"What does your sister have to do with the sword?"

"Maybe nothing! I don't know. Maybe Lady Henry has no idea that her brother was a diabolist—or at least, that he had a tainted sword. But at the same time . . ."

"What?"

Evadne took a deep breath. "I worry Lady Henry is *herself* a diabolist. I shook hands with her; we've come into contact a few times, and she also makes me feel . . . greasy. Unsettled. Do people —people like me, I mean—are we able to sense demonic taint in . . . other humans?"

George looked startled by the question. "I don't really know," he said. "I've never met anyone who was sensitive enough to do so, but I don't want to doubt your experience." He leaned in closely; her breath seemed to catch in her chest. "Have you felt this sort of sensation after touching anyone else?"

Evadne broke his gaze to look down at where her hands were folded in her lap, and nodded. "Lady Henry's companion, Jonas Fuller."

George said nothing, and she looked up. He was staring at her intensely; she was his entire focus. She'd never been looked at like that, not in all her life.

She liked it. She knew it was neither the time nor the place for such things, but she couldn't help but feel secretly thrilled by his glorious attention.

"What do you want me to do with this information, Evadne?" he asked, breaking the tension.

"I don't know," she said shyly, returning her eyes to her teacup and the cooling tea within. In spite of the summer's heat, she shivered. "I don't know what to do. I'm afraid. That girl we couldn't save, what if there really *is* something to worry about? What if Dorina . . ." She angrily dashed tears from her eyes.

"I see," he said gravely. "Well, I don't blame you for your concern. In my experience, it's not often that diabolic items are found in the houses of those who have nothing to do with demons. And your report of the experience of touching her . . ."

Evadne nodded. "That's what I was afraid of," she said. "And . . ."

"Yes?"

"Dorina, she said something odd. You see, there's a gathering that Lady Henry hosts every so often, and when I asked Dorina about it, she got very defensive. She said it was a group committed to art appreciation, which didn't make a lot of sense to me, but then she joked about them being demon-worshipers—"

"She *joked* about it?"

Evadne sighed. "I don't know. Maybe I just have this on my mind given . . . *everything* . . . but it seemed ghastly."

"Understandable. It's not a laughing matter. Or at least, it ought not to be." He looked thoughtful. "You're right. We must at least investigate this. Will you help me?"

"I'd do anything to help my sister." It was the only thing she was certain of.

"Then I'm afraid I'm going to have to ask you to do the hardest thing for people like us."

"What is it?" she said eagerly.

"I'm going to ask you to wait—to bide your time. Carry on as if nothing is wrong and nothing has changed. Be as natural as you can around your sister."

"But—"

"Then, the very next time you get wind of one of these meetings, I want you to come to me. *Immediately.*"

"What will you do?"

"I don't know yet," admitted George. "But have faith, Gray—I will know when the time comes. I promise you that. I have a lot of experience, and there's quite a lot at stake."

"Dorina's safety is my chief concern," said Evadne. "I will do whatever it takes to help her."

"I know how important she is to you. I'm sorry, I just need you to bear with me for a brief time while I come up with the best way of dealing with this information."

It was his frankness, his honesty that convinced Evadne she'd done the right thing as she nodded her assent. He was a professional; he'd dealt with demons before. Of course he needed time to think. But he would help.

"Thank you," she said, standing.

He got up, too. But, instead of showing her to the door, he stood over her. He was so much taller than her, and so broad in the chest. He smelled like fresh sweat and leather and the lingering hint of shaving soap. She inhaled deeply, not aware she did so.

"Don't thank me yet," he said. "I haven't done anything."

She looked up and saw that same intense expression on his face. Her cheeks felt warm.

"I feel better having confided in you," she murmured. "That's something."

"I'm glad," he said. "I only wish I could do more, right now."

His hand found her shoulder, and Evadne trembled. Something was happening, something she didn't quite understand, even if it was something she had longed for, terrified as she was by it. George—*Saint* George—was drawing her closer, closer . . .

He leaned in, leaned down, and kissed her.

Evadne had never been kissed—not by a boy at least, and not like this. His mouth tasted delicious, a little sweet, and his grip on her shoulders was tight, bordering on uncomfortable. But she did not cry out, or pull away; in fact, as she relaxed into his embrace, the pain became pleasurable. He was a forge, and Evadne metal that could be worked if she could but endure the heat and force. She felt herself shifting, changing. George always brought out the best in her, and this was just another way for him to shape her. She wanted this moment to never end, *never*—

A knock at the door came, and they sprang apart like startled deer. Evadne tried to gain control of her blushes, tucked a stray lock of hair behind her ear, and patted herself down, but when Mr. Perkins entered, he seemed to know *something* had been going on. Evadne made her excuses quickly, then fled the room, fled the studio, almost running into Trawless in her haste to be gone.

"All right, Miss Gray?" he called after her.

"Oh yes!" she said over her shoulder.

The day was fine, and it was still bright and sunny. Evadne decided to walk for a bit, before hailing a cab, enjoying the air and her sense of freedom. At some point it occurred to her that her face hurt, but when she raised a hand to her aching cheek, she realized it was because she'd been smiling.

2

What the gods give us, they quickly take away. What demons give us, they give forever.

— *On the Summoning of Demons*

WAITING WAS THE WORST TRIAL Evadne had ever endured, and that included that night on the rooftop. Time seemed to pass even more slowly than when she had been with Dorina and Lady Henry, talking of art and taste — and far less comfortably. Instead of feeling bored or annoyed or offended, Evadne simply felt wretched. Her body became a foreign thing, an enemy at war with her. Her stomach crackled like a pile of autumn leaves and heaved like the ocean. She retched every morning and had to get a cup of tea down before she could even consider breakfast — unusual, for she typically woke with an appetite. She shivered when she was warm, sweated when she was cold, and felt faint anytime she thought about what would happen when Lady Henry and her friends announced another meeting. Her skin hurt, her body felt weak and tired, and yet she could not sleep. She stayed up late, though she had nothing to do, and woke up early, only to lie in bed, tossing and turning — but getting up was to admit the day had begun, and she would have to find some way to fill the endless hours.

The only time she did not feel ill with worry was during fencing practice, though only when she was at the academy. She no longer felt able to practice at home, for there she was surrounded by reminders of Dorina, and overwhelmed by her worries. The effect of her new slackness was swift and noticeable. She became slower; her body no longer responded to her will as well as it had in the past. Mr. Perkins actually took her aside one day after practice to ask if everything was "quite all right," and the other students were very obviously concerned, too.

George, of course, knew exactly what was troubling her, but his only advice was patience; his only command her continued silence. She asked him once, after *that* afternoon, if he had a plan yet. He only shook his head, and squeezed her shoulder for comfort.

It hadn't been particularly comforting.

It wasn't that she expected another kiss. Evadne got the sense George was embarrassed for having betrayed himself that afternoon. She could understand that, accept it. She did not need to be kissed to be certain of his affection for her. She knew it by the way he kept training her. He would brook no protests, telling her privately that he knew she was struggling, but that was no excuse. That she would recover from whatever anxious malaise was making her limbs feel like iron and her joints, rusty bearings. That waiting did this to people, when they were like her—sensitive, and built for action.

It wasn't just the waiting, though. Evadne was also worried that after their row, Dorina wouldn't mention her friends' next gathering. To guard against missing it, she'd counted back the days, checking against a lunar calendar, but it didn't seem as if Lady Henry's group were bound to, say, the full moon, as the rooftop diabolist had been. The two meetings had been unevenly spaced. So she tried to ask discreet questions about what Dorina might be up to in the mornings, though usually the response was just Dorina throwing her interest back in her face.

In the end, Evadne needn't have worried—at least, not about that. In spite of her blossoming relationship with Lady Henry, Dorina had not spent another night at Lady Henry's house. When one morning she casually mentioned at breakfast that they ought not to expect her back that night, Evadne perked up, even if the announcement scarcely made their haggard uncle look up from his papers.

"Expecting to be out late?" he asked, as if letting a seventeen-year-old on her first visit to London stay out all night was a perfectly normal thing for a guardian to do.

"The last program went a little overtime," she said with astonishing cool, "and we're expecting a simply *marvelous* presentation tonight. I don't want to worry either of you, like I did last time, so I think it's best to just pack an overnight bag."

"Very good," said Basil.

"I hope you have a grand time," said Evadne, affecting as little interest as possible.

"You don't object?"

"Why should I?" Evadne's eyes flickered over to Basil. "You don't object to me going to the academy today, do you?"

"I . . . I suppose not," said Dorina. She stood up. "Well . . . goodbye. I'd better pack. Harry wanted me to come a bit early."

"I'm sure she did," said Evadne, allowing a bit of archness to creep into her tone. This actually seemed to reassure her sister, and after an impressive display of coordination—rolling her eyes and tossing her hair at the same time—she departed.

"I'll be gone too, this afternoon," Evadne told her uncle.

"Hmm?"

"I'm off to the fencing academy."

"Have fun," he said vaguely, and without another word, stood, and wandered off in the direction of his studio.

Really, Evadne didn't know what Dorina was so worried about. It was obvious the man didn't care at all what either of them did.

SHE'D INTENDED TO DROP IN to George's late class that afternoon, but when the clock struck five Evadne realized she had been dawdling, and then she had to rush. It was the need to hustle that propelled her out the door, oddly enough—as she hopped into a cab, bag with her weapons and fencing clothes bouncing against her side, she felt extreme reluctance to tell George what she knew. Perhaps it was just mixed feelings about "tattling" on her sister, as Dorina would surely call it.

Perhaps it was her memories of what had happened the last time she went chasing demons.

But none of that mattered. She was doing this for Dorina. Evadne had no desire to see Henry revealed as a monster like that rooftop diabolist, but neither did she want to see her sister end up as the victim in that scene. And if anyone knew how to prevent that, George did.

The school seemed so normal as she walked inside. There was Trawless, scribbling over something at the front desk—he nodded to her, smiling, as usual. Beyond the door, students practiced. The familiar smell of leather, sweat, canvas, and polish hit her nose, the ring of metal on metal, the squeal of indiarubber soles on the floor. There was Mr. Perkins, frowning over two boys sparring —and there Reid was, giving someone a lesson. Evadne was surprised not to see George out on the floor among them, and after watching for a moment, she slipped back into the foyer.

"Mr. Trawless . . . is Mr. Cantrell here?"

"No," he said, setting down his pen. "Why? You haven't a lesson today, Miss Gray."

"No . . ."

"Stockton is going to take over the class, if you came for that."

"I did . . . but mostly I came to see Mr. Cantrell."

"I'm afraid he's taken ill."

"Ill!" Evadne's overworked stomach flopped over. George couldn't be ill! It was the worst possible time for such a thing. "He can't be!"

"Oh, he'll be all right," said Trawless, avuncular and reassuring, as always. "Don't worry. He's just a little under the weather."

"But I must speak to him! Immediately!"

"I'm sorry," he said. "He's at home."

"What is his address?"

Trawless hesitated. "I'm afraid I can't—"

"Mr. Trawless," she said crisply, "I have information Mr. Cantrell *demanded* I relay to him the moment I came into possession of it." He still looked uncertain, so she added, "I believe you know me well enough that I should not need to reassure you of my character. Do I seem like the sort of woman who would visit a man at his private residence if it were not of the utmost importance?"

"No, I suppose not," he said slowly.

She looked at him for a few moments as he blinked at her. "Well?"

"Miss Gray . . . would you at least allow me to take you thither? George's residence is in a part of town with which you are not likely acquainted," he said, the very picture of delicacy.

Should she allow him to come with her? Evadne considered this. Yes, it would be better to have an escort, especially going into an unfamiliar part of London.

She nodded. "Thank you."

"Let me just tell someone I'm going out," he said, and disappeared into the school.

It took longer than Evadne had anticipated for Trawless to reemerge. She shifted from foot to foot as she waited, anxious and ready to be gone, but then at last he was by her side, and quickly after they were in a cab.

Their destination was indeed an unfamiliar part of town, still respectable but showing signs of shabbiness and degeneration. She looked out of the window in silence; Trawless did not press her about her troubles, nor did he make conversation. Once, when she hadn't realized how long she'd been staring at her folded hands, he reached out and patted them. The gesture, though familiar, brought tears of gratitude to Evadne's eyes, rather than offending her.

When the cab halted before a seedy boarding house, Evadne thought the driver must have made a mistake, and almost re-marked on it—then, she remembered that Freddie had long ago said something about George being a scholarship student. Sneered about it, really, the snob. Evadne blushed, remembering Dorina criticizing her for the same thing as regarded Jonas, and resolved to not betray any alarm or dismay over George's circum-stances.

Trawless paid the cabdriver over Evadne's protests, and led her up the front steps. They were let in by a suspicious landlady, but escaped quickly by climbing a flight of stairs to get to George's set of rooms. Evadne almost bumped into Trawless in her haste to knock on the door.

Evadne assumed the frail man who opened the door must be George's servant, but on second look she saw with a start that the sickly, wracked-looking fellow was wearing a housecoat, that his limp hair was not gray, but sandy. It was George, even if he didn't look like himself at all.

"My God, George, what's happened to you?" she exclaimed.

She didn't mean to be insulting, but she was appalled. Normally, seeing George filled her with joy, an effect he'd had on her even before his romantic overtures. This evening, however, she felt only horror. It was uncanny, his appearance—he was possessed of none of his usual vigor. He was even leaning heavily on a cane!

She felt a strangely protective rush of emotion for him—George quite obviously needed someone to look after him right now. How he must have suffered, all alone and so ill!

"What are you doing here?"

This chilly welcome snapped Evadne out of her momentary fantasy of feeding George mugs of Bovril and stroking his brow. Well, she deserved it, after her outburst. Then again, George seemed unaccountably annoyed at Trawless, too . . .

"Miss Gray was very insistent—said she had to see you immediately," said Trawless nervously in the face of George's displeasure. "She said you wanted her to come and tell you something . . . said it was urgent. I didn't know what, ah . . ."

Evadne nodded, desperate to justify her intrusion. "Tonight. They're meeting—she told me so this morning. Dorina, I mean." Evadne couldn't quite put a name to his expression as she spoke, but surprise and annoyance were both featured. Desperate to please him, she continued, "I know Mr. Trawless said you weren't feeling well . . . but I thought you would still want to know."

George nodded. "I see. Well, you'd better come in," he said, hobbling out of their way. "Forgive my rudeness . . . I was surprised."

They followed him inside. Evadne, though worried for George —and for her sister—was composed enough to note that in spite of their exterior shabbiness and location within London, George had rented a very comfortable set of rooms. The things in them were nice enough; in particular, a pair of crossed rapiers over the fireplace caught her eye—fine pieces, though the roaring fire beneath them seemed out of place, for it was already so very hot.

"I'm in no state to offer you anything," he said, his voice gravelly and hoarse. Poor thing, he really was ill—he didn't even sound like himself! "I'm sorry."

"Can I get *you* anything?" asked Evadne. The notion of traipsing into his kitchen to make tea seemed awfully personal and definitely a little ridiculous, but this was George she was talking about. She'd do just about anything for him.

"No, no. Thank you." George eased himself onto a settee; Evadne took a chair, as did Trawless. An awkward silence descended. Evadne's toe tapped against the faded Turkish rug. She was full of nervous energy, split between eagerness to help her sister and genuine concern for the health of one for whom she had come to care very much.

"I'm sorry I surprised you," she said after a moment or two. "But forgive me ... time is of the essence. After all, she is there now ..."

George nodded, and managed a smile. "Yes, that is so."

There was something queer about George's manner, something Evadne couldn't quite parse. "Yes, I know it is so," she said. "So what are we going to *do* about it?" To her annoyance, George and Trawless exchanged another look. She finally lost her temper. "Look at me, not each other!" she snapped, springing to her feet. "Dorina is my sister! So please, tell me—do we have a plan? Any idea what we ought to do? You've had *weeks* to think at this point!" Realizing she was gesturing animatedly as she paced back and forth, Evadne took a deep breath, and made a conscious effort to keep her hands by her sides. "You must give me something to do," she said somewhat more calmly. "Please, or I'm sure I shall go mad!"

"We have to tell her," said Trawless, again to George ... and there was something about his tone that gave Evadne pause.

"What?" she said. "Tell me what? *Someone* tell me what is happening!"

Her voice sounded high, shrill, not at all like her own—more like a teapot's whistle. To be fair, she had been under a lot of pressure: worrying over her sister, being put off, told to wait. She felt she might crack, being treated like an outsider by people she had trusted, people she had fought beside; it was too much, receiving a cold welcome from one who had at one time been so warm toward her. One who inspired similar feelings of warmth.

George sighed and winced as he rose slowly. Evadne was once again struck by how frail and ill he was, and doubted herself. She ought not to be so frustrated with someone who was clearly suffering. This was Saint George, after all—*her* George. The George who trained her to be the best fencer she could be, who had held her in his arms, who had promised to help her sister ...

"This will not be easy," he said, "but I hope you understand the need for the deception once I explain."

Evadne stopped pacing. Deception?

He held up a trembling hand, asking for silence; he needn't have worried, her voice was frozen in her throat. "Hear me out. I did deceive you . . . at least in part. You see, I was already aware of the meeting tonight."

Evadne sat down—she had to, or she risked falling to her knees. She felt so disappointed in herself. What had she done to make George distrust her?

"I have been anticipating this evening as keenly as you have, Gray. And I am glad you told me—glad you insisted on coming to tell me. It shows your strength of character. That's one thing I've always admired about you—your integrity. Oh come now, don't look so cross. Aren't you a little glad to know I knew?" He gave her a queasy smile. "It means I've had time to formulate a plan."

Evadne felt no surge of relief. She felt disillusioned and betrayed. To her mind, this wasn't a deception *in part*. George had known, intimately, how these past few weeks had affected her, had noticed their effect on her fencing, her general health, and had done nothing about it. What a fool she had been to think him so different from Freddie—Freddie, who had been aware of her affection, but let her cling to hope as he courted another. Both had allowed her to suffer for their own arcane purposes.

She hadn't asked Freddie why he'd strung her along, but she wanted answers from George.

"Why didn't you tell me?"

"I felt it was safest. As you just said, Dorina is your sister. You are very close, both in terms of proximity and your familial relationship. The risk that you might let something slip, however inadvertently, and tip her off—tip *them* off—was simply too great. And there is the fact that this meeting has been planned for weeks. You never mentioned it, and I thought that meant perhaps you knew, but had had second thoughts about telling me. I had to be careful, Gray. This is bigger than any of us."

So much was vying for her attention, but one thing was first and foremost in her mind.

"Does this mean they are really . . . that they are . . ."

"I've long suspected that Lady Henry's organization was no honest society, but rather a den of demon-worshipers who have colluded to summon and serve something unspeakable." He favored her with a smile. "What you told me the other day cleared away any lingering doubts. Something *must* be done about them. And quickly."

Despair claimed Evadne. She had so longed to be proven wrong. Dorina had been her responsibility, and in a fit of pique over feeling excluded she'd allowed the girl to run wild—or rather run straight into the arms of someone who might well be planning to use her to perform some unholy act of unspeakable horror.

"I see," she said, keeping her voice calm. "When exactly were you planning on telling me?"

"Tonight, of course," he said, a bit of his old warmth creeping into his voice. "We're planning to interrupt their meeting after it is underway—not before."

"Once it is underway?" Evadne was shocked. "So we can witness another scene like we saw on that rooftop? I cannot allow that!"

"Calm yourself," said George, steel returning to his voice. "There will be no 'scene' like last time. I've been able to infiltrate their organization. I shall be inside, monitoring the proceedings and waiting to give the signal for the rest of you to come to my aid."

Evadne frowned as something struck her. She had not given a second thought to how Dorina had believed she knew George from somewhere, when they met in front of their uncle's . . . but now . . . she had to know.

"How long ago did you infiltrate their group?"

"It doesn't matter."

He didn't meet her eyes. That, rather than his words, told her all she needed to know.

She had trusted him, had been so honest with him—had opened herself to him, shown him more of herself than she had ever shown anyone. She didn't blame herself for that. How could she have resisted? He had made her feel like she was worthy of his attention, of his affection. Of perhaps even his love. And all the while he had been playing her, using her. Lying to her about who he was in order to get what he wanted from her.

He had seduced her. Unconventionally, and to unconventional ends, but that was what it amounted to.

"Gray. The important thing is that we're poised to catch Lady Henry and her colleagues. We're in a position to stop them from doing more harm!"

There it was. *The important thing.* Lying to her, isolating her . . . that was inconsequential to him. It hurt to hear, but it also liberated her.

"Of course," she said, burying her fury deep. Dorina was in very real danger—and to help her, Evadne needed more information. "I'm sorry, I'm just so worried. I want to get my sister away from these people. If we can do that, I'll be grateful forever, no matter how it was done. It's time for us both to go home and have our lives go back to normal."

"I sincerely hope that happens. But of course you understand . . . if it turns out that your sister has already become one of them, we shall have to deal with her as we deal with the rest."

Evadne broke out in a cold sweat. "What do you mean by *deal* with her? Surely she is the victim here?"

George shrugged. "Who can say? I do not especially care; it is irrelevant if she has been tainted by that demon. Once I described us as a knife that cuts away at a cancer . . . It is not the duty of the knife to discriminate, or even regret. Only to carve away what is rotten."

"Carve!" Was his 'plan' to simply *murder* them all? Up until this point, she'd assumed they would get Dorina away from
Lady Henry and her cabal, and maybe alert Scotland Yard as to
what was really happening in Curzon Street. "You can't mean . . .
George! We don't know for sure if they're really *evil*, like that man
on the rooftop!"

"This isn't about good and evil." George's laugh was a dry bark.
"Rather, it is about something far more complex."

"What do you mean?"

"I mean that good and evil are abstracts, of course."

"Is that an 'of course'?" asked Evadne cautiously.

"Think of it like fencing. We—you and I, Trawless, everybody,
really—when we fence, we aren't men and women holding swords.
We *are* the swords. We must be, to excel."

"All right," allowed Evadne. This was nothing new; it was
something Perkins often said. And yet, the same words took on
new meaning as George spoke them.

"Well, a sword is neither good nor bad, by itself. Only when it is
wielded with strength and conviction is it capable of great things.
Whether or not those things fit into what arbitrary individuals
might classify as *good* or *evil* . . ." He shrugged.

"I'm afraid I don't follow you." Evadne tried to keep her tone casual, unaffected, in the hopes that he would not sense the mounting disquiet within her, but in truth Evadne's heart was pounding
as if the fencing she was currently engaged in involved an epee, not
words. "When you first introduced me to your mission, you spoke
of serving the greater good."

George stood and limped over to the fireplace, warming his
hands before the blaze. That was when she saw it on the mantelpiece, set out among other items: the dagger from the rooftop.

He had kept it! But *why?* After what it had shown her, that he
had brought it into his home . . . put it out on display like it was a
conversation piece.

Or a trophy?

"I spoke of what *I* consider to be the greater good, of course," he said softly. "Each man's is different."

"And what sort of good might yours be?" she asked, still hoping for confirmation that George didn't intend to beat down Lady Henry's front door and kill them all.

"What all people think of as *good* is that which helps them achieve their goals."

"Excellent. Our mutual goal is to protect the innocent, isn't it? So . . . shall we go?"

George glanced at the clock. "I shall depart in just a few minutes. As for you . . ." He shook his head. "I'm afraid *you* won't be going anywhere."

Evadne had been concentrating so intently on George that she had almost forgotten Trawless was in the room, but when George's evening scarf caught her around the chest and she found her arms pinned to her sides, she remembered him quickly enough.

"Let me go!" she cried, thrashing. But he had trussed her too neatly, too quickly, too perfectly, and all she managed to do was tip her chair. Trawless managed to catch her before she hit the ground, lowering her to the floor as easily as a child might a doll.

Though she had a lot on her mind, between George's betrayal and struggling to get free, Evadne still managed to be astonished by Trawless's reflexes and sheer strength. As he bound her wrists with the ends of the scarf, and her ankles to the legs of her chair with his necktie and belt, she reflected that of all the students within George's little group, she would not have assumed Burton Trawless would be the one who would overpower and manhandle her so effectively. But he had her knotted up tight, and by the time he had righted her, and she had recovered enough to speak again, she was quite effectively immobilized.

"Why are you doing this?" she demanded. "I want to come with you!"

"You put on a good show," said George, watching her struggle with detached amusement, "but you must think me a simpleton if you believe I could be fooled so easily."

Evadne squirmed, but found no give in her restraints. "Who's trying to fool you?" she demanded. "Didn't I come here? Didn't I tell you what you wanted to know?"

"Yes, and I was most pleasantly surprised and gratified when you did. But while you proved yourself loyal in one way, I saw your face when I mentioned the possibility of your sister meeting the same end as Lady Henry inevitably will tonight. You would do anything to see her spared—even betray me."

He was going to kill them. Kill them, and burn them, and leave everyone who knew or loved them to draw their own conclusions . . .

"You're wrong! I would never betray you!" She lied, desperate to convince him to let her go. She could not help Dorina, bound, here in his rooms! She tried one last appeal, speaking words she had lately hoped to say to him under very different circumstances. "I love you!"

He chuckled, and it turned into a cough. When he recovered, he croaked, "Even if that is true, Gray, I cannot risk this mission. Perhaps, if Dorina remains innocent and uncorrupted, you and I may yet have a fruitful liaison . . . but until I ascertain her heart, I cannot trust yours."

The clock chimed—it was seven. He glanced up at it, surprised.

"Time flies," he remarked. "I am expected . . . I must hurry if I'm to get there on time. Trawless, you'll have to stay with Gray here, I'm afraid. Don't worry—I'm certain the rest of us should be able to handle these fops."

"But—"

"If the girl gets loose, it could ruin everything we've worked for. I wouldn't ask you to stay behind unless I thought it was of the utmost importance. You know that, don't you?"

Trawless looked annoyed, but nodded.

"A shame I shall be forced to go scarfless," said George. He had the nerve to wink at Evadne, and she blushed, furious and humiliated. "Ah well. When one serves the greater good, one must make sacrifices I suppose . . ."

He winced as he shrugged into his evening jacket, and shuffling to the door, he collected his top hat and walking stick.

"It's a shame you proved weak at the crucial moment, Gray. I cannot abide weakness," he said over his shoulder. He touched the brim of his hat as a final mocking gesture, and was gone.

Evadne didn't have time to mourn, or even spend a moment mulling over George's treachery. Trawless was furious.

"Bloody hell," he swore, after the sound of George's footsteps had faded away. "Leave me here, will he? *The utmost importance* indeed." He whirled, turning on Evadne, stalking toward her, his face a rictus of frustrated rage. She trembled as he loomed over her. Not only were they alone, but no one knew where she was. She was completely helpless, and he was acting totally unlike himself. Gone was the pleasant, affable man she had come to like very much. "You! This is all your fault."

"How?" she asked, before she could stop herself. It hardly seemed wise to antagonize him.

"By . . . by . . . it doesn't matter!" He picked up a cushion from the settee and hurled it across the room, like a child having a tantrum. "You're just a silly girl, and you have no idea what you're doing, you know that? No clue of what you're meddling in, or what your meddling has done."

"I've rather begun to suspect that," she replied. "But if you cared to enlighten me at all . . ."

"As George didn't think you a fit custodian of our secrets, I shan't tell you anything," he said, beginning to pace like a caged tiger.

"Secrets . . ." Evadne desperately tried keep him talking. She couldn't think of any way to get him to untie her, so learning what she could seemed like her best option, for now. "You mean se-

crets beyond being demon-fighting vigilantes? Or rather diabo-
list-fighting vigilantes?"

"You really are a stupid girl," sneered Trawless, stopping in his
tracks. He was so totally unlike his usual self.

She shook her head as realization dawned.

"Yes, I am stupid—stupid not to think of it earlier," she said.

She'd thought it was nervous energy, back on that terrible rooftop, but now she realized that she ought not to have been able to
do all she had done, ought not have been able to drive her sword
through the eye socket of that creature and out the back of its skull.

"You ate one of those wafers a few moments ago, didn't you?
There's no way you could have overpowered me so easily just now
without it." Trawless didn't look pleased by this, but said nothing.
"What's in those?" she asked. "George said they were for protection, but as I'm not a demon . . ."

"Never you mind what's in them," he said, beginning to pace
again.

"Is it drugs?" Evadne thought back to how she'd felt after eating
one. "Some sort of stimulant that increases strength?"

"It's not *drugs*," said Trawless with what Evadne felt sure he
meant to be an air of superiority.

"It must be drugs," she mused. "The reaction I had, the day after . . . I could scarcely move—my body didn't feel like it belonged
to me."

"Really?" Trawless looked at her curiously. "That's never happened to me. Well, George did say you were particularly sensitive . . ."

There it was. That phrase. The puzzle piece she'd been missing.

George had said she was *particularly sensitive* to demonic presence or influence . . . and what else had he said?

*Demons give their followers gifts. Rewards for their service. Every
demon's is different . . . sometimes it is unnatural beauty; sometimes it
is something more advantageous in a fight . . .*

Extraordinary strength and increased agility certainly were useful in a fight, as was rage, if channeled against one's enemies . . . Could it be that for all his seeming hatred of demons and diabolists, George could have succumbed to the same sort of influence he claimed to want to stamp out?

"What?" asked Trawless, peering at her. He must have realized he'd let on something he shouldn't have. She decided to act the innocent—he thought her a stupid girl, so it shouldn't be too difficult, she assumed, to convince him she really was one. The less she pretended to know, the more he might tell her.

"Nothing." She squirmed, began to fidget. "I'm sorry, I just . . ."

"Sorry?" Trawless looked at her curiously. "For what?"

"I . . ." She looked down, to hide her lack of blush. "I need . . ."

"You need what?"

"I don't know how much longer I can hold it." This time, her blush was real. Even as a deception, it felt too personal a thing to say.

Trawless looked appalled; he clearly hadn't considered this unpleasant aspect of having to mind her while George was gone. "Forgive me," he said, his former politeness returning momentarily, "but I cannot unbind you."

"You don't mean to say you'll make me . . ."

"I'm sorry, but George said I had to keep you restrained."

"He doesn't have to know," she said, putting urgency into her voice. "*Please,* Trawless, don't do this to me. It's too much. I promise I'll be good if you just let me use the—"

"Oh, all right," said Trawless, annoyed now rather than embarrassed.

He unlaced her legs from the chair, but once he'd loosened her wrists he bound them together behind her back. Hauling her to her feet, he marched her to the WC.

"You'll just have to manage like this," he said shortly, and shut the door behind her.

Evadne's need for the facilities wasn't as bad as she'd made it out to be, but for verisimilitude's sake she stepped through her bound wrists, an awkward proposition in skirts in the little room, and then sat down on the convenience. She heard Trawless shift from leg to leg beyond the door, and it was awful knowing he was listening to everything . . . but at the same time, the sound of her water at least provided some noise to cover the rustling of her tearing at George's evening scarf with her teeth. Trawless had tightened the knot cruelly, and when at last she felt it give, her lips were torn and her teeth ached.

"About done in there?" he asked.

"Yes," she said. "Just one more moment. It's a bit difficult with my hands . . ."

"Just finish up."

Finally free, she got into position just behind the door. As far as Trawless knew, her hands were bound behind her; he would have to open it for her. As soon as he did, she would give it a push, hopefully knocking him one of the best on the forehead or nose. Some manner of deceit was needed, given that she knew he was either high on drugs or something more arcane, and would be more powerful than usual.

"All right," she called. "I'm sorry, I can't manage to flush it . . ."

He made a disgusted noise and opened the door. As it swung inward, trapping her against the wall, she gave it a hearty shove with her shoulder. It worked. He was hurled off balance and staggered into the wall opposite.

Evadne leaped out after him. She had never thrown a punch in her life, but she managed the basics well enough, aiming for and catching him on the jaw. Her knuckles slid slightly, weakening the blow, but her furious fist grazed his eye and the bridge of his nose.

As he staggered back, shouting and clutching his face, she lurched past him and then sprinted down the hall to grab one of the rapiers from above the fireplace. In his current state, she knew too well her only chance of besting him was with a sword in her hand.

The rapier's pommel was of a decent size; it was a longer weapon than she was used to, and not recently sharpened, but it would do. She silently thanked Lady Henry for her gift of Lord Oliver's swords; having practiced with a real weapon all summer meant she had the strength to wield this blade, now that it really mattered.

Trawless came around the corner, one eye looking a little twitchy. He frowned when he saw Evadne standing there, rapier in hand, the sofa between them.

"Foolish girl," he growled. "You may think I'm soft—everyone does—but I assure you, I am not. You'll regret defying me."

"For what it's worth, I've never thought you soft." Evadne saluted him with the blade, and sidestepping the sofa, she charged him.

Attacking an unarmed man was neither a brave nor a moral act, to Evadne's mind, but the circumstances were extenuating. Additionally, calling Trawless unarmed didn't quite account for whatever was coursing through his blood, giving him the advantage in nimbleness and strength.

He tried to get out of her way, but her first jab found its mark; she stabbed him in the right shoulder. The tip sank in a few inches, and she made sure to twist it as she withdrew it, deepening and widening the injury. Blood bloomed, soaking his shirt and jacket.

"Lucky," he snarled, lunging clumsily at her as she retreated. She stepped out of his way but crashed into an end table she hadn't remembered being there. Tail over teakettle she tumbled, avoiding stabbing herself with the long blade by releasing it; it skittered away over the floor, coming to rest close to where she did, but point first. She was just about to climb to her feet and make a grab for it when Trawless fell upon her, pinning her. She grasped for the point of the rapier, but no matter where her hand landed, it was the wrong place.

"You've made a grievous error," he said, and delivered a punch of his own to her face.

Stars bloomed from the blackness as Evadne felt the back of her head slam into the floor. A tooth felt odd; it had loosened. Thankfully, he was using his left, and Trawless was right handed, but with his increased strength this hardly mattered. When his second blow came, to her gut, she was suddenly very glad she'd actually taken the time to empty her bladder. She gasped, but there was nothing for her to gasp.

"Stupid girl," he said as she choked. "What were you thinking?"

"I was thinking," she groaned, "about saving my sister." The rapier had to be close; she kept feeling around for it. Unfortunately, Trawless noticed and swatted her hand away just as her fingers touched the tip.

"I don't think so," he said, and wound up for another punch.

Desperate, Evadne rocked herself violently, pitching Trawless into the sofa. He tried to steady himself with his injured arm, but it crumpled under him. Evadne pulled herself from under his weight and grabbed for the rapier. Her hand closed around the forte of the blade. She felt it cutting into her palm, but she did not pause or stop to shift it. Instead, she leaped atop Trawless, knees on his chest, as she grabbed it tighter and clobbered him in the temple with the pommel, really whipping him to get the most out of the strike.

He slumped, eyes rolling back in his head.

"Bloody hell," he said weakly, his body losing much of its tension beneath her.

Evadne was disappointed; she'd hoped to knock him out, but apparently that took more than a crack to the temple. Well, maybe it was better this way—she had the upper hand now, and might be able to get him to explain a few things before she went after George and the rest. The more she knew going in, the better.

"All right, Trawless," she said, trying her best to sound dangerous as she adjusted her grip on the sword and pointed the tip at his throat. She hoped he wouldn't notice how freely her palm was bleeding and assume quite rightly that she couldn't hold it if he chose to resist. "Tell me what's really going on!"

He spat in her face. She slapped him with her left hand.

"Talk, damn you!"

He winced. "Why should I tell you anything?"

"Because I'll kill you if you don't! If you won't talk, you're useless to me." Trawless looked genuinely shocked, as well he might — he didn't know how serious she was. Neither did she, for that matter. "In a few moments I'm going to Lady Henry's, and I'd prefer to know what I'm getting into. If I have to go in blind, so be it, but if you choose that, then know I'll face George and the rest having already killed a man!"

She must have seemed very scary indeed, for Trawless had gone pale. "All right! What do you want to know?"

"Do you serve a demon?"

"Yes." Trawless's eyes flickered to a wooden box on the mantel. "The wafers help us channel it."

"Channel . . ."

"One cannot just speak to a demon, one must *commune*, usually through taking a sacrament of some sort. Ours is the wafer, but George keeps it a secret — what it really is."

"What do you mean?"

"How he makes them. One must conjure a demon into something like a plant and consume it, in order to communicate with it. For example, Lady Henry's a botanist, and we suspect she uses the ginger she grows, given the motif in her home."

Evadne nodded as she thought about the smell of Lady Henry's cigarettes, perfume . . . everything. "Yours makes you stronger — what does hers do?"

"We suspect it makes them more receptive to aesthetic experiences."

Becoming more sensitive to beauty was scarcely as sinister as what the dagger on that horrifying rooftop had suggested to Evadne. Even so, the idea of her sister smoking those noxious cigarettes just to see a bunch of pretty pictures in a different light didn't exactly thrill Evadne. Who could say what the future plans of the demon truly were? And even if it had none, by exposing her to a demon, Lady Henry had put Dorina in terrible danger from George and others like him, be they vigilante demon-hunters or other servants of the unspeakable . . .

"How did George manage to infiltrate their group? What's going on tonight?"

"Ever since he fenced with Lord Oliver, George has suspected that group of consorting with demons. His face being familiar to the lady, he had to disguise himself . . . and then had to engineer himself an invitation via another member, as they are so secretive."

"Yes, but my sister didn't recognize him when he came to call . . . She thought he looked familiar, but scarcely seemed to consider him an intimate acquaintance, as one might expect."

"*You* scarcely recognized him, and you've been acquainted with him . . . intimately, even," sneered Trawless, earning himself another slap. "Ow! What I mean to say is only that there is always a price. Those who would traffic with such powers are granted physical boons, but it takes a heavy toll. George has gone further down the path than any of us, and if he doesn't take his pastilles — no, they are not for his digestion — then, well, you saw him, did you not?"

Evadne nodded. "That makes sense. But why now? Why tonight, I mean, for the . . . the everything? He didn't want me to come, kept the plan from me." She considered for a moment. "Was it the sword I told him about?"

"Yes and no. George has a weakness for trophies, like that dagger, and Lord Oliver's sword will be a lovely addition. But it's more that you confirmed his suspicions by condemning Lady Henry and her manservant with your sensitivity to demonic essence." He paused; Evadne prodded him with the tip of the sword, urging him to go on. "Stop that! Fine! The demon we serve . . . it is pleased when we eliminate the servants of others of its kind. As far as I understand it — George is the expert — it draws strength in its own world from such sacrifices, and shares that increased power and strength with us, in ours. Diabolists very often work alone — we are the exception, as is Lady Henry's little coterie. So far, we've only been able to take down individuals. But *this* night our power will be exponentially increased by the deaths of so many at once! I have been with George for many years, and long has he hungered to uncover a group of this size, a sacrifice of this magnitude . . . So you see, we had to be certain. A mistake would mean a lot of bodies, which aren't easy to dispose of — the fire he wields by the grace of our patron will only burn that which has been touched by their world."

Recalling her confusion over seeing George seem to light the oil with a word, Evadne nodded.

"It's strange, though . . ." he continued.

"Eh?"

"You've touched me — and I *know* you've touched George, though not as much as you would have liked to." Trawless smirked as she blushed, but she did not react any more than that — she resolved not to show that his sneering wounded her. She had always worried about others laughing at her behind her back; this barb just served as a confirmation for her. "And yet you didn't notice anything *off* about us."

Evadne hadn't thought of that, but now that Trawless mentioned it, it occurred to her just how good she felt after contact with George, and even Trawless himself, in the cab. Not greasy, not unclean, like when she touched Jonas, or Lady Henry. Just . . . *wonderful.*

What did that say about her? About them? She would have to puzzle it out later.

"Well. Thank you, Trawless," said Evadne. "You've been *most* helpful."

He eyed the rapier still pointing at his throat. "So . . . you're going to let me go?"

"I'm not going to kill you," she corrected him, and brought the pommel down on his temple again.

This time he went slack, thank goodness. Climbing off him, she dropped the rapier, and after a quick look at her bleeding hand, she bound it with George's scarf and then set to tying up Trawless so he wouldn't be able to warn anyone if he awoke. She wasn't strong enough to lift him anywhere, so she left him on the floor, on his back, far away from anything he could use to cut himself free.

After that, Evadne hesitated, considering taking the wafers in the box on George's mantelpiece. He and the rest of her former companions would be under the influence of the demon. She could use like against like—take a dose or two to augment her strength and endurance to combat whatever awaited her that night.

No. The idea of ever again communing with the demon that George served—a demon that grew stronger through murder— disgusted her. And anyway, she couldn't believe that a demon that had invested so heavily in a cause like George's would help her undermine it. What reason would it have to aid her?

She felt an overwhelming sense of despair. How could she possibly face them? Even without demonic essences that made them stronger and faster, it would have been an impossible task. They had been waiting long for this night; they were prepared. She would fail if she stood against them.

She needed help.

The police? She considered them, but they would be too slow. She had to get to Lady Henry's, and quickly. She had no idea how quickly George would begin his slaughter.

But she could ask for help elsewhere. Help beyond what any human could give her.

Her stomach clenched as she realized the clear course before her. She would just have to trust that Lady Henry's demon would be invested in saving those it had collected—including Dorina. If she could but speak to it, perhaps she could ask it for advice—what to do, how she ought to prepare. What she should expect. It would know what was happening to them in the moment, whereas she could only guess and barge in . . .

Right or wrong, her sister was in danger. *That* was what mattered.

She loved Dorina. She always had. And not in spite of her being headstrong, selfish, thoughtless, but because of it. She couldn't imagine a world without her sister in it. She would not let that light go out, not while she could still lift a sword or draw a breath.

It was this that got Evadne to her feet and let her ignore the ache in her jaw and the blood dripping from her palm, the pain from Trawless's strike to her gut blossoming as she walked out of George's rooms. She didn't lock the door behind her.

3

When one summons a demon, out of the shadows of life shines a new light, and by it we come to see a world fashioned for our pleasure, where things have fresh shapes and new colors, where we ourselves are changed, and are able to keep new secrets. A world in which our past has little or no place, and obligation and regret are mere myth.

— *On the Summoning of Demons*

A s much as she had been looking forward to her first evening as a full member of Lady Henry's secret society, Dorina could not shed her sense of disquiet over how Evadne had not objected to her staying the night. Dorina had been expecting a pitched battle, and had received an indifferent shrug. Her sister's calm lack of interest seemed extremely out of character.

The new presence in her mind stirred gently, soothing her. In only a short time, she had come to listen to it, to trust it. It told her without words not to worry, to accept that she could not understand everything all the time, especially where humans were concerned. She appreciated the reminder, and wondered how she had ever managed without the guidance of this generous and ancient entity. It made her a bit sad, actually, to think of how many out there were alone, as she had once been. Their thoughts and their lives were limited by their individuality, their distinctiveness from every other thing. They were only themselves, especially if—like

Evadne—they refused to open themselves up to the perspectives of others.

Dorina felt around in her bag for the ginger candies that Henry had given her. They weren't there; that's right—she'd finished them. With a sigh, she stood, fidgeting, flitting from window to window, looking out for she knew not what.

"Dorina," said Henry, looking up from her book. "Are you in need of something?"

"A cup of tea, perhaps." Dorina didn't want to tell Henry about her issues with her sister; to always be complaining about one's sibling was tiresome, and tiresome was the last thing she wanted to be.

"I'd be happy to prepare some," said Jonas.

"Bring those ginger biscuits, too," advised Henry as she lit a cigarette.

As much as Dorina desired to draw nearer the spicy smoke, she forced herself to turn away. Henry still denied her the pleasure; she had smoked before she began lacing her cigarettes with ginger powder, and didn't think it an appropriate habit for Dorina to cultivate—not at this point in her life. As she pointed out, their demon might enhance their appreciation of the world around them, but it wouldn't keep her teeth white.

"What's gotten into you?" Henry was sprawled lazily across a couch, legs thrown over the arm, cigarette dangling from her long fingers. "Are you nervous about your interview with Dr. Sauber?"

"Oh!" Dorina had forgotten, but Dr. Sauber was hosting the gathering that evening, and as he needed to be there early to set things up and sign for deliveries, it had seemed most convenient. "No, not really."

"Brave creature," remarked Henry. "Well, if it's not that, I'm all out of ideas. If you feel like sharing, I'm here—oh bother, there's the door. I'll just go tell Jonas to make a bigger pot, and bring out more biscuits. The doctor enjoys them so."

Dorina nodded, resigned. Truth be told, she was not really of a mood to discuss her sexual experiences and preferences back to her earliest memories, but she *had* promised, and vowed to make the best of it.

"Miss Gray! Ah!" said Dr. Sauber, bounding into the salon like a satyr. All he needed was a flute and an honor guard of women in robes. "And unchaperoned! Good, good . . ."

"Why is that good?" she asked, feeling alarmed for the first time.

"I have found," he said, setting down his bag on a low table and making himself comfortable on a chair with uncanny speed, "that people are more forthcoming when alone with a doctor."

"I see," said Dorina, forcing herself to sit down. "Well, never fear," she said as Henry returned with Jonas, bearing tea and biscuits, "Henry knows all my secrets."

"Does she!" exclaimed Dr. Sauber, looking sharply from her to Henry. Henry smiled sheepishly, a charming blush coming to her alabaster cheeks. "I had suspicions, of course, but I must say I'm delighted!"

"Of course you are, you prurient bastard," said Henry, handing him a fragrant cup.

"Life is short, and happiness is in short supply in this world," said Dr. Sauber. "While I might admit some *professional* interest in your relationship, my personal interest is completely due to enjoying both of you as people, and hoping for an increase in your happiness."

"That's very sweet," said Dorina, warming to him a bit. "Well, what do you want to know, Doctor?"

Talking about sex usually cheered Dorina, but there was just something she could not shake from her shoulders that day. The engaging conversation of the doctor, the excellent biscuits, and the prospect of a very good dinner, which she began to smell long before leaving the doctor to don her caftan, should have thoroughly invigorated her had she been herself. And yet she had a strange sense of foreboding that even the friendly presence in her mind could not ease with its gentle nudges and sense of wry amusement over various remarks and questions put to her by Dr. Sauber.

She put on her best face when the guests began to arrive, but all too soon her temper was tried by Mr. Walmsley, the sight of whom put her even more out of sorts. Something about his appearance bothered her, nagged at something in the back of her mind, but she couldn't get away from him to think about it, for he had not left her side since he'd joined her in the salon. Of course, the last two meetings they had had much to speak of, both being outsiders, but now that she had been inducted into the inner circle, she dreaded him noticing and making his typically arch remarks. She sensed he would take it poorly that she had been invited to become a full member after he had been waiting for so long—and honestly, if he did, she couldn't blame him. She just didn't want to hear it.

Of course, this was what he did, *immediately*, upon seeing Jonas hand her a cocktail that looked ever so slightly different from the one he himself received. Dorina sipped it, detecting Jonas's proprietary ginger bitters, but before she could even so much as swallow, Mr. Walmsley made a comment.

"I see you have been honored with initiation," he remarked. "You must be pleased." He, however, sounded anything but.

"I beg your pardon?" she said. "Initiation? Why, Mr. Walmsley, you make it sound so . . . *ritualistic*."

"Was it not?" He smiled wanly into his own beverage. "I wouldn't know. How did they let you know you'd met their exacting standards? Was it after the last meeting? You stayed . . ."

"Of course I stayed. Lady Henry always makes sure her coach takes me home. It's not safe for a young lady to traipse about London late at night in just any old cab."

"For fear of worse than death?" She stared at him, shocked by his language. "Come now, Miss Gray. You needn't act like such an ingénue. We both know you're no innocent."

"Pray excuse me," she said, and left his side.

"Everything all right?" asked Henry. "I know I keep asking you that, but Dorina, really, you look as if your pet had died."

"I'm sorry," she said. "Mr. Walmsley is just so tiresome. He made some rather inappropriate comments after noticing I was now . . . one of you."

"Mr. Walmsley hasn't been our most successful recruit," admitted Henry. "Truth be told, we've been talking about not inviting him back. None of us feel he really understands what we do, who we are . . . Of course, he's enthusiastic, and has proven a strong desire to join us, but sometimes that's simply not enough. It's a shame, but what can you do?"

"Perhaps he senses he's about to be given the boot."

"Just ignore him and have a good time," advised Henry. "All you can do, really. Here, have another cocktail. Later, when we ask Mr. Walmsley to wait outside for a moment, you'll love what we have prepared. I know how much you enjoyed the ice cream we ate together, that day we went to the gardens at Kew, so I had some specially churned."

"Ginger?" asked Dorina, and Lady Henry winked at her.

Dorina felt a bit like a child, but this did indeed please her; mollified, she mingled with the other guests, who all congratulated her on joining them. Unfortunately, her pleasure was alloyed, for she felt Mr. Walmsley's eyes on her the whole time. He was watching her, even when he pretended as if his attention was elsewhere. Whenever she moved, he repositioned himself so she was in his line of vision. It bothered her, and she sensed he knew this.

"Tonight, the program should be exquisite," said Henry. "Dr. Sauber, would you mind telling us a bit before we break?"

Dorina was startled; she'd scarcely noticed they'd sat down to dinner, much less finished eating it. Her mind had been so completely elsewhere . . .

"I should be delighted!" cried the fellow, leaping to his feet in excitement. "Why, my friends, I am so glad you made it tonight. It was a challenging thing, designing a program around *touch*, for of course, it is potentially the rudest of the senses." He laughed in his bouncy, good-natured way—his cheerfulness was infectious, and Dorina felt her mind relocate to the present, to the demon's delight. "I of course am wondering if this is why our gracious hostess, Lady Henry, assigned this one to me? But do not be disappointed when I say that while I hope you find my program sublime, and of course sensual, it will not be salacious. I want to engage our sense of touch, not exploit it . . . not to say that the more carnal uses for the sense of touch are exploitative, necessarily . . ."

Henry put her hand on Dr. Sauber's shoulder, which seemed to recall him.

"Ah! The philosophizing can also be done during the program, of course. Mr. Walmsley, if you would not mind . . ."

"Of course," he said, casting a look at Dorina that, had they been dealing with taste, not touch, would have been as sour as any lemon.

His absence felt like an immediate relief, like a pressure being lifted from her shoulders. She sighed, and glanced at Henry, who was smiling at her.

"Welcome, Dorina," she said. "We're so glad to have you join us."

"What is it tonight, Henry?" asked Mr. Seward, who was also more animated than Dorina had ever seen him.

"In honor of our newest member: ice cream. Jonas and I churned it ourselves—for hours, it felt like . . . though he assures me that was not the case." Henry comically mimed a wince as she rotated her elbow. "I made it with that divine ginger spread you preserved for us, Mrs. Dhareshwar, as well as some fresh root we shredded this morning."

Beth brought in small dishes, each with a single perfect sphere of ice cream. Dorina longed to tuck in, but fearing seeming childish she waited, to see if any words were spoken, or a ritual intoned. Indeed not; Henry said "Bon appétit" and they all dug in.

Eating the sweet was the single most sublime experience of Dorina's life. The candies Henry had given her had been delightful, and the biscuits, too, but both were meant for everyday consumption—to keep the demon's essence gently regulated in the bloodstream. They enabled Dorina's connection to the demon that now dwelt in her mind, but did not allow her to experience it fully.

The ice cream, on the other hand . . . the moment it melted over her tongue it was like discovering a new world, very similar to the first time she had tasted the sacramental ginger, and her eyes had been opened to all that had been hidden from her. And yet, this was unlike that, in terms of the intensity of the experience. She felt the demon's awareness growing in her, as the earth's shadow slides across the moon during an eclipse, darkening it, and yet revealing it in a different manner. She did not lose any part of herself; she simply became more than she had been. She knew she would never, ever be the same after feeling this, never feel wholly able to appreciate the world without coming back to this place, occasionally, to experience it.

She looked over at Henry, and in her limpid eyes saw . . . well, it was difficult to explain. It was almost as if she saw herself in Henry, but her lover's face hadn't changed. It was just that Dorina was aware that on some level they were the same, had always been, but were now more than ever. They were connected by a will not their own that loved them both equally and sought to add their uniqueness to its understanding of the world.

Her rumination was cut short by a brisk, loud knock on the door. Time seemed to quicken as she looked around, surprised— none of them were finished with their portion; it hadn't been very long at all. What could Mr. Walmsley be thinking, barging in during this part of the evening?

Then the door burst open and four men swarmed into the room, all armed with swords and some with daggers. The largest of them, a big brute with a gorilla's brow, went straight for Henry. Before anyone had any idea what to do, he had a knife at her throat. Dorina leaped up, upending her chair in her haste, but the gorilla pointed at her with his free hand and told her to sit down.

"Whatever funny stuff you try will be the last thing she sees," he grunted. "No one's coming. You're quite alone."

Unwilling to endanger Henry, Dorina righted and sat back down in her chair. Henry stared at her, thanking her with her eyes for her obedience.

"Miss Gray, that was very wise," said Mr. Walmsley, hobbling to the front, just beside where Henry sat. "Your spunk and impetuousness will not help you tonight."

"Mr. Walmsley. You are not permitted to join this portion of our evening," said Henry, with astonishing calm given how close that knife was to her neck. "If you will go back outside, I would be most grateful, and once we've concluded our business we will join you for the program."

"Shut up," he spat at her. "There will be no *program*, my lady. At least, not one hosted by Dr. Sauber. Instead, *you* will be the entertainment."

"What have you done?" Jonas, who also had one of the thugs behind him, yelped as his assailant tightened his grip.

"I'm so glad you asked!" Walmsley cried, happier than Dorina had ever seen him. Then he turned serious. "I've betrayed you," he said, stage-whispering.

"To whom?" asked Mr. Seward. Of all of them, he looked the most appalled; then, Dorina remembered that he was the one who had invited Mr. Walmsley in the first place.

"Ah, Mr. Seward. Thank you. I should clarify . . . I have not *yet* betrayed you. I shall betray you later." He chuckled hollowly. "And to one more powerful than any of you fools could possibly ever imagine."

"You have rather desperately tried to become a member of our group of *fools,* as you say," said Mr. Seward coldly. "It is childish, Mr. Walmsley, to revenge yourself upon us simply because you were never the fit I once thought you might be."

"Oh, you think I'm piqued because you didn't let me into your little club?" Mr. Walmsley laughed, then began to cough. "No, no," he said when he had recovered. "The only reason I pretended to so ardently desire inclusion was to ascertain whether you lot really were diabolists."

The silence that followed this pronouncement was incredible. No one knew what to say or do; even the demon in Dorina's mind reeled in shock.

Henry recovered first. "Diabolists! How fantastical. Really, Mr. Walmsley, where do you—"

"*Stop,*" he said. "I know the truth. Long have I suspected, but it was finally confirmed for me . . . by Miss Gray's elder sister, actually."

"I don't believe you!" Dorina almost jumped out of her skin; she was reeling, hurt and mostly confused as to the whys and hows of Evadne's alleged betrayal, but it was Jonas who seemed the most upset by this insight.

"Miss Gray would *never* do such a thing!" he snarled.

"*Would* has nothing to do with it; she *could,* and *did,*" said Mr. Walmsley. "Your devotion is charming—what a shame she did not feel you were deserving of the same. Let me be clear: this is a calculated assault. Your—and I mean the collective *your,* not just you, Mr. Fuller—choice to meddle with things you do not understand has exposed and condemned you. Your only choice now is whether you will choose to make your last moments as pleasant as they can be, or less so."

Mr. Walmsley produced a small pouch from his pocket, and after swallowing two pastilles, changed before Dorina's eyes. His back straightened; his limbs eased from their locked and cramped position. The lines of his face smoothed and filled in, revealing an all-too-familiar visage.

"George Cantrell," said Dorina in horror, recalling him from their brief meeting on the doorstep of Uncle Basil's townhouse. "From the fencing academy! You're Evadne's teacher." Tears welled in Dorina's eyes at the undeniable evidence. "The two of you really have been planning this together . . ."

Anger was one thing, but a real betrayal, like this . . . it seemed incredible—so out of character! After all, Evadne had once jumped into the ocean to save her; Dorina thought about that incident often, both when she was cross with Evadne, and feeling affectionate toward her. The sister who did that would never send strangers after her, to threaten her with death and torment! And why hadn't she come with them? Evadne was not one to hang back and let others do her work for her . . .

"After a fashion. Miss Gray revealed to me that this house holds at least one demonically tainted object . . . and is home to one or two who traffic directly with such beings." He winked at Lady Henry.

"I wonder how she knew." Henry managed to sound both bored and intrigued; she certainly was cool under fire. Dorina couldn't help but admire her, even now, when she felt she might start screaming or fly to pieces at any moment. "More importantly, I wonder what demon it is *you* worship? Something that privileges strength, brutality . . . I have seen it all before. Just remember, Mr. Cantrell, the soft will always overcome the hard."

"Spare me," sneered Cantrell. "I have no time for the philosophies of the weak." He turned to Jonas again. "Reid! Have Mr. Fuller take you up to Lord Oliver's bedroom. There, you will find a Chinese sword. Retrieve it for me."

Jonas struggled as he was hauled to his feet, but just a little—there was still a blade dangerously close to his neck, after all.

"I don't know what sword you're talking about," he said calmly.

"Well, you're both fairly bright. Go and see if you can figure it out," drawled Mr. Cantrell. "We'll be waiting."

"What shall we do while we wait?" asked Henry as Reid hustled Jonas out of the room. "Shall we proceed with Dr. Sauber's program, or . . ."

"Sadly, there's just no time," said Cantrell. "This will be a *very* busy night. In fact, I'd say it's past time we got started. Boys, let's get their hands bound and herd them into the salon. I think that will be the best place for it . . . We can clear away the furniture to make sufficient space."

"Space for what?" asked Mrs. Dhareshwar. She was afraid; Dorina could hear how tight her voice was.

"Oh, I can't tell you *that*," said Cantrell, smiling savagely. "That's information I can share only with full members of our society. You know how it is."

His making jokes frightened Dorina more than shouting and rage. *Fear not,* said the presence in her mind, the first time it had communicated in anything like words to her, likely due to her recent, intense infusion of ginger. She marveled at what it said. Well, *it* wouldn't suffer were she injured.

The demon protested this thought, even seemed a little offended, but she pushed away the sensation. She could worry about a demon's hurt feelings later, when she was safe.

Safe! Safe from *what*, though? That was the question. The idea of her parents crossed her mind—what would they say? Would Cantrell torture her, or kill her outright? Either way, how would Evadne explain what she had wrought?

Would she regret it?

As for Dorina, perhaps it was the ginger flowing through her body, or just that she knew her own heart, but she didn't feel any regret. She was afraid, especially when one of the men bound her wrists with rough hemp cord, but even if the past few weeks of her life turned out to have been her last, she wouldn't have traded them for anything, not even a longer life. She had literally tasted something divine, and she would never be the same, whatever happened, because of it.

The demon wholly approved of this sentiment, and for the first time Dorina wondered just how much of an influence on her its will had . . .

"Get them into the salon," said Cantrell. "I want to get started." His eyes flickered to Dorina. "I'm *so* sorry this is happening your first night as a full member, Miss Gray . . . really, I am. You were very kind to me, well, before your initiation at least. If only things had gone differently, you might not have become the victim you will soon be. But, then again, you did want to deal with demons." A dark smile turned up his lips only at the corners. "I suppose we're all getting what we want, eh?"

4

What demons teach us is to never squander the gold of our days. We must live—we must let nothing be lost upon us. We must always search for new sensations. We must be afraid of nothing.

—On the Summoning of Demons

BASIL'S HOUSE WAS INFURIATINGLY FAR AWAY, and cabs were scarce in George's neighborhood. When at last Evadne managed to catch one, she spent the whole ride fuming.

It had taken her too long to get free. George was so direct, so efficient. What if he had already dispatched Dorina, Lady Henry, and the rest? She clung to the hope that it would likely take him some time to set up the ritual sacrifice, but it was cold comfort.

Hopefully she wouldn't have to wonder for much longer. She wasn't quite sure what would happen when she deliberately tried to talk to the demon through the sword in her room. She just had to trust that her particular sensitivity would prove to be of some use.

Rage flared inside her, mostly anger at herself. How could she have been so stupid? She knew George's betrayal wasn't her fault, no . . . but she was at fault for trusting him so quickly, so blindly. She had allowed her heart to overrule her reason, and now others would suffer—perhaps die—just because she had been so hungry for what he had to offer her. She should have known better. The sensation of feeling special, unique, and valued . . . mere illusion. She vowed never to fall for such again.

Evadne's hands balled into fists, seemingly of their own accord. She winced as her injured palm throbbed. The cut was not deep, but it was nasty—she'd have to take the time to bind it properly before doing anything else. Another delay! It made her want to scream, but she choked back the cry as they pulled up to her uncle's house in Chelsea.

"Thank you," she grunted, pushing some amount of money into the driver's hands before sprinting away and through the front door.

Her first stop was the washroom, where she bathed her hand in hot water. It throbbed as she dabbed at the jagged cut with a clean washcloth, and it started bleeding anew as she loosened the dried blood, but she gritted her teeth and forced herself to do it correctly.

Once she was satisfied, she repaired to her room, where she ripped apart an older petticoat to dress it in clean muslin, binding it tightly in the hopes of stanching the fresh blood.

Then she went to retrieve the sword.

The box was right where she'd shoved it, a lifetime ago it felt like. She tore into it and extracted the tainted blade, shuddering as the odd feeling of pleasure hit her. Dizzy, she dragged herself to her bed and sat, trying to concentrate. Clutching the pommel of the Chinese weapon with both hands, she closed her eyes, waiting.

There it was. A nudge, in the back of her mind, like a small animal waking up after a long hibernation. Her eyes popped open in surprise, and she noticed her vision had changed slightly. Color seemed more intense; light and shadow were more distinctly contrasted. The loveliness of everything seemed to increase dramatically, not just the pattern on her coverlet or the pictures on her walls; she even saw the beauty of the small cracks in a rather ugly porcelain vase and other common objects. She tried not to be too distracted by this, and directed her thoughts toward the actual consciousness behind this shift, nudging it back, thinking one message over and over again.

I want to help them.

The response was less like language, and more like a series of feelings that conveyed a message. Evadne was surprised but pleased to find it was genuinely eager to hear from someone who wished to aid those it loved. *Loved* might not be the right word, in all fairness, but that was the best she could come up with to describe the sensations it conveyed.

The next part of what it said to her was more complex. She had to clear her mind, focus on the meaning. It began by congratulating her on connecting with the sword, but warned her that their ability to communicate would be severely limited. It felt surprise that they were able to speak so easily just through the sword, but was insistent that she needed to open herself more to it—and she needed to do it quickly. Dorina and the rest were in terrible danger, and it could help Evadne save them . . . but not without a deeper connection.

How?

Evadne almost swooned as images flooded her mind. The back door of Lady Henry's townhouse in Curzon Street, which flew open; then she was inside, up the stairs. A picture on the Lady's bedroom wall, of ginger of course, and behind it, a safe full of Lady Henry's supply of ginger-infused substances: cigarettes, snuff, candy, and so on. Dizzyingly, the vision shifted to Jonas's bedroom, to where the safe key was secreted away in the false bottom of his shoe chest. Evadne was appalled by the idea of sneaking into his private chambers, which amused the demon—but she would have to do it. She needed to deepen her connection to the demon by actually consuming something. By letting it inside her.

The demon correctly interpreted her revulsion toward the tobacco products, and expressed that there would be enough of the edible material to facilitate what needed to happen.

What needed to happen . . . Meaning, of course, when she had to face George, and the rest of them.

The answering sensation seemed to be questioning her resolution to do this. Evadne answered with her own feeling of puzzlement: Dorina was her sister. Of course she would do this. She would do anything for her.

Then she understood. It was telling her that there would be a price.

I will pay it, she said without hesitation. After all, her sister wouldn't be in this situation but for her. She hadn't told their mother Dorina was in danger, hadn't insisted they go back home. She had let Dorina run wild, out of a combination of spite over the unfairness of life and distraction in the form of the fencing school. Not only that, but she had handed off her responsibility regarding Dorina to someone else. If her character had been stronger, none of this would be happening. She had to make that right, no matter the cost.

The demon heard her thoughts, but fascinatingly, she felt no judgment from it. It did not chide her over her betrayal of its pets to George; it did not admonish her for being resentful and stubborn regarding Dorina's relationship with Henry. It was merely interested in her and her feelings—it wanted to know more about her, not less. This total acceptance . . . she felt absolved by it.

And then she realized that was exactly why someone would risk everything to commune with something like this demon. What had Henry said, weeks ago?

Why else would anyone agree to traffic with such a being? Surely no one would if it were boring, or annoying, or unpleasant.

Now she knew.

Once I get the ginger, where must I go? she asked.

She saw a scene she sensed was happening as they spoke. She saw George, looking like his usual self, directing Stockton as he shifted furniture in Henry's golden salon.

"They're there?" she said aloud, startled. "At the house? How can I possibly sneak past them?"

To this, it had no answer. It only conveyed that she must. George was going to soon begin a ritual and kill them. She resigned herself to being as quiet as she could. If she went in through the servants' door . . .

Then an image of her uncle came to mind.

"Oh," she said aloud. It hadn't occurred to her that her uncle would be any help at all. In fact, she was fairly certain he wouldn't be, but when needs must and all that.

A devil was certainly driving.

At least she now had a plan, knew what to do. Mostly. With a mental farewell, Evadne let go the sword. The feeling of connection disappeared instantly.

She undressed, and then put on her fencing ensemble. Socks, bloomers, skirt. Shirt, breastplate, plastron. She tied on her shoes, and tucked her gloves inside her jacket. She tied back her hair, grabbed her mask, and finally felt ready to do what she needed to do. It might be a Chinese sword she'd be wielding that night, but she would know what to do with it. She was *particularly sensitive*, after all.

While this knowledge had caused her horror before, she was now very grateful indeed.

She had no scabbard that would fit the blade, which was unfortunate — save that it was a relief to make contact with the demon again. Sword in hand, demon in mind, Evadne left her room, calling her uncle's name.

He did not answer.

She checked his bedroom, only peeking in, but he was not there, nor was he in the sitting room. The third time was the charm — he was in his studio, sitting before his favorite painting, doing nothing, merely staring at it. Perhaps it was the light, but she thought he looked even worse than when she had left that afternoon; he was huddled in a blanket in the stifling room as if it were midwinter and not high summer.

As for the painting, it looked more glamorous, more beautiful . . .

"Uncle, you must help," she blurted, not taking the time to compose herself. "They're going for Lady Henry, and Dorina's there."

He turned, slowly blinking at her like an owl. He didn't even seem surprised to see her dressed for a fight, with Oliver Wotton's Chinese sword in her hand. "They?" he asked, only politely interested at best.

"My fencing teacher and his associates. They're also diabolists, and they're—"

Basil stood then, backing away from her and staring as if she'd grown another head. She realized he must be ever so surprised she would know anything about the matter at all. She took strength from the presence in her mind, and tried again.

"I know all about it," she said, plunging ahead. "And . . . and I assume you do too, being friends with Lady Henry . . . and with Lord Oliver, too." Her eyes darted to the painting as she spoke the name aloud. "The important thing is, we have to help them!"

To her surprise, Basil shook his head.

"There's nothing to be done," he said, turning away and shoving his hands in his pockets as he wandered toward a stand of ferns. "If they're already under attack what good can we do? They're lost to us, sacrificed on the same altar as my dear Oliver. I *told* Harry, but she wouldn't listen. And old fool that I am, I didn't think she would involve Dorina. At least, not like that," he said when Evadne gave an incredulous snort. "I thought I could hide it from you girls . . . Dorina wanted to come so badly and as I'm your family's only London friend or relation . . ."

"None of that matters!" said Evadne, unwilling to be distracted by a broken man's handwringing, not now, of all times. The demon approved of this, even as it felt a bit wounded by Basil's allegations. "The time for regrets is over; we must act."

"You can't save them," he said. "Aren't you listening to me? I couldn't save Oliver . . ."

"I'm not you, and the situations are very different," she snapped. "I have to try—can't you see that? I can't just sit here and do nothing!"

"No. There will be no sitting. You must go home. Immediately. I'll escort you. We'll both go."

"Go! And leave them!"

"Wiser to leave. If they betray us—"

"*They* betray *us?*" Evadne shook her head, knowing she was the betrayer, not her sister. The demon reassured her, but she pushed aside its comfort. "You don't believe that, do you, uncle?"

"It doesn't matter," he said, deflecting her question.

"It does! Your friend is in trouble." He winced, turning his back on the painting; Evadne decided to appeal to his odd obsession with the image. "It's *his* sister, you know! And Dorina is your niece. She worships you—you know that, don't you? Maybe things have been strained between you of late . . . but she is seventeen. Things are strained between her and everyone who thinks she ought to have concerns beyond exactly what she wants to be concerned with."

"She made her choice," he said, looking down at his hands, avoiding Evadne's eyes.

"Of course it was a choice. What person her age, with her interests, would not choose glamour and novelty and intrigue over . . . over anything, really?" Evadne silently rebuked herself for not acknowledging this about Dorina's motivations before this very moment. "I can't believe you'd have me sit by just because . . . because what? You're frightened? Hurt? Angry at someone who can't respond or defend himself?"

Basil looked genuinely shocked, as well he might, but he said nothing. Evadne, finally sick to the teeth of her uncle—his attitude, his inaction, his moping and weeping—adjusted her grip on her sword with a wince, and pointed it at the face of Oliver Wotton. Her bandaged palm ached, but she kept the blade still.

"What would he want?" she asked, glad to see some display of dismay from her uncle at last. "Do you think he would have you sit by and let his sister be killed?"

"What would you have me do?"

"Do you have any ginger left?"

He shook his head, eyes flickering to the painting. "I put it in the paint. I didn't want it ..."

"The paint ..." She stared at the portrait, despairing. Such waste, such foolishness! "Then ... come with me. I need a distraction to keep them occupied while I sneak in the back ..." She trailed off as he looked at her with increasing incredulity. "I know it's dangerous, but they're your friends, and Dorina is—"

"They're *not* my friends!" he cried. "Perhaps they once were, but no longer. I have no need of them—look at them! They're a danger to themselves, and to me. I have everything I need in this house!" Once again, his eyes were drawn to the painting.

Evadne had finally had enough. Furious and frustrated, she slashed it in half with one swoop of the blade. The canvas made a satisfying ripping sound and then peeled apart, right through Lord Oliver's perfect face.

Basil rushed forward, pressing his fingertips to the ruined painting, trying to press the edges together. "Oliver!" he cried.

"It's *not* Oliver!" she shouted. "It's just a painting of him—a painting you made! It's not real!"

Dropping the sword, she tore the canvas from the frame. Pushing past her uncle's weak attempt to stop her, ignoring his entreaties to cease, she hurled the remnants into the fireplace. After a brief but intense flare of golden sparks, it was gone.

"You burned it," he said, kneeling before the blaze. He turned to her, his eyes wild and full of tears. "It was all I had left of him, and you burned it!"

"No!" Evadne knelt beside him, and putting her hands on his shoulders, shook him gently. "You have his sister; you have his friends; you have his memory! He is more a part of those things than any static image, no matter how lovely. And more importantly, you have *your life,* which you can choose to live, if you would only leave this sorrow behind you!"

After a long moment, Basil nodded, and rose. Was it just her imagination, or did he look better—steadier—already?

"Evadne," he said. "I'm sorry. I haven't been a good guardian, to you or to Dorina. Let me make it up to you. Tell me what you need."

Looking over him, Evadne decided it would likely be better to put him into some other role than "distraction." The man was an absolute wreck. Thankfully, she knew of someone who might be able to help . . . and he didn't live too far away . . .

"If I am successful tonight, we will need to get out of town, and quickly," she said, thinking of what she would likely have to do at Lady Henry's house, and with Trawless, when he woke up. "Go and get enough train fares for all of us, out of town. Is there anywhere you all discussed going, if something like this occurred?"

"Actually, yes," said Basil, his eyes focusing fully for perhaps the first time since she'd come to London. "I can do that. And pack some bags, with things we might need . . ."

"Good. Maybe it won't be necessary, but just in case."

"I'll see it done."

"I have to go," she said as she picked up the sword to find the demon anxious for her, urging her to extricate herself.

"Go, and be safe," said Basil. He did look better, and she smiled at him, grateful for his sincere encouragement. One brief nod, and she turned, heading into the night, to face she knew not what.

5

It is dangerous to traffic with demons, but only in danger can we really experience delight.

— *On the Summoning of Demons*

H ENRY HAD ALWAYS BEEN PLEASED that her parlor was among the most comfortable in London. The furniture had been built to her specifications — elegantly, of course, but her primary concern had been for it all to be plush and supportive. Unfortunately, she had not possessed the foresight to design it to accommodate persons with their hands tied behind their back and their ankles bound together. Every time she tried to adjust herself on her sofa she only managed to sink down farther and lose circulation somewhere else.

Not that her discomfort was her most pressing concern ... Walmsley — George Cantrell — that utter fiend, had dispatched his minion Bourne after getting them into the salon; the man was allegedly bringing back Evadne and one more of their number. It was intolerable, watching him and the one called Stockton shift tables and furniture and rugs so Cantrell could chalk some obscene diagram on her lovely mahogany floors, all while listening to the stomping they occasionally heard from upstairs, for the gorilla-like Reid and poor Jonas had not yet returned.

"What can they be doing?" Cantrell paused to look at his pocket watch. "I do hope your friend isn't attempting to dissemble with him. Reid has many excellent qualities but patience and understanding aren't among them."

Jonas, of course, knew exactly where the sword was. Something must be going on. Henry was worried about him; the only thing keeping her calm was the demonic presence in her mind. The massive dose of ginger from her dessert would keep her connected for a time, but it wouldn't last. It never lasted.

"I think it's time to fetch the servants," said Cantrell, getting up off his knees. He dusted his palms on his trousers, leaving inelegant white smears. "They should have drained well enough by now."

"Drained?" The sound of Dorina's voice, usually so delightful to Henry, made her heart sink. She ought to keep quiet. "Drained of what?"

"What do you think?" he asked, one eyebrow raised. "How many substances can be drained out of a body, you stupid girl?"

"You *killed* them?" Dorina looked horrified. Henry was astonished—Cantrell had betrayed them, ambushed them, bound them, and was clearly planning to murder them all to please his patron demon, and Dorina was surprised they'd dispatched her servants? "That's monstrous!" Her voice rose in both volume and pitch. "They were innocent!"

Cantrell picked up his cane from where he had set it against the wall, and turning it over in his hands a few times, walked to Dorina. Before she—indeed, before any of them realized what he might be thinking—the man struck Dorina on the kneecap sharply. The crack of the metal top against bone was nauseating; Dorina's answering shriek, heartrending. Henry lunged at Cantrell before she remembered she was bound like a rabbit, and fell to the floor, hard, on her face. She felt blood gush from her nose as pain blossomed.

"*Ungh,*" she mumbled, twisting herself to try to get onto her back, but then Cantrell was there, looming over her.

"That was foolish," he said. "The two of you are well matched. Or *were,* rather."

He picked her up. His strength was incredible; she felt like a doll in his arms as he lifted her and dumped her back onto the couch. She cried out—she couldn't help it. Her back hurt, her bones felt misaligned, her face was sticky with blood still flowing over her lips, but all she could think about was what his strike had done to poor Dorina, who was weeping, almost choking as she squirmed on her chair, tears running down her cheeks, into her mouth as she heaved and convulsed. She had failed Dorina. Differently than how she had failed Oliver, but she had doomed them both.

Mr. Seward apparently felt the same way. He couldn't even look at Dorina, or Henry. "I'm sorry, I'm sorry," he said, but Henry couldn't tell if it was to himself, or the rest of them.

"Yes, you really are. All of you. I played *you* like a fiddle, Mr. Seward . . . when I came into the bank, and later when I came in . . . Well, I don't like to tell tales out of school."

"You're disgusting," said Henry, desperate to reach out to Dorina, who was still whimpering in pain. The demon inside her told her it was helping the girl as much as it could, but that was little comfort to Henry. Her darling Dorina was in pain, and she could do nothing.

"And here I thought you approved of catamites," said Mr. Cantrell, eyes flickering to the weeping girl. "Or, whatever the feminine equivalent might be, I suppose."

Henry couldn't speak, she was so heartsick. Poor Mr. Seward, who had only acted in good faith.

Cantrell laughed. "Ah, but it's *such* fun to make the insufferably arrogant question themselves."

This she could not brook. "You think *I* am arrogant?" Henry's voice sounded thick in her ears, with the blood filling her nose. It hurt to speak, but she knew, too, that the longer she kept him talking, the longer she lived. She loved living so much . . .

"Unquestionably so. All of you, actually. When I joined your little group, you did not seem like discerning, mature aesthetes, but rather cliquish schoolchildren pretending at sophistication. It was awful, attending so many meetings . . . like experiencing Oxford all over again. You're just a lot of snobs who think you're better than everyone—assuring one another that the choices you've made are so rarified, so unique. Well, they're not. Anyone can do the things you do, as I have proven."

"All you have proven is that jealousy can consume a heart as a worm gnaws at an apple," said Mr. Seward. "You have not done what we have; you have given yourself wholly to hatred and rage. The power you think you have gained is an illusion."

Cantrell approached Mr. Seward, but did not strike him as he struck Dorina. Instead, he spat in his face.

"I pity you," said Henry as Cantrell turned his back on Mr. Seward, knowing well she might be opening herself to more ugliness, more violence.

"Oh?" Cantrell's amusement was unaffected.

"Yes," she replied. "I chose to walk this path out of a desire to experience more of the beauty of the world. It seems you take pleasure only in its horror and ugliness."

Cantrell actually looked annoyed by this. "Perhaps it is because I know something of horror and ugliness, whereas you—a pampered pedigreed bitch if ever I've seen one—have never suffered."

"You are mistaken," said Henry.

"Ah, Lord Oliver you mean," said Cantrell. "Yes, I can see how that would sting. And yet, I have known more of pain than you ever will. I have had to scramble and scrape for everything I have. Even before I met that which guides me now, I knew strength and power were the only two things that mattered—the strength to endure scorn, the power to overcome my opponents . . . and I was correct. Your guide through this world, meanwhile, encouraged you to laze about, staring at paintings . . . Where has that gotten you?"

Help will come, said the fading presence in Henry's mind. She marveled at this. From where? Of what sort?

Patience, it counseled, and said no more. That was probably for the best. She had no idea how much Cantrell might be able to divine. He had a demon within him, too, and other than strength she had no idea what abilities it had gifted him so that he might carry out its will.

A sharp knock at the door perked them all up. "Stockton," barked Cantrell. "Go see who that is. Bourne would just come in. Be careful."

Henry heard the door, then heard Stockton exclaim in surprise. Cantrell noticed, too, and turned to see the last person any of them were expecting. In fact, it took Henry a moment to recognize the fellow—it had been a long time since she'd seen him, and never in evening dress.

"What the deuce are *you* doing here?" said Cantrell.

"Stopping by to call on an old friend," said Mr. Perkins casually— *too* casually, for he just bowed to Henry instead of seeming alarmed that she was, after all, tied up and bloodied, sitting on a couch in her own salon with eight of her closest friends. "Good evening, Lady Henry. How are you?"

He'd known! But how had he known?

"I am well, Mr. Perkins," she said as evenly as she could manage. "Lovely to see you. How are you?"

"Oh, can't complain," he said. "Keeping fit."

"And the missus?"

"Stop that," snapped Cantrell. "Perkins, what—"

"*Mr.* Perkins, to you, George Cantrell," he said. "I must say, I'm surprised to find you here, along with another of my academy's finest. It seems rather a strange sort of party, though, doesn't it?" He looked around as if noticing the situation for the first time. "What is going on here? Seems awfully unkind not to offer the lady a handkerchief for that nose. Looks nasty—my apologies, my lady. I do not mean to imply your appearance is uncouth, merely my student's behavior."

"No apology necessary," she said as he walked over, handkerchief in hand, but Cantrell sprang between them.

"Stay away from her," he demanded. "What's your game, old man?"

"Old man?" Mr. Perkins chuckled as he tucked away his handkerchief. "Oh, George. There's no game. I really did just stop by on a whim. I was in the area, and—"

"How stupid do you think I am?" said Cantrell, looming over the smaller man. "Who told you we were here?"

Perkins turned his back on Cantrell as if the younger man were not armed and dangerous, and ambled toward the dry bar. "Lady Henry, might I help myself to a drink?"

"Of course," she said automatically.

He poured himself a whisky and shot a bit of soda into it. "Ah, that's better," he said, after taking a sip.

Henry was impressed. Mr. Perkins was brave—everyone who wasn't tied up in this room was armed, save him, unless he had a knife or firearm concealed on his person. That was entirely possible, but neither a pistol nor a dagger would be particularly effective against young, edgy, violent men with swords—especially ones who were also under the influence of a demon that granted them extra strength and speed.

Not that Mr. Perkins knew that. Or did he?

She was so nervous, craved a cigarette badly, eager for its steadying effects, but there was nothing for it. She would have to endure the early symptoms of withdrawal.

"I must say, George, I'm not entirely sure I approve of the ways you're using my teaching . . . tying up respectable citizens in their own homes. Where did you ever learn such disrespect? Such rudeness?"

He was stalling, Henry realized. Her demon, only a faint presence in her mind now, agreed. But why?

"Fencing is supposed to build a person's character," said Perkins, taking another sip. "I'm surprised at you. You've always been concerned about seeming gentlemanlike, and here you are—"

"Shut up!"

It was the first time she'd seen Cantrell angry that night. Something Mr. Perkins said had infuriated him. His face had gone beetroot red and he was now walking toward his master.

"How dare you," he snapped, pointing at the older man with his sword tip. "I'm as much of a gentleman as anyone!"

"Oh, I don't know about that," said Mr. Perkins amiably. "You see, George, *real* gentlemen aren't defined by where they go to school, or even where or to whom they were born. A real gentleman is revealed by his actions."

"Watch out!" screamed Dorina as Cantrell finally lunged—but it was unnecessary. Perkins sidestepped the incoming attack as nimbly as a man half his age and suddenly, impossibly, was behind George.

"No, a gentleman isn't defined by *where* he learns, but *what* he learns—just like a swordsman isn't defined by having a sword," said Mr. Perkins gaily.

The old man was enjoying himself! Henry was astonished by his composure, but felt despair as both of his students bore down on him, murder in their eyes. His bravado was impressive, but it would not save him.

It wouldn't save any of them.

6

The natural diabolist is he who can allow his impressions
to change.

— On the Summoning of Demons

I T HAD TAKEN SURPRISINGLY LITTLE effort to convince Mr.
Perkins to accompany Evadne to Curzon Street. She had despaired over needing to persuade him she was not mad, along
with getting him to agree to a possibly dangerous mission to rescue her sister and friends — but that hadn't proven to be the case.

"I warned Oliver that his peccadillo would endanger not only
him, but those he cared about," said Perkins as he changed. Evadne,
pacing nervously beyond the cracked door of his bedroom, paused.

"Peccadillo?" A horrible, anxious giggle escaped her throat. "Is
that really how you'd describe summoning a demon?"

"Yes, well," he said, coming out as he finished tying his white
tie, "when one teaches for as long as I have, especially the martial
arts, you meet people with all sorts of vices. I made a vow a long
time ago that as long as a potential student was honest, hard working, receptive, and not abusive or dangerous, I would teach them.
One of my best students was a prostitute, long ago; another had a
criminal past he was striving to put behind him. Neither of them,
to my mind, were unworthy of learning to fence — especially as
both of them volunteered the information when they became serious students."

Seeing Evadne's incredulous look, he smiled. "It happens all the
time. When a student truly commits to a master, they often feel

the need to bare their soul, submit themselves for judgment as a way of asking if they are worthy. When Oliver told me he was an occultist, I was inclined to laugh at first . . . but when I realized he was serious, I listened. I was shocked—and disinclined to believe him until he showed me a few, ah, *things* . . . But really, in the end it didn't seem like the sort of hobby that would disqualify him from learning, any more than him being a homosexual. Which is to say, not at all." Mr. Perkins frowned as he shrugged into his jacket. "I see now how unfortunate it was that I let my enthusiasm for talent color my judgment regarding George. We all make mistakes, but this one was inexcusable on my part."

Evadne was frowning, too. She was keenly aware that she, too, had made a grave mistake. She had let her attraction to George convince her that he was the teacher she'd longed for all her life; she saw now that Mr. Perkins would have been the wiser choice.

If she succeeded tonight—if she rescued her sister, and was able to continue taking lessons by virtue of being neither dead nor incarcerated, she would ask Mr. Perkins to teach her. It might even be worth living in London to learn from him.

This realization on her part allowed Evadne to focus on the task at hand, and they worked out the details of their plan as they trotted over to Curzon Street posthaste. Perkins would go through the front, stalling and distracting George and his gang as she snuck in through the servant's door to get to what she needed. After readying herself, she would come down, with an extra sword for her companion in case things got ugly—which they both agreed was likely, given who was there, and for what purpose.

"Two on three, with a possible fourth and fifth eventually," said Perkins, resigned, after the demon had relayed the situation to Evadne. "Not the best odds, but given that we are the two, it's not as bad as it could be. Especially if you're fighting using Oliver's style . . . That Chinese sword, in his hands, was one of the most effective weapons I've seen, and if you're in a position to replicate that . . ."

"We'll see" was all she could say before her throat closed up tight.

Lady Henry's house in Curzon Street was ablaze with light, and Evadne took a deep breath to try to calm herself. She said a final farewell to Mr. Perkins—hoping it was not really final—and she left him to go up the front stairs as she snuck down to the servants' entrance below street level. Those windows were dark, but fortunately the door was unlocked.

Less fortunately, the smell of blood made her gag as she stepped inside. As her eyes adjusted, she saw two bodies on the counter, heads hanging over the edge. Their throats had been slit, and the blood was dripping into buckets on the floor. Horrified, Evadne rushed through the kitchen, almost tripping in her desperate desire to get into the fresher air of the hall. There, she gave herself a moment to gulp several lungfuls and let her stomach settle.

The demon had told her that Reid was upstairs with Jonas, in Lord Oliver's old room, and the situation was not a safe one. Fearing for him, Evadne hurried upstairs. With her hurt hand, and knowing how strong Reid would be, she had decided to seek out the ginger reserve in Lady Henry's room first thing. But as she crept past Lord Oliver's door, she heard a sickening thud, as of a fist striking flesh, and a moan. She hesitated before turning the handle, readying herself, then eased the door open.

Jonas was on the floor, his arms tied behind his back, crushed painfully beneath him as Reid sat on his chest. He was winding up for another punch to Jonas's already bloodied face.

"Where is it?" he asked as Jonas wheezed through bruised lips. "Where is the sword? I know you know!"

"The sword is right here!" cried Evadne, horrified. "If you want it so much, fight *me* for it!"

Reid fell off Jonas, surprised, and Jonas curled onto his side, coughing. Scrambling to his feet, Reid got his rapier in hand and pointed it at her.

"The dried-up virgin comes to save the fat fop," he sneered. "What a mess you are—all of you!"

"Be that as it may, I *will* save him," said Evadne.

Her hand hurt, but she tightened her grip on the sword as the demon urged her to wait and watch. She obeyed. Observing Reid's face, his stance, she saw he was spoiling for a fight. He would make mistakes. He always did in class when he got hot or excited, and he was never genuinely angry then.

Reid charged her, feet slapping on the carpet. Trusting in the sword, she listened to it. Like the first time she'd used it in this very bedroom, it told her what to do. Up came her arm, and she deflected Reid's sloppy strike, sending him staggering past her. She turned, now facing his retreating figure, and with a little hop got herself close enough to slash him across his back. He howled and swung around, spraying her with blood, stabbing wildly at her. His motions were so big, so clumsy, that she easily avoided his blade.

Unfortunately, she hadn't thought he would fight dirty—they'd only dueled in class, after all—and so she didn't anticipate the left hook that hit her in the ribs. It dropped her. Her abdomen was already sore from Trawless's assault, and Reid was the strongest of their group. Aided by demonic influence, the power behind his fist was annihilating. As she staggered back several steps before collapsing, she was certain she felt something crack inside her. It was a struggle to stand while he stomped over to her, but she kept trying, her vision blurred from tears.

Her eyes fell on Jonas, who was in a sort of fetal position, arms still tight behind his back. Even so, he was looking at her. Through the bruises and blood, he smiled at her, and it was like stepping into a warm bath. She smiled back, and the surprise and joy in his eyes at her acknowledgment stiffened her resolve to finish the fight—and walk away from it.

She got to her feet, and raised her sword.

"You should have stayed down," said Reid, advancing.

"You should yield while you can still speak," she replied. "You will not win this fight."

Reid charged again. Dizzy from pain, Evadne knew she had to settle this quickly. His sword flashed, but hers sang in her hand. His strike was slapdash; her parry opened his chest to her, and she got her blade around quickly to stab him through the stomach. Two left fingers pressed to the pommel helped her push it all the way through his flesh.

This time, he dropped—to his knees, eyes wide as the light went out of them. She withdrew her blade, and he fell face-down, black blood pooling around him, soaking the carpet.

"Jonas," she said, racing to his side. "Are you all right?"

"Miss Gray," he mumbled, and she smiled. Even now, he was so polite. "You have my thanks. Untie me, and we . . ."

"We nothing. You need to rest." She cut free his arms, and he winced as he pushed himself into a seated position, rubbing the blood back into his hands. "You're in no condition to help me, and anyway, I have help. Is the key to Lady Henry's safe in your shoe chest?"

"What? Yes, how did you . . ." Jonas looked at her. "You're in touch with it!"

"Yes, and I plan to be in closer contact soon. It's the only way I'll be able to defeat them. That's the other reason you must stay away from the fight. Uncle Basil, he's getting train tickets so we can get out of town if . . . ah, depending on what happens." Jonas was staring at her in the most curious way, as if she had done something marvelous instead of simply fumbling her way through everything, trying to make things right after betraying him and his friends.

The intensity of his expression startled her; she wondered why she had never noticed how very handsome he was. Even bruised and bloodied, there was a pleasant elegance in his features. But she could not get lost in his wide eyes. Not now. She was here for more than just him.

"You can sneak out the back," she said crisply. "Then get to Basil, so if things go wrong, someone will know what happened."

"Miss Gray." Those were the words he said, but his tone spoke volumes more. "I will do as you ask."

"I have to go," she said. After squeezing his trembling hand with her good one, she gathered up her sword and Reid's heavier rapier, and left him. When she turned back, he was still sitting on the floor, bleeding freely from one nostril, but he looked happier than she had ever seen him.

Evadne knew it was ridiculous that even now, when the best chance for her and her sister's liberty and survival lay inside Jonas's bedroom, she had a hard time with this part of her task. Even if she had his blessing, it just seemed so invasive.

Once inside, she noted the perfectly made bed with crisp white linens and blue-and-gold-patterned duvet. Hurrying, she fetched the candle from his bedside table and after getting it lit went into his closet. The tidiness of it all made her smile, just for a moment. And the smell of his cologne . . . She inhaled, in spite of herself.

Poor Jonas, whom she had totally written off after his unfortunate quip in the National Gallery—well, and due to his choice of friends. Both reasons for pushing him away had been unfair. Especially the Athena remark . . . He hadn't intended to remind her of something he couldn't have known about in the first place. What a fool she had been!

The demon in her mind pointed out a low wooden chest, and she set down the candlestick and swords to open it, removing shoes pair by pair until it was clear. She felt around the edges of the container until she found a slight lip; pulling it up, she discovered a cache of all sorts of things. A cleverly made wooden boat, interesting coins from several nations, a few letters, and other odds and ends . . . a child's horde in a tuck-box, save for its meticulous organization and the absence of things like a coil of string and an old wad of chewing gum. It made her smile as she sifted through it, searching for a key, but when she recognized his copy of the museum guide she'd purchased for them all that fateful day, her smile disappeared. She picked it up, and turning it over in her hands, finally accepted what her sister had said and Jonas had tried to tell her: he cared for her.

He'd never desired anything from her other than friendship, never wanted her to be anyone other than herself. Why had she never seen that about him, never recognized it? Silly, how she'd been so eager for George's attention, and now she knew he'd never cared for her, not really. He'd only seen her as a means to an end.

Deliberately setting aside the museum guide, as well as her bruised heart, Evadne located the small key. Tucking it into her jacket, she left Jonas's room without cleaning up after herself— plenty of time for that later, if necessary—feeling very confused indeed.

Evadne found a carton of cigarettes in Lady Henry's safe, which she ignored. She'd never in her life tried tobacco, and filling her lungs with smoke just before facing down several expert swordsmen seemed foolish. Better to her mind were the candies, though the idea of swallowing some enormous amount of sugary sweets didn't sound much better. Her stomach rolled at the thought.

A small tin at the back held the likeliest candidate—powdered dried ginger. The only issue Evadne had with this was quantity. A candy, a cigarette . . . she had seen Lady Henry and Dorina dose themselves, she realized that now. But as for her, she had no tolerance built up in her blood, no defenses. It seemed too risky to swallow a bunch of demonically infused ginger powder without having any idea what it might do.

She would just have to take the risk, see it through. Perkins couldn't stall forever. She licked her finger, and dipping it into the powder, sucked it clean. Nothing happened immediately, so she dipped her finger in again, trying not to worry about time, or dose. She needed—

Ah. Reality intensified around her as the presence formed its first real words in her mind, not just sensations and images. *Good. They need you. George tires of Perkins. He is eager to begin his ritual.*

How many of them are there?

Still only two. Bourne is absent, and the one he was sent to fetch.

She stood, ready to face her fate, but it bid her wait.

Take more ginger. If you do, you will go into this with gifts given by your connection to me, it assured her. *As I said, there will be a price . . . but I assure you, you will go into this fight as strong as they are, if in different ways.*

I hope you're not referring to strength of character was her wry reply.

She felt its delighted laugher. *No indeed. There is strength in beauty—in swiftness and cunning, in subtlety and in grace, Evadne.*

Evadne recalled the sword form, the way the blade had moved, felt like an extension of her arm, and understood. She nodded.

How much must I take?

Quite a bit. An image of her putting several spoonfuls of the powder into a glass of water filled her mind. She headed to Lady Henry's attached bath and after finding a cup, started shaking powder into the bottom. *And I would suggest you take some with you,* it said as she worked, *in case you need to reinvigorate yourself. If you can stomach them, the candies will be more easily consumed.*

A little pick-me-up, eh?

It agreed.

I don't usually like candy, or ginger for that matter, but I see your point.

You ought to get used to it, it advised her. *After this ordeal, if you survive, you will always need a little.*

The *if* didn't bother her, but the *always* did. For the first time, she balked.

But Basil—

Never took this much, not all at once, not for this sort of thing. I am only telling you the truth, Evadne. I would not lie to you.

She heard a shout, faintly echoing up from somewhere deep within Lady Henry's house. It pushed her to her decision, and as she gulped the spicy, gritty concoction, she knew she would have chosen the same thing if she'd been given all the time in the world.

The warm taste of the ginger spread out over her tongue, coating her throat like butter on hot bread. She swallowed, and felt it bleeding into her, hitting her stomach lining like a glass of wine. The change it effected was as astonishing as it was instantaneous. Evadne felt her body *shift,* and she looked down at her own trembling hand. She saw through her own skin to the bones beneath, the muscles and tendons that held and pulled, and identified microscopic adjustments she could make to hold a sword yet more effectively. The vision was too much for her, and she had to look away, but her hand remembered when she picked up the sword.

She smiled.

Good, said the demon.

Her legs, too, she found were different. Her first few steps were wobbly, but once she figured out how to move, she found they were springier, more fluid. Yes—that was the word for it, her entire body felt like a liquid, able to melt into an ideal shape or form at will. *Her* will. The suppleness was intensely pleasurable; she was almost glad there was a reason to abandon her experimentation and do something productive. Otherwise, she might have lost herself, forever, deep within the warm waters of this sea of sensation.

Hurry, the demon urged her. *Your friends are in danger.*

"I'm hurrying," she muttered under her breath as she padded along the hall and down the stairs as quickly as she could, her legs supple as a cat's tail and silent as an owl in flight.

"I must be getting old," she heard Mr. Perkins say as she rounded the corner. "I never noticed how slipshod your footwork was, Stockton."

"A pity, too," Evadne announced, "as it's *so* fundamental."

Mr. Perkins was the only one who was expecting her, and he had wisely kept himself by the door of the salon. Without anyone in her way she was at his side in an instant. She noted the locations of the many immobilized bodies strewn about the edges of the room, on elegant Chinese-inspired couches and settees that circled an awful symbol drawn on the center of the floor, but she did not allow herself to look upon the faces of those whose lives depended on her success. She could not think of them as individuals right now, to do so would be a distraction she could not abide. In a way, they did not matter. What mattered was handing Perkins the sword and springing away to give him room to swing it.

"Evadne?" cried Dorina. Strangely, she sounded more dismayed than overjoyed to see her sister coming to her rescue.

George, too, was less than pleased. "How did you—where is Trawless? Where is Bourne?"

"I know nothing of Bourne. I defeated Trawless, and left him behind. Let them go, George, or you will force me to defeat you, too." Her voice had a strange quality to it, to her own ears—more resonant, more sibilant.

George was not impressed. "No," he said. "Why should I? You might not be outnumbered, for now, but you're certainly outclassed."

"Neither numbers nor experience will help you if you choose to fight me." The words were coming out of her, unbidden. She assumed the demon was speaking through her—she certainly had no practice making pretty speeches. She wasn't surprised; it was with her, inside her, a part of her—many times had she seen Lady Henry's parlor, but it had never looked like *this*. The golden wallpaper gleamed brighter than a saint's halo, and the trees painted upon it seemed to sway in an uncanny but clement breeze. The birds and monkeys also had the appearance of life; they rustled and shifted as if she were really in a garden somewhere, surrounded by nature and life and beauty, instead of a London townhouse where the dead were growing colder above and below where she stood.

"And you telling me you love me won't help you when I kill you along with the rest of this trash," said George. "I can tell you've gone over to the other side, Gray. Your death will only make me more powerful, when it comes."

She blushed to hear her words thrown back at her—even if she knew they had been a lie, those around her did not. But that scarcely mattered, not now. The time for pride was past.

She stepped forward, readying her blade, the tip pointed down.

"It's *Miss* Gray, if you don't mind," she said crisply.

It was then that George noticed the sword, and it was his turn to go red. She took a savage pleasure in his anger—even though she had never intended to lie to him about it, it pleased her to see he thought she had.

"I *will* succeed, and I *will* take that sword from you, *Miss* Gray," he snarled, jabbing at it with his own rapier. "You little liar—you had it the whole time!"

"I never said I didn't," she replied, actually smiling now. She had hurt him! It was a bit of her own back, at least. "It's just that by the time we got down to specifics, you'd already revealed yourself to be a liar and a cad."

"And *you're* a murderer!" Bourne barged into the room, and Evadne froze. "Trawless is dead," he said to George, whose face contorted in rage. "She bashed in his skull!"

Dead? She hadn't meant to do that. Reid had been necessary, but she'd thought she'd merely left Trawless unconscious . . .

"I had no choice!" she cried, to herself as much as anyone else.

Perkins finally spoke. "George! I'm *begging* you: give this up. Release these people—this is madness!"

Just then, something dripped onto George's aquiline nose from above. He wiped at it, and stared at the red smear on his fingertips in confusion. Then slowly, so slowly, he looked up.

Another drop of blood fell on him, from a stain above his head.

"Reid," he breathed, and looked to Evadne.

"Reid!" cried Bourne, and he charged her. It was a desperate move, but no feint. Aware Stockton was close behind her, Evadne slipped to the side, and instinct took over. Her blade was up before he reached her; her feet were in the right place, as if by magic.

Maybe it was, or something similar at least.

While always more confident with a sword in her hand, tonight Evadne felt different, as if she was observing and directing herself. But she was directing Bourne, too — she saw what he intended before he knew it himself, as though his motions were choreography in a play she'd seen a thousand times. A graceful upward swing of her blade sent his flying wide — away from Perkins — before her opponent could even react. Before she'd even realized *she'd* acted.

She did note Perkins's impressed look, but their eyes met for only a second — Stockton was charging toward him from one direction, George from the other, and Evadne had to go in for her riposte before Bourne recovered.

Her mind was focused; and her body was wholly responsive to her will and the tainted ginger coursing through her veins. With a lunge, she dipped below Bourne's windmilling arm and swept the Chinese blade upward. Bourne screamed as blood poured out of a thin vertical cut across his jacket and plastron. His chest was split open. It wasn't a deep wound, but it was a nasty one.

Bourne staggered back, but only for a moment; he got his sword back up faster than he ever did in class to go for her again, twice as ferocious this time. She despaired, wondering if this berserker's ability to ignore pain was a gift from his supernatural benefactor. If it had conferred such a boon upon them all, she and Perkins were doomed. Momentarily alarmed, she stepped back, but bumped into the arm of a sofa where two of Lady Henry's friends lay, bound and miserable. One said something to her as she silently cursed parlors and all their furniture, but she didn't hear what it was. She was listening to another voice.

Don't despair, the demon was urging her. *Use your environment. They will use force and anger; we will use everything else.*

Focus returned. She jumped, boosting herself with her left arm. For a brief moment she was flying, or at least jumping higher than possible, but her altered awareness of her body guided her muscles; her altered senses, her feet. One touched the arm of the sofa; the other, she placed on the blade of his rapier. Only for a moment —he cried out, her full weight tugging on his arm, but before he could collapse she stepped forward onto Bourne's forehead. She came down behind him, light on her feet. Whirling, blade upright and held close to her own chest, she sank down into her stance before he could even turn around, and lunged. Bourne screamed as she drove the blade through his back, sliding it between his ribs and into his heart, her left arm out behind her to steady her. The smell of ordure filled Evadne's nostrils. He was dead.

She yanked on her blade, but it was stuck in his meat. She kicked him off it with her right foot, and then turned while he fell limply to the floor. To her surprise, when she turned, she saw that she did not need to rush to Perkins's side to help —George, Stockton, and Mr. Perkins were all staring at her, motionless, mouths open.

She cherished the astonishment in George's expression, but it quickly turned to rage; she had, after all, taken out three of his acolytes all by herself—and while they were at their strongest. It was now down to two against two, much better odds than Mr. Perkins had predicted.

"How dare you," snarled George. "Tonight, of all nights!"

To Evadne's surprise, George did not go for her, but for his own master. Evadne cried out, but Perkins had his blade up and deflected the strike. His grim look and surprised grunt spoke to George's strength.

Perkins did something to free himself and danced back. He knew as she did that the best thing to do in a fight was to simply not get hit, but she knew he couldn't hold out alone against George forever. But he had to, at least until she took care of Stockton, who was now coming for her.

Popping a few candies into her mouth to suck on, Evadne brought her sword up and focused on her new opponent. As Perkins battled his star student, she found herself similarly engaged.

Stockton was a good fencer, but he miscalculated with his first attack, giving Evadne a good opening to press the advantage. She slithered closer and he roared as the tip of her sword caught him in the right armpit. Blood blossomed from the wound and he dropped his weapon. Fear came into his eyes when he looked at her, and Evadne felt her resolve to kill yet another man falter.

Her blade dipped down, even as her instincts and the demon within her screamed at her *get it up, get it up*. Then she heard the crash of steel on steel and her eyes tracked to where Perkins was fighting for his life against George.

They would not stop, so she couldn't.

"Don't," she said as Stockton's eyes went back to the rapier on the ground.

Stockton either heard the change in her voice or saw it in her eyes as Evadne raised her blade. He panicked, and turned to run, but in his haste he stepped without looking. The slipshod footwork Perkins had earlier noticed came back to haunt them both. He crashed into his master's right side, knocking the older man off balance.

"No!" screamed Evadne, but it was too late. It was the opening George needed. As Perkins shoved off the dead weight, his blade went down and George's went up—and through the older man's throat. Blood gushed as George pulled back, and Perkins went to his knees, gasping like a fish as Stockton collapsed atop him.

Move!

At the demon's prompting, Evadne realized she'd frozen again, staring in horror at the pile of limbs and blood, listening to Perkins rattle out his last.

Stockton was stirring, covered in gouts of his master's lifeblood. That he should be groaning while poor brave, wonderful Mr. Perkins lay there, no longer making any noise at all, brought her back to herself.

"You will not take any more lives tonight," she said, stepping back into a low stance as her arm curved up to bring the blade level with George's eyes.

"That isn't for you to decide," he said, sounding almost bored. "Get up, Stockton, you useless sack!"

He scrambled up, grabbing his sword before she could stop him. No matter—Evadne's eyes were dry; her muscles were warm. She felt the universe swirling around her like a cloud of golden dust, but saw nothing other than what she had to do. She knew Lady Henry and her friends were cheering her on, but she didn't register more than their sense of hope. Her ears only heard what her opponents were saying; her eyes saw only what they were doing.

She was ready.

As she ran at them, she decided to duel George first. He was the more dangerous of the pair, and she needed to take him out, if she could.

It was not to be. Stockton had put himself to her left. George did something with his blade, but it was an obvious feint. Shimmering between the two men, she spun around, sword extended, to slice at them both in one move. Stockton ducked; George jumped away. She'd drawn no blood, but she'd achieved her goal of further separating them. That was good, but now she had to make the same choice a second time: which to go for first.

Stockton made her decision for her, rushing in quickly enough that the tip of his rapier grazed her cheek as she bent backwards, her spine popping musically from the dramatic curve. Her face alight with pain and her stomach muscles screaming as she pulled herself upright, she leaned into her own riposte and slashed across Stockton's middle. It was a hastily considered gambit, but it worked. He howled as she opened his belly, then stopped howling when she slashed him again, marking him like a hot cross bun.

He fell back, but she did not watch what he did. George was now behind her, and she whirled, just barely blocking his attack.

"You've learned well, Miss Gray," he said, pushing her backwards and away. She went flying back, almost losing her balance. She silently thanked the demon that steadied her, guided her. George's strength was incredible, even compared to that of his compatriots. She would not have been able to stand against him without its help.

George pressed his advantage, striking again with terrifying power. She blocked him, but the vibrations along the blade of her sword made her arm go numb. A cross-body block and her shoulder burned like a fire. "You do realize what you have done tonight will only lead to your death?"

"Only," she gasped as she parried another strike, "if you win!"

He wasn't even winded. He jabbed viciously at her; she deflected it, but the point of his rapier sank into her thigh and she felt the leg go weak.

"Your success tonight indicates overdose, if I am any judge," he said. "As you were already—though very slightly—conditioned to receive the sacrament of my far more effective demon, you will certainly perish. I hope you still think it was worth it to defy me."

"Standing against wickedness is always worthwhile," she said, driven back another step by another strike.

"Wickedness! I'm no different from you, Miss Gray. We both now serve a master. Mine is simply greater than yours."

Evadne made the choice to give up ground to try to recover for a final charge. Her leg was wobbling; she would not last much longer against this juggernaut of power and rage. The demon within her tried to soothe her, but there was only so much it could do. Her body was working hard; she needed to dose herself again. Voluntarily retreating, she groped for her candies until the bag crinkled beneath her fingers.

"You're trying to frighten me," she said, before ripping into the package with her teeth and getting as many sweets in her mouth as she could.

"No, Miss Gray. I'm trying to kill you."

She felt nothing but scorn for this man. Perhaps it was the demon. Perhaps it was learning all at once how completely he had betrayed her. Perhaps it was knowing she was the only one who could save her sister. Whatever it was, George had no power over her—not anymore. With confidence, she raised her blade and saluted him as if it were an epee and they were just having a lesson together, as they had at the academy.

George smiled, mocking her by not answering her salute but instead withdrawing his box of pastilles. Flipping open the lid with his thumbnail, he knocked back a few before casting the rest aside; they bounced away over the floor.

"Foolish girl!" he croaked. One had lodged in his throat. "You didn't have to die like this, you know."

"I won't," agreed Evadne, and charged.

Her feet weren't her own; her arms belonged to something neither human nor divine. It felt as if gravity did not affect her as much as she expected it to. She felt guided, directed; all she had to do was give herself over—or rather give over everything she had, bone and blood, muscle and memory, determination and discipline.

Her first thrust was simply a test, to see what he would do. She thought he would counterattack, but he just blocked her. He didn't need to do more. When their blades met, it was like hitting a wall —well, a wall that kicked like a mule, for his parry tore something deep within her shoulder as it sent her spinning away. All the demon could do was help her cope with the pain.

"You stupid girl," he said, advancing on her. "You really thought you could beat me in a fight?"

She shook her head. "Never," she gasped, her arm bright with terrible sensation.

His blade met hers again, and not only did her muscles scream as they weakened yet further, it felt like the bones in her arm were cracking. She desperately wanted more ginger, but sensed—and the demon confirmed—that she was putting her survival at risk if she consumed any more. Once again, a quick end to this fight was her only chance of winning it.

George was ruthless, going in again before she had recovered. Desperate, she disengaged her blade with a sweep and looked around to see what she could use against him. She fled, tipping a table in his path, shattering a vase at his feet. It scarcely slowed him. He was on her again in the blink of an eye, his sword falling on her time and again as if she were an anvil and he wielded a hammer.

She couldn't take much more of this. His strikes were getting progressively heavier, but they were less frequent.

He's tired, said the demon. She agreed. As to how to take advantage of it, she did not yet know.

She watched him as he struck her yet again, and saw how stiffly he now held himself. He was a machine. One bent on killing her, but still a machine.

Not her. She was a living, breathing, thinking creature, a luminous being not bound by reality.

"*Oh,*" moaned Evadne, blocking yet another blow and staggering back more than she needed, clutching dramatically at her injured shoulder.

George grinned. "Surrender," he said. "You can't outlast me, Miss Gray, but you *can* choose to live."

"I choose," she gasped, gathering herself as she pulled an agonized face, "to defend my sister!"

He only laughed, and charged.

She waited, watched. Only when he was close enough to stab her did she move, stepping with her uninjured leg into a far wider lunge than she could have managed had the demonic ginger not turned her body into malleable jelly. But even that could only do so much for her. Tendons ripped as her muscles screamed; she shifted her weight, actually dipping between George's legs. Jabbing upward, Evadne sent the blade through the underside of his stomach. It stopped in his spine; she had not the strength to drive it farther.

She didn't need to. Abandoning the blade, Evadne fell as her legs gave out from under her. He collapsed atop her, twitching, impossibly heavy.

"You've made a grave mistake," he said through a mouthful of blood, his eyes dimming. "It will find you. *We* will find you. I am not its only servant, and now you've revealed yourself . . ."

She pulled herself out from under him, and scrambling to her feet, she ripped the blade from his body. She felt it widen the incision, and his eyes popped open in surprise and pain. Blood gushed from the bottom of his guts, but she paid him no mind, just cleaned the blade on his shirt and left him there.

She'd killed five men in one night. She had no energy left to feel anything about it. As for the demon inside her, it felt no remorse. Only a sense of satisfaction at the sublime execution of its will—and gratitude to her for saving its servants.

Coming back to herself, Evadne slowly straightened and looked around for the first time to see her sister and her colleagues. She found them looking at her with expressions ranging from admiration to astonishment. Dry-mouthed, she knew not what to say.

"I'm so sorry," she croaked. It seemed like the best choice, under the circumstances.

"Why are you sorry?" said a small, rather satyric man with a Germanic accent.

"I betrayed you," she said, astonished.

"I believe you *saved* us, Evadne," said Lady Henry.

"I'd like to be untied, however," suggested another woman.

"Of course." Evadne turned to the person closest to her.

It was Dorina.

"My hero," her sister said as Evadne cut her free. There was no irony, no mockery in Dorina's words. Evadne smiled at the younger girl, helping her to her feet, but then her body seemed to melt away—or perhaps it re-formed into what it had been before. She felt her awareness of the demon fade as she became more cognizant of how her body felt, and it did not feel good. She was keenly aware of her shoulder wound, and her leg muscles were as fragile as wet paper. She could barely walk, and her arms were not strong enough to hold the sword. It clattered to the ground as she collapsed.

"Evadne!" shrieked Dorina. "Are you all right?"

Evadne shook her head. She was too busy trying not to vomit to speak. The demon expressed a sincere regret at what she was experiencing, but could do nothing for her. Embarrassing tears leaked from her eyes as Dorina cradled her in her slender arms.

"Rest," she said. "I'll get the others free."

Evadne nodded.

"I have to say," said one of the men, "that was the worst evening I've spent in a long while."

"My apologies," said the German. "It was not the program I intended . . ."

"It could have been worse," said Lady Henry sternly. "No lasting damage done, at least not to any of us. As for our savior . . ."

It pained Evadne to be referred to as such when she was the cause of so much death and pain. She moaned, shaking her head.

"*Shh.*" It was Dorina; she had returned. Even with the diminishing potency of the demonic ginger in her blood, the sight of Dorina alive, and smiling, was the most exquisite thing Evadne had ever seen in her life.

"We must be gone from here," said Lady Henry. She was just across the room, but it sounded to Evadne as if she were very far away. "We cannot stay here even tonight—who knows what the neighbors heard, and he said there were others . . ."

"I told . . . Basil . . . to pack things. Just in case," Evadne managed.

"Very thoughtful," said Lady Henry. Evadne winced again at the sincerity in the lady's voice. The woman was very possibly on the brink of losing everything she had in the world, and she genuinely seemed to appreciate what Evadne had done to remedy her error.

"I'm so sorry," she said, to herself, and then to her sister. "Dorina . . . can you forgive me?"

"*I'm* the one who should apologize," said Dorina, running her cool fingers over Evadne's aching brow. The others were getting to their feet, stretching, but Evadne had eyes only for her sister. "I doubted your love."

This seemed entirely reasonable to Evadne. "Why wouldn't you?"

"You've never given me a single reason to, not really. That's why. I'm so sorry, Evadne . . . After I mocked you, belittled you for your passion . . . without it, we'd . . . we'd all . . ." She wiped a tear from her eye. "You were magnificent. And if you hadn't spent all that time practicing . . . I'm no expert, but that man, those men I mean, they all seemed like very good fencers indeed." Evadne would have laughed, but it hurt to move. "What I mean to say is . . . maybe you told Mr. Cantrell about us, but he would have come for us one day, regardless. He told us so. Really, your fencing . . . it *saved* us. All of us. You couldn't have done it if you hadn't been you. Thank you."

Evadne closed her eyes as tears spilled over her cheeks. She was astonished at herself. Mr. Perkins lay dead on the floor, and the corpses of the five men she'd slain were not yet cold. Her body was ruined and yet she felt insanely, deliriously happy. Dorina had just said, unasked, the only thing Evadne had ever wanted to hear.

EPILOGUE

Those who find ugly meanings in beautiful things are corrupt without being charming. This is a fault. Those who find beautiful meanings in beautiful things are the cultivated. For these there is hope. They are the elect to whom beautiful things mean only Beauty.

—*Oscar Wilde*

ONE YEAR LATER

NEARLY TWO HUNDRED MILES from London, the little community nestled in the green hills outside Wath-on-Dearne was thriving.

The kitchen garden, overseen by Lady Henry, was nothing short of extraordinary. It was high summer, and cucumbers were bursting from their vines. Summer squash was abundant, as were the asparagus, peas, beans, strawberries, and cabbage. The tomatoes were ripening on the vines, and the potatoes under the earth. Lady Henry had never grown crops such as corn or wheat, but her extensive knowledge of root, leaf, and stem had served her well. If the yield was as grand as she expected, next year she had designs on brewing and distilling for the community.

As for preserving the less potable portions of their crop, Miss Travers, in spite of her years writing a women's column, had proven herself to be a terrible homemaker. While she was fantastic at carding and knitting the wool from the few sheep and goats they'd purchased (Dr. Sauber had been a herder in his youth, and had been happy to jump back into the role), Mr. Blake and Mrs. Hill had taken over the kitchen, canning what Lady Henry grew so that they might have fruit and vegetables to enjoy during the winter and early spring. Mr. Seward kept the accounts, and Mrs. Dhareshwar inventoried what was brought in and went out.

It wasn't just in these ways that they were doing well. Mr. Seward had at one time been apprenticed to a carpenter, and remembering the skill had made several improvements to the sprawling but picturesque farmhouse in which they all now dwelt. Through enthusiasm and diligence he had improved so much over the last year that he was thinking of adding a second barn so that they could start keeping cows along with their goats, sheep, and placid workhorse that Dorina had improbably named Pegasus. He also wanted to improve the chicken coop so they could accommodate a larger flock. And Mr. Blake, when not busy in the kitchen, had adorned the plain walls of the common rooms with beautiful murals, and all the bedrooms and the parlor had Basil's paintings to ornament them.

Paintings new and old, for Basil was working again. The change of scenery and pace had done him well. He was more cheerful, more engaged since the destruction of his lover's portrait, and his newer works—while still darker in tone than those he used to paint before Lord Oliver's passing—suggested hope as well as death.

Jonas had felt a bit useless for a time, given that everyone else had some hidden talent or skill that added to the community, but soon enough he'd realized that bringing people what they needed, when they needed it, was as noble an occupation as any other. To that end, he could always be found concocting cooling or warming beverages, and delivering them at the very moment someone breathed a sigh and sat back from their labors, or fetching a shady hat or extra sweater when it was needed.

Evadne had not known most of these people before that fateful night, and felt enormous guilt over their needing to pick up and move on her account. Or as Dorina would insist, on account

of needing to disappear after the assault by George and his associates. Dorina, of course, had known them well, and when Evadne
asked, a few months into their new situation, her sister had sworn
to Evadne that in spite of their different circumstances, everyone
was just as happy at Innisfree—a name that had occurred to Miss
Travers not long into their residency—as they had been in London. Differently happy, to be sure, but still happy.

This pleased the demon that yet lived in Evadne's mind more
than it pleased her, but she had come to accept both her guilt and
the obvious pleasure of those who surrounded her. Today, as she
and Dorina sat together in Lady Henry's rose garden, the bees
buzzing about them and the breeze casting spent blossoms into
the grass, she thought back on that conversation . . . and smiled.

Dorina was sprawled on a blanket, making tea, her bad leg out
to the side. It had healed, after George Cantrell's knocking it so
badly, but she carried it differently. It didn't matter; to Evadne's
mind, she looked lovelier than she ever had in the loose, comfortable caftans she wore now that she needed a bit of extra mobility.

Evadne was also dressed for comfort rather than style, but that
had always suited her. Wrapped in blankets, though the day was
warm, she nestled deep in the wheeled wicker chair she made use
of on days when her legs didn't seem to want to carry her very far.

"Dorina," she said, the new low, husky rasp of her voice still a
surprise to her ears, "I miss our parents."

"I do too," admitted Dorina. "I wish we could have let them
know where we'd gone. They must be *so* worried. But . . ." She
sighed. "We're not the only ones who gave up our families, and we
all made a pact . . ."

In the wake of that terrible night, they had retreated to Basil's
house—but only temporarily. With Evadne having slain five men,
and George's alleging that others would come, and soon, they had
all agreed to disappear.

They had spent only enough time in London to withdraw the

money from their accounts—Mr. Seward's influence as a banker was terribly helpful with that aspect of their departure—and no one went out in public, save to collect what they could from their homes without it being too evident they were planning to be absent for more than a few days. Heirlooms had been left, art abandoned, wardrobes pared down into only what could be easily packed. Miss Travers had managed to bring her five cats, which had yowled all the way on the train—but they, too, had settled in nicely, and grown fat and sleek on the rats in the barn.

"How badly do you resent me for taking you from them? Our parents, I mean?" asked Evadne softly.

Dorina handed her a cup of tea. "Not at all. You know, Evadne, I wouldn't change a thing about you, save for your insisting on saddling yourself with the responsibility for us being here in Wath-on-Dearne. *I* chose to pursue Henry. *I* chose to join her—to join with . . . well. And while it makes me a bit of a monster, I admit I'm happier than I've ever been." She looked serious for a moment, but it only gave her a quiet dignity. "I never thought I could be happy, living in the country, away from London . . . but as it turns out, I've found *peace*. And really, it is possible that one day, I'll— *we'll*—be able to visit them, visit London. Just not now. Harry says we must give it time."

Evadne sipped at her tea, spiced lightly with ginger. It soothed her throat, eased the pains coming back into her joints.

"Time," she mused. "I wonder how much I have left."

Evadne knew she still looked the same. She was, at first glance, a woman of not quite thirty years. But the longer she looked at herself—or anyone else looked at her, for that matter—the more it became evident that *something* was wrong. It was impossible to avoid the impression that she was older, far older than she would be by any conventional reckoning. And it wasn't just her appearance—she *felt* like an old woman most days, too.

When it became apparent just how much she had damaged herself that night, Evadne had felt humiliated. She valued strength, but she could now barely walk without assistance; she craved independence and was now forced to rely on others. And for the rest of her life, this was how she would be.

But soon enough she found there was no need to feel embarrassed. Asking for help when she needed it was a form of strength, and needing that help did not mean she wasn't independent.

"You mustn't think about things like how much time you have," said Dorina. "Why, any of us might have only an hour left—lightning might strike me dead here as we speak, for example. The important thing is to live happily, *beautifully,* every moment."

The demon within her—within them both—agreed.

"You're right," said Evadne, even though she was, truthfully, unsure if Dorina was. "Do you feel you are living beautifully? I know your desire to become an art critic has been . . . delayed."

"Oh, I delayed it before we even thought of moving here," said Dorina, with a wave of her lovely hand. "I hadn't the stomach for it, not really. Anyway, once I began to *live* in art, I found I simply wanted to enjoy it, for myself, instead of telling others what to think about it." She sighed. "I still think it was a lazy decision . . . So many critics put me on to art, and culture. I wanted very badly to do that for others, but I'd rather *be* than *do.*"

"Not both?"

"Maybe when I'm older. I still have so much to learn . . . and I ought to learn it, at least before I try to tell anyone anything."

"I can't argue with that." Evadne smiled down at her sister. "I have a decade on you and I don't feel I could tell anyone anything. Perhaps it won't take you as long."

Dorina put her hand on Evadne's knee, and squeezed it gently.

"You know, Evadne, even though it was an awful thing . . . everything that happened, it got us here, together. And for that, I feel only gratitude."

Evadne's throat was so tight that no words could get out. Dorina understood. She leaned her head against Evadne's knee. She sighed happily, and they lapsed into a companionable silence.

The light faded as they sat together. Evening would come soon. Supper tonight was to be an informal affair, which suited Evadne just fine. Afterward, Miss Travers had promised to read to anyone who wished to listen. She had a lovely voice and was in the middle of reading to them from *The Strange Case of Dr Jekyll and Mr Hyde,* which, while too terrifying for Dorina, Evadne was enjoying very much.

Evadne became aware of the sound of footsteps behind her. A moment later, Dorina looked up.

"Harry!" she cried — and the delight in her voice made Evadne's eyes well. It seemed incredible that at one time she had considered the two of them ill suited. They loved one another so much; how could she feel anything but joy for them?

"Supper's almost ready," she said. "Hello, Evadne. Are you having a fine afternoon?"

"Delightful, Lady Henry." She had never been able to drop the woman's title.

"And Jonas is here too," said Dorina. "Good evening, Jonas."

"Good evening, Dorina." Evadne craned her neck, eager to see the young man, but he thoughtfully stepped around the side of her wingback chair so she needn't risk a cramp. "And good evening to you, Miss Gray. Forgive me, but I must say, you look remarkably well this evening."

"I *am* well, thank you."

She smiled at him, grateful as always for his respectful courtesy . . . though of course it was more than courtesy. She and Jonas had become very close over the past year, and she had decided he was a delightful person in every way. He was so intelligent, perceptive . . . even handsome. That he enjoyed her company, and had desired more of it ever since their first meeting in Lord Oliver's chambers still never failed to astonish her.

Several months ago, as they lay in bed together late into a chilly winter morning, he had shyly asked how he had once managed to offend her so thoroughly; she had done him the courtesy of replying honestly. It had been awkward to admit her reaction had so much to do with her anger toward one whom she had once hoped would be a lover, but Jonas had been understanding, even apologetic. No apology was needed—he could not have known, and anyway, every day she was more grateful to Freddie Thornton for choosing to marry someone else. Jonas was a better man than she could ever have dreamed of; he had loved her. Still loved her. And she loved him.

"I had hoped you would let me escort you back to the house," he said, glancing at where Lady Henry and Evadne were murmuring to one another in the shadow of a rosebush.

"Nothing would delight me more," she said. "Thank you."

"Let's pack up the things and go, then," said Dorina, who didn't bother to hide the fact that she had been eavesdropping. At least it was obvious that what she had overheard pleased her. "We're expected."

Evadne watched them put away the tea things and fold the blanket, regretful that she had not the strength to help them—but also happy to watch the way they all moved and spoke with one another, laughing at this and that. Jonas's eyes found hers more than once as they worked, and she saw something in his gaze that still made her blush and look away.

It wasn't the life she had imagined for herself, that of a devoted wife. Nor was it the life she had craved to return to, back with her parents, with its order and security providing the illusion of control.

But that didn't matter to her. Not anymore, at least. She had found peace—and to her mind, that was a better thing by far.

Acknowledgments

It's never easy for me, writing my list of acknowledgments. I'm a highly social person—people inspire me; they make a difference in my day, every day, whether they're regulars (or randos!) at the coffee shop where I work, coworkers, friends, family, or lovers. It's hard selecting a handful to draw out as being especially important to a project, but here goes: My editor, John Joseph Adams, who also acquired this book for Houghton Mifflin Harcourt; my agent, Cameron McClure, whose insights always make my books better; my copyeditor, Rebecca Jaynes, who improved this book tremendously with her knowledge of grammar, art, and history; Wendy Wagner, who is basically this book's Jane Austen novel–style aunt in that she helped get it in front of the individual who would eventually acquire it; Selena Chambers and Gina Guadagnino, whose emotional support, in addition to their knowledge of the nineteenth century, helped me so much, and in so many ways; Jared Shurin and Anne Perry, who kindly let me stay with them as I trotted all over London in the November rain, looking at streets and houses and museums as research; Max Campanella and Carrie Vaughn, whose pamphlet on fencing helped me get a toehold in the theory of the sport; and the friendly athletes and coaches at Northern Colorado Fencers who helped me with the practice: Gary Copeland, Scott Permer, Brian House, and all the students, as well. Friends and associates are also essential to my process (though I'm lucky to call many of those listed above friends, as well), so I'd like to thank Yaz Ostrowski, Cristal Dávila, Tim Wieneke, David Ardanuy and Rachael Zeitz Ardanuy, John Gove, Jesse Bullington, Adam Locy and Melissa Sauer Locy, my mother, Sally Tanzer, and my cat, "the Toad." And of course I must thank the attendees of the 2015 Starry Coast Writers' Workshop, where I received many truly amazing revision notes. Marissa Lingen, Chris Cevasco, and Michael DeLuca I must thank in particular, as they read the entire manuscript, but everyone that week helped me with this project: Grá Linnea, Jennifer Linnea, David Mercurio Rivera, Desirina Boskovich, Terra LeMay, Robert Levy, and Barbara Krasnoff. Thank you all—and that "all" includes everyone I've forgotten. You, too, are remembered in these pages.